Women and Industry in the Balkans

Women and Industry in the Balkans

The Rise and Fall of the Yugoslav Textile Sector

Chiara Bonfiglioli

I.B. TAURIS
LONDON • NEW YORK • OXFORD • NEW DELHI • SYDNEY

I.B. TAURIS
Bloomsbury Publishing Plc
50 Bedford Square, London, WC1B 3DP, UK
1385 Broadway, New York, NY 10018, USA
29 Earlsfort Terrace, Dublin 2, Ireland

BLOOMSBURY, I.B. TAURIS and the I.B. Tauris logo
are trademarks of Bloomsbury Publishing Plc

First published in Great Britain 2020
Paperback edition first published 2021

Copyright © Chiara Bonfiglioli, 2020

Chiara Bonfiglioli has asserted her right under the Copyright,
Designs and Patents Act, 1988, to be identified as Author of this work.

For legal purposes the Acknowledgements on p. viii constitute
an extension of this copyright page.

Cover image: A film still from the movie Od 3 do 22 by Krešimir Golik, 1966.
Courtesy of Croatian State Archives, Zagreb.

All rights reserved. No part of this publication may be reproduced or
transmitted in any form or by any means, electronic or mechanical,
including photocopying, recording, or any information storage or retrieval
system, without prior permission in writing from the publishers.

Bloomsbury Publishing Plc does not have any control over, or responsibility for,
any third-party websites referred to or in this book. All internet addresses given
in this book were correct at the time of going to press. The author and publisher
regret any inconvenience caused if addresses have changed or sites have
ceased to exist, but can accept no responsibility for any such changes.

A catalogue record for this book is available from the British Library.

A catalog record for this book is available from the Library of Congress.

ISBN: HB: 978-1-7845-3960-3
PB: 978-0-7556-3600-6
ePDF: 978-1-8386-0075-4
eBook: 978-1-8386-0076-1

Typeset by Deanta Global Publishing Services, Chennai, India

To find out more about our authors and books visit
www.bloomsbury.com and sign up for our newsletters.

Contents

List of figures	vii
Acknowledgements	viii
Introduction	1

1   Industrializing Yugoslavia: Market socialism and textile workers' structure of feeling — 21
    Textile factories in the interwar era — 22
    'Factories to the workers': From shock-work to self-management — 26
    Biking to the night shift: Women's emancipation through labour — 32
    The factory as a socialist microcosm: Work, welfare and leisure — 40
    Balancing welfare and productivity: Paternalist management in socialism — 46

2   Being a seamstress in Yugoslav times: The 'working mother' gender contract — 55
    Re-conceptualizing the double burden in the Yugoslav context — 56
    From 3.00 am to 10.00 pm: The seamstresses' endless working day — 61
    'What do you get from being a party member?': On the 'triple burden' — 67
    Women 'made of granite': Workers' portraits in the factory press — 74
    Seamstresses on screen: Workers' representations in popular culture — 81

3   Labour after Yugoslavia: Post-socialism and deindustrialization in the textile sector — 87
    Post-socialist transformations in the textile sector — 88
    'Before it was different, it was easier': Work across generations — 95
    'Only duties and no rights': The subcontracting limbo — 103
    Trade unions in post-Yugoslav states — 112

4   Workers' structure of feeling after deindustrialization: Loss, nostalgia and belonging — 123
    Deindustrialized landscapes across the post-Yugoslav space — 124
    Threads of belonging: Remembering the factory as a second home — 132

    Missing the future: The end of intergenerational solidarity   138
    Feeling Yugoslav: Nostalgia for brotherhood and unity   146
    Matters of gender and class: Critical Yugo-nostalgia   153

5 Beyond nostalgia: Workers' struggles for social justice and everyday resilience   161
    Industrial workers' struggles in the cultural, artistic and academic realm   163
    Heads up: Textile workers' strikes and collective organizing   169
    Do it yourself: Everyday survival strategies   179

Conclusion   185

Bibliography   195
Index   213

Figures

1	Work at the Arena knitwear factory, Pula, 1970s. Reproduced with permission from the Arena factory archive in 2015.	8
2	Work at the Dalmatinka spinning mill, Sinj, 1950s. Courtesy of Muzej Jugoslavije, Belgrade, and Dalmatinka Project, Sinj.	38
3	The Metka factory in post-war Celje. Courtesy of Zgodovinski Arhiv Celje.	44
4	The canteen in the Arena factory, Pula. Reproduced with permission from the Arena factory archive in 2015.	51
5	Arena's director Ivan Škrinjarić with leading communist politician Milka Planinc. Reproduced with permission from the Arena factory archive in 2015.	52
6	Anica's portrait in the newspaper of the Vuteks factory, Vukovar.	76
7	A photograph from the shooting of *Vera i Eržika*, Pančevo. Courtesy of Želimir Žilnik.	85
8	A portrait of Tito in what remains of the Makedonka factory, Štip, 2013. Photo by the author.	98
9	Arena collections, design by Marija Vareško. Reproduced with permission from the Arena factory archive in 2015.	127
10	The abandoned Golden Deer, Arena factory, 2015. Photo by the author.	128
11	The Dalmatinka factory in 2016, before its demolition in 2018. Photo by the author.	143
12	The Konzum supermarket in the former Sana factory, Novi Grad, 2014. Photo by the author.	150
13	Kamensko workers' protest, Zagreb, 2010. Courtesy of Tomislav Medak.	171
14	'Catwalk on strike' in support of Arena workers, Pula, 2014. Courtesy of Dejan Štifanić.	177
15	The kindergarten in Prvi Maj, Pirot. Reproduced with permission from the Arena factory archive in 2015.	186

Acknowledgements

In 2012, while designing a new postdoctoral project on gender and citizenship in the Balkans, I started to research the current living and working conditions of textile workers in the former industrial towns of Leskovac, Serbia, and Štip, Macedonia. Little did I know that the project would keep me occupied for the next five years, and that I would engage in a quest for factory tales across the post-Yugoslav region. Workers' narratives of factory life challenged me to go back in time, and to tell the untold story of textile workers' lives both during socialism and in its aftermath. I am profoundly indebted to the women and men who made it possible for me to record their words, emotions and interpretations. I hope that the book will do justice to the narratives I was so generously entrusted with.

This book was made possible by transnational institutional support. The research started in 2012 within the Edinburgh-based project on the 'Europeanisation of citizenship in the successor states of the former Yugoslavia' (CITSEE), where it continued for an additional year thanks to a Rubicon postdoctoral grant awarded by the Netherlands Association for Scientific Research (NWO). I wish to thank Professor Jo Shaw for her long-standing support and feedback, which extended well beyond my stay in Edinburgh, as well as Dr Igor Štiks and all my colleagues within the CITSEE project. Dr Stef Jansen also provided valuable suggestions and support in the early stages of the project. Subsequently, I could count on a NEWFELPRO postdoctoral fellowship, based at the Centre for Cultural and Historical Research of Socialism (CKPIS) at the Juraj Dobrila University of Pula, which allowed me to conduct more extensive ethnographic fieldwork across the region. My gratitude goes to Dr Andrea Matošević, Dr Igor Duda, Dr Boris Koroman, Dr Lada Duraković and all my colleagues at the CKPIS for making me feel at home in Istria. Special thanks also to Zorana Barišić at the NEWFELPRO office in Zagreb, and to Barbara Unković at the International Research Office in Pula. Finally, a European Institutes of Advanced Studies (EURIAS) fellowship, held at the Institute for Human Sciences (IWM) in Vienna, allowed me to focus exclusively on book writing for ten months. The IWM staff and fellows deserve praise for making my stay so pleasant and productive. I also wish to thank Professor Rosi Braidotti and Professor Francisca De Haan for their support, over the course of several years, with postdoctoral applications.

Acknowledgements

The narrators quoted in these pages could not have been reached without the help of numerous friends and colleagues, who kindly put me in touch with their relatives, neighbours and acquaintances. When hearing about the research, many appeared to have a mother, grandmother, aunt or neighbour who used to work in textile. I wish to thank Adriana Zaharijević for contacts in Leskovac, Pavlina Pikova for contacts in Štip, Milorad Kapetanović for contacts in Novi, Maja Hodošček for her help in Celje and Julija Sardelić for her help in Murska Sobota, as well as for her insightful feedback on the manuscript. In Sinj I am grateful I could rely on the contacts previously established by Nikola Križanac, Dragana Modrić, Jelena Pavlinušić and Silvia Milić, who also provided me with additional archive material and photographs. In Pula, I wish to thank Manuel Angelini, Sonia Angiolin, Marta Baradić, Tanja Habrle, Ivan Kraljević, Ena Krožnjak, Edna Jurcan, Maja Maksić, Jasmina Mihajlović, Ana Orsag and Dejan Štifanić for providing contacts, additional archive material and overall support with the project. In Zagreb, I am grateful to Jelena Miloš, Andrea Milat, Katarina Jaklin, Igor Lesar, Tomislav Medak and Sabina Sabolović for helping out with contacts and photographs. Thank you also to Andrew Hodges for the cat sitting opportunity and to Agata Juniku for her hospitality and friendship. In Belgrade, Marijana Mitrović was there for me with logistic and archival support, and Miloš Jovanović helped me with last-minute archival queries. Fieldwork across Croatia would have been way lonelier without the company of Nikolina Hrga, who also offered additional contacts in Varaždin. Thank you also to Željka Ljubičić Berić for her assistance with transcriptions. Želimir Žilnik and Sarita Matijević generously provided a copy of the documentary *Vera i Eržika* and a photograph for the book. Heartfelt thanks also to the narrators who went the extra mile, suggesting additional contacts, organizing meetings and providing archive material and private photographs.

A major source of inspiration for this project was the 2014 conference *Deindustrialization and its Aftermath: Class, Culture and Resistance*, organized by the Centre for Oral History and Digital Storytelling (COHDS) at Concordia University in Montréal, Québec, and by the Scottish Oral History Centre at Strathclyde University in Glasgow. I am grateful to Professor Steven High and his collaborators at COHDS, and to Professor Arthur McIvor and Dr Jackie Clarke for further discussions on gender and deindustrialization in Glasgow. I also greatly appreciate the critical feedback on the manuscript given by friends and colleagues engaged in post-Yugoslav labour history and social history, namely Rory Archer, Ljubica Spaskovska, Goran Musić and Vladimir Unkovski-Korica. Thomas Stottor from I.B. Tauris has been an exemplary editor. His suggestions, together with the constructive comments of the anonymous reviewers, greatly improved the book. All errors are, of course, mine alone.

Most of all, I am grateful to my family in Italy, for their unconditional love and support, and for sustaining me in this journey. My partner Alkiviadis Zevgaridis also deserves to be thanked, for embarking with me into the ups and downs of academic nomadism, and for reminding me that there is life – and joy – beyond academia.

Introduction

> *For us it was much better, for us personally, for people it was much better during socialism than it is today, in any case. In every way. From interpersonal relations, to the rights we had, to the protection we enjoyed as workers, it was a hundred thousand times better for us than today. Today you have no right to oppose anything. 'If you don't like it, you can go.' That's the phrase that you will hear everywhere, that's it. Before, you had the right to fight for something, to ask for something, and to have that taken into account. Things were seen very differently than today, today it is very different.*
>
> Sanja, former blue-collar worker, Pula, Croatia, May 2016.

Sanja retold her story in a café in front of the former Arena knitwear factory, now bankrupt. Sanja worked at Arena from the late 1980s until 2014, when she resigned from work after wages stopped being paid, shortly before the bankruptcy that led to the closure of the factory and to the dismissal of its last sixty-two workers. After a short period of unemployment, she now works full time as a cleaner in a local company. Even if she only experienced a couple of years of work under socialism and before the privatization process started, Sanja knew of earlier working conditions at Arena through her contact with older generations of workers, and particularly through her mother-in-law, who had started her work in the knitwear factory in the 1960s. Sanja is by no means alone in her feeling of having enjoyed better labour and welfare rights during socialist times. Rather, this feeling is a shared *leitmotif* among the over sixty women and men currently or formerly employed in the textile sector that I interviewed across the post-Yugoslav region, from Slovenia to Macedonia and from Croatia and Serbia to Bosnia-Herzegovina.

The uneven performance of the Yugoslav socialist system in terms of keeping up to its promises of class and gender equality are by now widely discussed.[1] How is it, then, that working-class citizens in the post-Yugoslav space often retain a positive image of their working lives during the socialist

---

[1] Rory Archer, Igor Duda and Paul Stubbs (eds), *Social Inequalities and Discontent in Yugoslav Socialism* (Farnham, 2016).

era, and that this positive image is also widespread among working-class women? Why is socialism, in the eyes of many citizens formerly employed in industrial jobs, consistently equated with 'normality', namely, with good working relations, job security, state sovereignty vis-à-vis of the global market economy and a functioning welfare state? And why is factory work associated with dignity, interpersonal connections, interethnic coexistence and solidarity? The book argues that this post-Yugoslav nostalgia for labour and welfare rights is rooted in the specific structure of feeling that was created in industrial workplaces during the socialist era, at the intersection between ideology, socio-economic transformations and workers' everyday lives, as well as in the process of deindustrialization that accompanied the collapse of socialism.

For the very first time, this book tells the ongoing story of textile workers[2] in the Balkans, investigating how the manifold legacies of the socialist, industrial past persist in the post-socialist and deindustrialized present. The book retraces the ways in which female workers experienced both the process of socialist industrialization after 1945, as well as the process of post-socialist deindustrialization that followed the break-up of the Socialist Federative Republic of Yugoslavia in the 1990s. These processes entailed very different gender regimes, from the 'working mother' gender regime typical of socialism to the 'mother of the nation' regime promoted by the seven new nation states that emerged out of the Yugoslav break-up. Social and economic transformations, therefore, were profoundly gendered. Simultaneously, the position of female garment workers was shaped by gender as much as class. Industrial workers occupied a strong symbolic place in the Yugoslav self-managed economy, and feminized textile factories were seen as a site of gendered modernization through productive labour. For textile workers, factories often became 'second homes', through which they could access job security, welfare entitlements and sociability networks – these elements became an integral part of workers' structure of feeling across Yugoslavia.

The garment industry flourished in socialist Yugoslavia from the mid-1950s onwards: thanks to Western economic assistance after the

---

[2] In this book, I use the terms 'textile workers' and 'garment workers' and the terms 'textile factories' and 'garment factories' interchangeably, given that the production of yarns and of ready-to-wear clothing was often carried out in the same factories. The local terms 'tekstilne radnice', 'tekstilna tvornica' and 'tekstilna industrija' usually include both types of production (for garment production, the term 'konfekcija' or 'modna konfekcija' is also used). This book, it should be noted, does not encompass workers in the shoe and leather industries, even if these sectors are traditionally represented by the same trade unions in the post-Yugoslav region.

Soviet–Yugoslav split and also due to the introduction of a mixed market economy founded on workers' self-management, Yugoslavia stood among the fastest growing economies in post-1945 Europe. Yugoslav policies of industrialization gradually spread across what used to be a mainly rural region, opening up new possibilities of work, welfare and consumption across four decades. The industry covered over 10 per cent of total manufacturing in the 1970s and 1980s, exporting its garments and textiles worldwide. New factories appeared in the main cities and peripheral towns of the Federation, mainly employing young rural women, for whom factory work became a way to achieve economic independence and a host of welfare rights such as health care, cheap housing and subsidized holidays. The Marxist idea of workers' councils was combined in original ways with a Fordist vision of work, not only determining individual workers' wages according to their productivity, but also allowing for general redistributive welfare mechanisms within factories – especially when it came to 'working mothers', who represented the majority of the workforce in textile.

In contrast, the closure of many textile and garment factories in the 1990s and 2000s as a result of the collapse of socialism and the Yugoslav Wars, with the subsequent loss of 350,000 jobs, as well as the precarization of labour in the industry due to global competition, fundamentally altered workers' Fordist imaginary shaped during the socialist era. Adding to the recent literature on deindustrialization and oral history in Western Europe, Eastern Europe and North America, the book provides the first in-depth study of the deindustrialization process in the Balkans and of its effects on workers' lives in different communities across the post-Yugoslav region.

Key contributions

Deindustrialization and oral history in the Balkans

Deindustrialization – and its wide-ranging impact on citizens, communities and societal values – has been mainly studied in the context of Western Europe and North America. Existing historical and sociological studies have long privileged processes of post-Fordist industrial transformations in capitalist settings, particularly in relation to male-dominated heavy industrial sectors.[3]

---

[3] For recent accounts of deindustrialization and transformations of work relations, see, notably, Steven High, Lachlan MacKinnon and Andrew Perchard (eds), *The Deindustrialized World: Confronting Ruination in Postindustrial Places* (Vancouver, Toronto, 2017). See also Jefferson Cowie and Joseph Heathcott (eds), *Beyond the*

Works dealing with deindustrialization in non-Western, non-capitalist contexts or with deindustrialized sectors dominated by a female workforce have been emerging only recently.[4] Next to such studies, a number of ethnographers of post-socialism have also been addressing transformations in class relations and in the position of industrial workers since the collapse of the Eastern bloc, at times considering parallel transformations of class and gender relations.[5] Scholars of deindustrialization have been increasingly relying on the concept of 'structure of feeling' developed by cultural theorist Raymond Williams to discuss how the ways of life shaped by industrialization are challenged by processes of deindustrialization and factory closures.[6]

Ruins: The Meaning of Deindustrialization (Ithaca, 2003); Steven High, '"The wounds of class": A historiographical reflection on the study of deindustrialization', History Compass, 11/11 (2013), pp. 1–14; Steven High and David Lewis, Corporate Wasteland: The Landscape and Memory of Deindustrialization (Toronto, 2007); John Kirk, Sylvie Contrepois and Steve Jefferys (eds), Changing Work and Community Identities in European Regions: Perspectives on the Past and Present (Basingstoke, 2012); Arthur McIvor, Working lives: work in Britain since 1945 (Basingstoke, 2013); Tim Strangleman, Work Identity at the End of the Line. Privatisation and Culture Change in the UK Rail Industry (Basingstoke, 2004).

[4] Kinga Pozniak, Nowa Huta: Generations of Change in a Model Socialist Town (Pittsburg, 2014). Even if it is focused on the legacy of the steel industry, Pozniak's Nowa Huta presents a number of similarities with the post-Yugoslav context. Alice Mah, Industrial Ruination, Community, and Place: Landscapes and Legacies of Urban Decline (Toronto, 2012) presents a very useful comparison between the United States, the United Kingdom and the former Soviet Union. On deindustrialization and gender, see Jackie Clarke, 'Closing time: Deindustrialization and nostalgia in contemporary France', History Workshop Journal, 79 (2015), pp. 107–25; Valerie Walkerdine and Luiz Jimenez, Gender, Work and Community After De-Industrialisation: A Psychosocial Approach to Affect (Basingstoke, 2012).

[5] On workers' experiences of post-socialism, see David A. Kideckel, 'The unmaking of an East-Central European working class', in C. M. Hann (ed.), Postsocialism: Ideals, Ideologies, and Practices in Eurasia (London and New York, 2002); Alison Stenning, 'Re-placing work: Economic transformations and the shape of a community in post-socialist Poland', Work, Employment and Society, 19/2 (2005), pp. 235–59; Alison Stenning, 'Where is the post-socialist working class? Working class lives in the spaces of (post-)socialism', Sociology, 39/5 (2005), pp. 983–99. On labour relations and trade unions, see Stephen Crowley and David Ost, Workers after Workers' States: Labor and Politics in Postcommunist Eastern Europe (London, 2001). On gender and class transformations, see Frances Pine, 'Retreat to the household? Gendered domains in postsocialist Poland', in C. M. Hann (ed.), Postsocialism: Ideals, Ideologies, and Practices in Eurasia (London and New York, 2002); Elizabeth C. Dunn, Privatizing Poland: Baby Food, Big Business, and the Remaking of Labor (Ithaca, 2004).

[6] David Byrne, 'Industrial culture in a post-industrial world: The case of the North East of England', City, 6/3 (2002), pp. 279–89; Steven High, 'Beyond aesthetics: Visibility and invisibility in the aftermath of deindustrialization', International Labor and Working-Class History, 84 (2013), pp. 140–53; Tim Strangleman, James Rhodes and Sherry Linkon, 'Introduction to Crumbling cultures: Deindustrialization, class, and memory', International Labor and Working-Class History, 84 (2013), pp. 7–22; Tim Strangleman,

Williams used this term to investigate 'a particular quality of social experience and relationship, historically distinct from other particular qualities, which give the sense of a generation or of a period'. The term 'feeling' was chosen to indicate 'meanings and values as they are actively lived and felt', as opposed to more formal definitions such as 'world view' or 'ideology'.[7] Building upon Williams, British sociologist David Byrne notably argued that 'industrial systems were more than just systems of economic production. They were also systems of social production and reproduction,' and that the effects of industrialization persisted as 'structures of feeling' after deindustrialization.[8] The concept of 'structure of feeling' has also been used for the Yugoslav socialist context in Breda Luthar's and Maruša Pušnik's edited volume on the culture of everyday life in socialist Yugoslavia. According to them, 'the structure of feeling of a period is grounded in the everyday, the rigid and the habitual, in the mundane details of the ordinary life and in the grey zone of semi-official practices.'[9]

Oral history has been singled out as an important source for the recollection of industrial structures of feeling in industrialized and deindustrialized communities.[10] In the post-Yugoslav space, the existence of several generations of ordinary people who happened to live through both socialism and post-socialism is indeed what makes oral history so relevant and poignant when investigating memories of industrialization and deindustrialization.[11] As Ljubica Spaskovska has noted, when writing about Yugoslavia, one is confronted with the fact that 'the Yugoslav time is historical, while the (post)Yugoslav space and the many people who inhabit(ed) that time and space still exist. One faces the challenge of writing about a phenomenon that qualifies as "not-yet-entirely-past" and "partially-still-present".'[12] Alongside the persistence of the Yugoslav legacy, another important legacy shaping oral history in the region is the one of the Yugoslav Wars. According to feminist activist Žarana Papić, the war fundamentally

---

'Deindustrialisation and the historical sociological Imagination: Making sense of work and industrial change', *Sociology*, 51/2 (2017), pp. 466–82.
[7] Raymond Williams, *Marxism and Literature* (Oxford and New York, 1978), pp. 131–2.
[8] Byrne, 'Industrial Culture in a post-industrial world', p. 280.
[9] Breda Luthar and Maruša Pušnik, 'The lure of utopia: Socialist everyday spaces', in Breda Luthar and Maruša Pušnik (eds), *Remembering Utopia: The Culture of Everyday Life in Socialist Yugoslavia* (Washington, 2010), p. 15.
[10] High, MacKinnon and Perchard (eds), *The Deindustrialized World*; Alessandro Portelli, *They Say in Harlan County: An Oral History* (Oxford, 2012).
[11] Tanja Petrović, 'Towards an affective history of Yugoslavia'. *Filozofija i društvo*, 27/3 (2016), pp. 504–20.
[12] Ljubica Spaskovska, 'The Yugoslav chronotope – histories, memories and the future of Yugoslav studies', in F. Bieber, A. Galijaš and R. Archer (eds), *Debating the End of Yugoslavia* (London, 2014), p. 241.

destabilized the balance between perceptions of past, present and future: 'it is not the past we thought we knew, nor the present we thought we had been living, nor the future we thought we could foresee and expect'.[13] Ordinary citizens' narratives, therefore, tend to be shaped according to a 'then' and 'now', 'before' and 'after', with the collapse of socialism and the Yugoslav Wars constituting a discursive watershed.

Similarly to war, deindustrialization has been described in the literature as a traumatic event that disrupts conceptions of past, present and future, generating forms of ruination and enforced forgetting.[14] In the post-Yugoslav space, deindustrialization was shaped simultaneously by post-socialist and post-conflict transformations. The disruptive character of economic changes was often accompanied by warfare, genocide and ethnic discrimination against those that did not fit with the new national communities, causing job losses together with human losses and displacement. The enduring consequences of both deindustrialization and violent conflict are very visible and very pervasive, determining the outlook of urban settlements and the life opportunities of their inhabitants. Former industrial towns are literally 'dying out', as a result of the process of de-development that followed post-socialist and post-conflict transformations.[15]

At the same time, when it comes to the textile sector, deindustrialization went hand in hand with labour intensification and a worsening of social rights in existing factories, as a result of the global 'race to the bottom' for production costs which characterizes the industry. While exploitation of garment workers in Asia is a well-known phenomenon, many sweatshops are also located in Central, Eastern and South-Eastern Europe, just a few hundred kilometres away from major European capitals.[16] The widespread discontent with the new geopolitical order that can be felt across the entire post-Yugoslav space has as much to do with the neoliberal precarization of welfare and labour as it has to do with the feelings of disruption of previous multicultural and multinational communities in which ethnic identities were superseded and counterbalanced by socialist values. As a white-collar female narrator from Croatia summarized: 'We had brotherly exchanges

---

[13] Žarana Papić, 'Women in Serbia: Post-communism, war and nationalist mutations', in Sabrina Petra Ramet (ed), *Gender Politics in the Western Balkans: Women and Society in Yugoslavia and the Yugoslav Successor States* (University Park, 1999), p.157.

[14] High, 'Beyond Aesthetics'.

[15] See, for instance, Igor Spaic, 'Bosnia's "hero town" dies on its feet', *Balkan Insight*, 23 October 2017. http://www.balkaninsight.com/en/article/bosnia-s-hero-town-dies-on-its-feet-10-20-2017 (last accessed 20 January 2018).

[16] See the various reports by the Clean Clothes Campaign cited in this volume, and particularly in Chapter 3.

among different factories because it was the Socialist Federative Republic of Yugoslavia then, *brotherhood and unity*, that old socialist system. No matter what people would say now, – she stated – we lived well, we socialized nicely, we visited each other, it was really good.'

The possibility to access labour and welfare rights, as well as social mobility, brought citizens of different ethnicities and genders together, especially in factories and new urban settlements, contributing to build an inclusive multinational state decentred in different republics and communes. The omnipresent comparison between 'then' and 'now', therefore, is a way for many middle-aged citizens to express their agency, their visions and their hopes for yet another better future, since the future they got was not the one they could foresee and expect. It is also a way to adapt to the new context, to 'make do', to survive day by day through hard work and sacrifice, as most seamstresses – and women – did anyway during socialism, and as they continue to do these days for themselves, their families and their communities. This book tells their stories through their voices and narratives, striving to portray both their hardships and their endless resourcefulness and resilience.

Gender history between socialism and post-socialism

The generations of working-class women who came of age or were born after 1945 witnessed both the industrial expansion of the socialist era and the industrial decay of post-socialist times. They also went through a constant, persistent struggle in combining productive and reproductive work, since women's hard work and self-sacrifice outside and within the home have been foundational in both socialist and post-socialist societies. Garment workers, both during socialism and during post-socialism, have been subjected to a strict piece-rate regime of labour measurement (the so-called *norma*[17]) as well as to night shifts in most of the factories I analysed (Figure 1). In this book, however, I argue that the main difference in garment workers' experiences of the socialist and post-socialist era lies in the greater symbolic and material recognition of women's labour during socialism, in the space for empowerment and socialization provided by the factory, and in their ability to enjoy greater welfare rights, job security and purchasing power in the heyday of socialist modernization.

---

[17] The *norma* indicated the specific piece-rate measurement that had to be reached by each worker in a certain amount of time. See Chapter 1.

Figure 1 Work at the Arena knitwear factory, Pula, 1970s. Reproduced with permission from the Arena factory archive in 2015.

Consequently, the book strives to demonstrate that the study of socialist gender politics in Yugoslavia needs to go beyond existing interpretations which tend to emphasize state control over women and women's lack of agency.[18] The socialist gendered legacy, in fact, appears to be more complex than a legacy of passivity that extends from 1945 to the present days.[19]

---

[18] Transformations of gender relations in the socialist era are generally treated in reductive terms in two influential and otherwise very valuable edited volumes: Sabrina Petra Ramet (ed.), *Gender Politics in the Western Balkans: Women and Society in Yugoslavia and the Yugoslav Successor States* (University Park, 1999); Christina Hassenstab and Sabrina Petra Ramet (eds), *Gender (In)equality and Gender Politics in South-Eastern Europe: A Question of Justice* (London, 2014). For a similar interpretation of the socialist era, see also Ulf Brunnbauer, 'From equality without democracy to democracy without equality? Women and transition in southeast Europe', *South-East Europe Review for Labour and Social Affairs*, 3 (2000), pp. 151–68. The most balanced and complex account to this date on the issue remains the one by Susan L. Woodward, 'The rights of women', published in 1985, which I cite in Chapter 1 and 2. For a critique of 'common knowledge' on gender relations during the socialist era, see Kristen Ghodsee and Kateřina Lišková, 'Bumbling idiots or evil masterminds? Challenging Cold War stereotypes about women, sexuality and state socialism', *Filozofija i Društvo*, 27/3 (2016), pp. 489–503.

[19] In a recent editorial, feminist writer Slavenka Drakulić attributed young women's current post-socialist 'passivity' to the legacy of the 'emancipation from above'

Concepts such as 'state patriarchy', 'emancipation from above' and the 'double burden' are often used as shorthand judgements about socialist gender politics, but tell us little about women's complex life experiences. Gender regimes in socialism were as different as the various socialist regimes across Eastern Europe, and women's life choices were not only shaped by their gender, but also by their class, ethnic and national background.[20] When it comes to seamstresses in socialist Yugoslavia, the book shows that female industrial workers were empowered up to a certain degree, not only as a result of the official discourse which posited both industrial work and women's work as central to the socialist project, but also thanks to a number of welfare arrangements and to the existential security attached to factory work. Rather than passively accepting the closure of their factories and the devaluation of their labour after the end of socialism, industrial workers fought to keep their jobs and welfare benefits, as was witnessed in the case of the Kamensko textile workers' strike of 2010, which I analyse in this book.

Similarly, as in other socialist regimes, the 'working mother' gender contract stemmed from Marxist ideology, which saw women's emancipation as dependent upon women's equal entry into the labour force.[21] Women's reproductive tasks as mothers and caretakers, at the same time, were to be socialized by the state through collective welfare services such as canteens, kindergartens and laundries, which would enable women to integrate

---

experienced by their mothers and grandmothers: 'Ultimately, young women in the former communist countries have also been "emancipated from above". Like their mothers and grandmothers, they enjoy, at least formally, the rights that women in the western democracies had to fight hard for. But on the other hand, it is exactly this kind of emancipation that makes them so passive.' Slavenka Drakulić, 'How women survived (post-) communism (and didn't laugh)', *Eurozine*, 5 June 2015. Available at: http://www.eurozine.com/how-women-survived-post-communism-and-didnt-laugh/ (accessed 20 January 2018).

[20] On gender relations in other socialist and post-socialist contexts, see, notably, Krassimira Daskalova, Caroline Hornstein Romić, Karl Kaser and Filip Radunović (eds), *Gendering Post-socialist Transition: Studies of Changing Gender Perspectives* (Vienna, 2012); Elizabeth C. Dunn, *Privatizing Poland*; Eva Fodor, *Working Difference: Women's Working Lives in Hungary and Austria, 1945–1995* (Durham, 2003); Malgorzata Fidelis, *Women, Communism, and Industrialization in Postwar Poland* (Cambridge and New York, 2010); Susan Gal and Gail Kligman, *The Politics of Gender after Socialism: a Comparative-Historical Essay* (Princeton, 2000); Shana Penn and Jill Massino (eds), *Gender Politics and Everyday Life in State Socialist Eastern and Central Europe* (Basingstoke, 2009); Jacqui True, *Gender, Globalization, and Postsocialism: The Czech Republic After Communism* (New York, 2003); Joanna Regulska and Bonnie G. Smith (eds), *Women and Gender in Postwar Europe: From Cold War to European Union* (New York, 2012); Lisa Rofel, *Other Modernities: Gendered Yearnings in China After Socialism* (Berkeley, 1999).

[21] Leontina M. Hormel, 'A case study of gender, class, and garment work reorganization in Ukraine', *Gender. Journal for Gender, Culture and Society*, 1 (2011), pp. 10–25; Tatiana Zhurzhenko, 'Free market ideology and new women's identities in post-socialist Ukraine', *European Journal of Women's Studies*, 8/1 (2001), pp. 29–49.

themselves in the labour force and to combine productive and reproductive work.[22] This type of gender contract certainly did not question women's main role as caretakers in the private sphere, but nonetheless empowered some women in the public sphere and guaranteed a certain degree of independence in personal choices. Contrary to widely held assumptions, the double burden faced by women was not overlooked, but rather frequently discussed and acknowledged by socialist authorities, and, in turn, by female workers themselves.[23]

The extent of such discussions meant that women could negotiate their productive and reproductive time in flexible ways up to a certain extent, particularly in the late socialist period, when maternity leaves were extended up to a year and part-time work for working mothers with small children was allowed up to the third year of age. Abortion was also further liberalized and widely available from the late 1960s onwards. Yugoslav seamstresses can be thus compared to their Polish counterparts, who, through their work, 'were able to realise a kind of individual value which transcended, without excluding, the prescriptions of kinship and gender located in the domestic domain'.[24] While working-class women's productive and reproductive labour provided a useful buffer to the dysfunctions of the fragmented and uneven socialist market economy, Yugoslav authorities nonetheless valued and made visible both women's labour outside the home and women's role as mothers and caretakers in the home, as testified both by workers' narratives and by archive material from the socialist era.

In contrast, post-socialist deindustrialization brought a general devaluation of industrial work in general, and of women's industrial work in particular. Labour and welfare rights rapidly deteriorated, pushing working-class women towards an increasing dependency on informal work and on family networks. In the areas of former Yugoslavia most affected by violent conflict, gender-based violence and displacement contributed to worsen women's living and working conditions. The existing feminist literature on gender relations in the Balkans focuses very much on ethnicity, nationalism and borders, but very little on class, as a result of its conditions of production during the Yugoslav Wars and in their aftermath, when feminist activists

---

[22] Chiara Bonfiglioli, 'Women's political and social activism in the early Cold War era: The case of Yugoslavia', *Aspasia*, 8 (2014), pp. 1–25.

[23] For a historicization of the double burden in Poland, see Fidelis, *Women, Communism, and Industrialization in Postwar Poland*.

[24] Frances Pine, 'Retreat to the household? Gendered domains in postsocialist Poland', p. 104.

were among the few to oppose gendered warfare and nationalism.[25] As underlined by many scholars, the socialist 'working mother' gender contract was undone and a new 'mother of the nation' gender contract came about.[26] While scholars in the 1990s and 2000s stressed the ways in which new nationalist discourses emphasized women's role as reproducers of the nation and threatened women's reproductive rights, contributing to the symbolic retraditionalization of gender relations in the post-socialist era, the material backlash brought about by factory closures and layoffs, especially among working-class women, was neglected.[27]

On the basis of textile workers' narratives, I argue in this book that the retraditionalization of gender roles had as much to do with the precarization of welfare and labour rights as with nationalist rhetoric in the public sphere. Behind the giant nationalist flags and the tailor-made suits of ethnic entrepreneurs stood the labour of overly exploited, precarious seamstresses on the brink of hunger and poverty, as recounted by some of my narrators. It would be mistaken to believe that working-class women wholeheartedly complied with the new state of affairs and that they were only interested in family life and ready to go back home, as some scholars of post-socialism anticipated in the 1990s.[28] As my informants make clear, instead, by harking

---

[25] For a brief critical overview of the existing literature, see Chiara Bonfiglioli, Katja Kahlina and Adriana Zaharijević, 'Transformations of gender, sexuality and citizenship in South East Europe', *Women's Studies International Forum*, 49 (2015), pp. 43–7. About feminist activism during the Yugoslav Wars, see the extensive study by Ana Miškovska Kajevska, *Feminist Activism at War: Belgrade and Zagreb Feminists in the 1990s* (London and New York, 2017).

[26] Among the vast literature on the subject, see, notably, the anthology edited by Rada Iveković and Julie Mostov, *From Gender to Nation* (Ravenna, 2002) as well as Papić, 'Women in Serbia'. See also: Jelisaveta Blagojević, Katerina Kolozova and Svetlana Slapšak (eds), *Gender and Identity. Theories from and/or on Southeastern Europe* (Belgrade, 2006); Dubravka Žarkov, *The Body of War: Media, Ethnicity and Gender in the Break-up of Yugoslavia* (Durham, 2007); Elissa Helms, *Innocence and Victimhood: Gender, Nation, and Women's Activism in Postwar Bosnia-Herzegovina* (Madison, 2013).

[27] Chiara Bonfiglioli, 'Gender, labour and precarity in the South East European periphery: The case of textile workers in Štip', *Contemporary Southeastern Europe*, 1/2 (2014), pp. 7–23. Chiara Bonfiglioli, 'Gendered citizenship in the global European periphery: Textile workers in post-Yugoslav states', *Women's Studies International Forum*, 49 (2015), pp. 57–65.

[28] This thesis, notably, is put forward in the widely quoted text written by Katherine Verdery, 'From parent-state to family patriarchs: Gender and nation in contemporary Eastern Europe', *East European Politics and Societies*, 8/2 (1994), p. 253. Verdery writes: 'There is considerable evidence that many women are eager for this restoration and do not resent the loss of their place in the labour force and political life. For many, work was a necessity, not something they sought. ... For many, the home was always a haven from an oppressive state; they are content to return there now, if only their husbands can earn the proverbial family wage.' Similar views are expressed by Joy B. Reeves, 'Women, work and family in former Yugoslavia', in Barbara Łobodzińska (ed.), *Family, Women, and Employment in Central-Eastern Europe* (Westport, CT, 1995).

back to their memories of the socialist past, and to their class consciousness, former garment workers used their past experiences of welfare and labour to express resilience, agency and personal dignity in a new mutated context which pushed them into invisibility, precarity and exploitation.

Social and labour history after Yugoslavia

While providing fresh perspectives on gender and women's history in the Balkans, this book also contributes to a recent wave of scholarship in social and labour history, which has been spurred on by the 2008 economic crisis and by the wide range of new social mobilizations taking place across the region in the 2000s and 2010s.[29] New scholarly works openly challenged the predominant interpretative framework of South-Eastern European societies based on nationhood, nationalism and ethnicity, which had crystallized during the Yugoslav Wars.[30] Several publications have highlighted scholars' renewed interest in Yugoslav social history, labour history and the history of everyday life, as well in transformations of class and labour in the post-socialist era, alongside transformations in national and ethnic identities.[31] Working-class women's experiences, however, have remained marginal within these recent studies. A notable exception is the case of textile workers in post-socialist Slovenia studied by Nina Vodopivec.[32] While Vodopivec's

---

[29] About recent mobilizations in the region, see Srećko Horvat and Igor Štiks (eds), *Welcome to the Desert of Post-Socialism: Radical Politics after Yugoslavia* (Brooklyn, NY, 2015). Igor Štiks, '"New Left" in the post-Yugoslav space: Issues, sites, and forms', *Socialism and Democracy*, 29/3 (2015), pp. 135–46.

[30] For a reappraisal of the existing scholarship, see Florian Bieber, Armina Galijaš and Rory Archer (eds), *Debating the End of Yugoslavia* (London, 2014).

[31] On everyday life in socialist Yugoslavia, see Luthar and Pušnik, *Remembering Utopia*. On tourism, consumption and leisure, see: Hannes Grandits and Karin Taylor, *Yugoslavia's Sunny Side: A History of Tourism in Socialism (1950s-1980s)* (Budapest, 2010). On the generations that lived during the socialist era, see Ljubica Spaskovska, *The Last Yugoslav Generation: The Rethinking of Youth Politics and Cultures in Late Socialism* (Manchester, 2017). On labour history in South-East Europe see Sabine Rutar, 'Towards a Southeast European history of labour: Examples from Yugoslavia', in S. Rutar (ed.), *Beyond the Balkans, Towards an Inclusive History of Southeastern Europe* (Vienna and Berlin, 2014). On social inequalities and social history during late socialism, see Archer, Duda and Stubbs (eds), *Social Inequalities*; on transformation of labour and class after socialism, see Tanja Petrović, '"When we were Europe": Socialist workers in Serbia and their nostalgic narratives', in. M. N. Todorova (ed.), *Remembering Communism: Genres of Representation* (New York, 2010).

[32] Nina Vodopivec, 'On the road to modernity: Textile workers and post-socialist transformations in Slovenia', *History*, 97/328 (2012), pp. 609–29; Nina Vodopivec, 'Past for the present: The social memory of textile workers in Slovenia', in M. N. Todorova (ed.), *Remembering Communism: Genres of Representation* (New York, 2010).

work dealt with a number of local case studies in the Slovenian setting, this volume adopts a comparative, post-Yugoslav perspective, making use of different case studies of garment factories in Croatia, Bosnia-Herzegovina, Serbia, Slovenia and Macedonia. This comparison testifies to the lingering presence of the Yugoslav legacy in workers' memories, thirty years since the beginning of the 'transition' from market socialism to neoliberal market capitalism.[33] It also shows that garment workers' post-socialist nostalgia for the work relations and welfare benefits experienced in the socialist era is something that can be found across national borders and across the borders of what used to be the different Yugoslav republics, despite all their differences in economic development, politics and culture.

While addressing post-Yugoslav social and labour history from a gender perspective, this book also intervenes in the discussion on post-socialist nostalgia, in particular Yugonostalgia, which has been the object of much scholarly attention in the field of popular culture, cultural studies and anthropology.[34] For ordinary people in post-Yugoslav states, as Ivana Spasić has argued, the Yugoslav Federation still functions as a 'model of normal life', not just in social and economic terms, but also in cultural and moral terms.[35] While nostalgia has been singled out as a defining feature of post-Yugoslav societies, less attention has been paid to nostalgia for welfare and labour rights among working-class citizens, and among women in particular. As Woodward argued, during socialism, 'the employment status defined the identities, economic interests, social status and political loyalty of Yugoslav citizens. One's place of work was the center of one's social universe.'[36] Through the different chapters, I demonstrate that this centrality was strongly internalized and appropriated by textile workers, also thanks to the decision-making possibilities offered by self-management organs

---

[33] Given that the term 'transition' is highly contested for its deterministic and teleological undertones, the book more frequently uses the term 'post-socialism' to investigate the persistence of the socialist legacy in current times, following other anthropological studies of Central and Eastern Europe. See Nicolette Makovicky, *Neoliberalism, Personhood, and Postsocialism: Enterprising Selves in Changing Economies* (London and New York, 2016), p. 3.

[34] See, for instance, Svetlana Boym, *The Future of Nostalgia* (London, 2001); Maria N. Todorova and Zsuzsa Gille (eds), *Post-communist Nostalgia* (New York, 2010); Olivia Angé and David Berliner (eds), *Anthropology and Nostalgia* (New York, 2014); Mitja Velikonja, *Titostalgia: A Study of Nostalgia for Josip Broz* (Ljubljana 2008); Mitja Velikonja, 'Lost in transition: Nostalgia for socialism in post-socialist countries', *East European Politics and Societies*, 23/4 (2009), pp. 535–51.

[35] Ivana Spasić, 'Jugoslavija kao mesto normalnog života: sećanja običnih ljudi u Srbiji', *Sociologija*, LIV/4 (2012), pp. 577–94.

[36] Susan L. Woodward, 'The political economy of ethno-nationalism in Yugoslavia', *Socialist Register*, 39 (2003), p. 76.

within the factory. In socialist legislation, factories were defined as social property (*društvena svojina*), namely, they were the property of workers and of society, and they were mostly perceived as such by workers themselves, who had the feeling of working both for their interest and for the interest of the entire collectivity. During socialism, factory life provided workers with meaning and structure, not only in the productive sphere but also in the sphere of welfare and leisure.

Post-socialist articulations of power and statehood, instead, were enmeshed with processes of deindustrialization, privatization and economic accumulation performed by the new nationalist elites at the expenses of ordinary working citizens across the post-Yugoslav space, who often had to witness the closure of the factories they so strongly had identified with. So-called 'criminal privatization' practices have been rife in the past decades, giving rise to forms of capitalist accumulation by dispossession throughout the Balkans.[37] Class analysis, which had been such an important part of socialist rhetoric, both in the formerly socialist East and in the formerly Keynesian West, was shunned in the new hegemonic discourse, founded on neoliberal, post-Fordist capitalism and on the rebirth of nation states.[38] As the book makes clear, denouncing social inequalities in post-Yugoslav successor states was often seen as an open contestation of nationalist elites and nationalist discourse in war times, and was equated with national treason. As in other post-socialist contexts, but perhaps even more so during the Yugoslav Wars, '*Not* discussing class seemed to many as a patriotic obligation.'[39] That is perhaps why many of my narrators, before denouncing today's social inequalities, and before comparing the past to the present, often make use of formulas like 'I am not Yugo-nostalgic, but', or, alternatively, 'I am glad we got *our* nation-state, but ...'.[40] This is followed by staggering accounts of unpaid wages, poverty wages and precarious working conditions since the onset of post-socialism. Similarly to industrial workers in other post-socialist and capitalist deindustrialized settings, post-Yugoslav industrial workers became

---

[37] See David Harvey, 'The "new" imperialism: Accumulation by dispossession', *Socialist Register*, 40 (2009), pp. 63–87. I am using the term 'criminal privatization' throughout the book following my informants' perceptions of this phenomenon and of its consequences on workers' lives, and also to indicate the non-neutral character of the privatization process.

[38] David Ost, 'Class after communism: Introduction to the special issue', *East European Politics and Societies and Cultures*, 29/3 (2015), pp. 543–64.

[39] Ibid., p. 545.

[40] Pozniak discusses similar narratives in the Polish context, arguing that 'all these carefully worded "buts" are an attempt to stretch these discursive frames, to make it possible to remember good things about the past without being accused of nostalgia for socialism'. Kinga Pozniak, *Nowa Huta*, p. 189.

greatly marginalized both on a symbolic and material level after 1989. This book strives to counter textile workers' invisibility in public and scholarly discourse, further contributing to the ongoing political, cultural and artistic initiatives that aim to preserve and valorize the local industrial heritage across generations.

Sources and methodology

This book is the result of several years of empirical research. Oral history interviews represent the bulk of the research material, as I conducted over sixty oral history interviews with former and current workers in the textile industry in Croatia, Serbia, Macedonia, Slovenia and Bosnia-Herzegovina over the course of four years, from the autumn of 2012 to the spring of 2016. After a round of short field trips to the towns of Štip and Skopje (Macedonia), Leskovac (Serbia), Bosanski Novi/Novi Grad (Bosnia-Herzegovina) in 2013 and 2014, during which I collected fourteen interviews in total, I moved to the city of Pula, Croatia, at the end of 2014, and resided there until the autumn of 2016. While I lived in Croatia, I collected the bulk of my empirical material, mostly in Pula, but also in Varaždin, Osijek, Zagreb and Sinj, gathering forty-seven interviews across Croatia in 2015 and 2016. I also conducted two interviews in the town of Celje, Slovenia, in 2016, and another two interviews in Murska Sobota, Slovenia, in 2017. Besides a majority (two thirds) of former and current blue-collar female workers, my narrators also include a minority (one third) of former managers, designers and technical staff, including male workers. I also conducted a round-table with Croatian trade unionists working in the textile sector.

I conducted interviews in Bosnian/Croatian/Serbian, the former common official language in Yugoslavia, which is also spoken and understood by the older generations in Macedonia and Slovenia, who were exposed to it through the media and in the public sphere (younger generations of Macedonians and Slovenes are generally only passive speakers of the language). Interviews were collected through a process similar to participant observation, in a variety of settings, such as a bankrupted factory, an informal garment workshop or the narrator's home. Besides individual interviews, where I was alone with one narrator, it often happened that I interviewed two or three former colleagues simultaneously, or that I interviewed one or more workers in the presence (or alternate presence) of family members, gatekeepers and representatives of cultural associations and trade unions through which I contacted the narrators. In Sinj, the interviews were conducted together with the members of the Dalmatinka Sinj team, while in Osijek and Varaždin I co-interviewed most narrators together with filmmaker Nikolina Hrga.[41] The average single interview duration was of an hour in length, but in the case of collective interviews, with groups up to five workers prompting each other's memories, the interview became obviously longer. In the case of collective interviews, I would still collect each participant's biographical data and individual comments on a specific theme.

When conducting the interviews I followed a semi-structured or 'flexible' approach,[42] starting with general questions about the narrator's biographical path and experience of factory work and then letting the informant speak as freely as possible. I usually asked additional questions on specific welfare and labour rights, such as maternity leaves, canteens, healthcare facilities, sick leave and holidays, as well as working time and wages, during the socialist era. The theme of factory closure and the comparison between the socialist and post-socialist era would usually emerge quite spontaneously, but at times, depending on their previous answers, I prompted the narrators with additional questions. All interviews were recorded, transcribed and anonymized to guarantee the privacy and safety of the narrators. During the interviews, I spoke to workers who were employed as early as the mid-1950s, up until those who started only in the post-socialist era. This meant that the eldest workers I talked to were in their mid-eighties, whereas the youngest were in their early or mid-fifties. Even if my narrators had different life paths, most of them, including the retired and unemployed, experienced work both during the socialist and the post-socialist era – thus they could explicitly compare working conditions, wages, living standards, power relations within the factory and welfare rights.

In order to balance oral history recollections of socialism with data from the socialist era, I also collected archival sources, notably workplace periodicals published under socialism, located in the national libraries of Ljubljana, Belgrade and Zagreb. I could collect periodicals for most of the factories studied through oral history, but I also reviewed the periodicals of several other companies across former Yugoslavia, in order to obtain a broad overview of the geographical and industrial diversity of the region. Factory newspapers are excellent sources for the study of industrialization and welfare during socialism.[43] They often contain several pages of workers' individual testimonies and offer insights into workers' subjectivities, sense of belonging and discontent within the factory. Besides workplace periodicals,

---

[41] Throughout the book I indicate if the interview was conducted with one or several narrators and if other interviewers were present.
[42] Alan Bryman, *Social Research Methods* (Oxford, 2008).
[43] Rory Archer and Goran Musić, 'Approaching the socialist factory and its workforce: Considerations from fieldwork in (former) Yugoslavia', *Labor History*, 58/1 (2017), pp. 44–66.

I consulted documents and reports on the garment industry contained in some of the archival collections of state socialist women's organizations in Yugoslavia, as well as published secondary literature on women's workplace status and sociological and statistical reports published before 1989. Together with archival sources from the socialist era and oral history interviews, I also make use of contemporary press material about the garment industry (generally reports on single local cases of 'mismanaged privatization' and deindustrialization), which highlights regional trends in the deterioration of workers' social rights and in the devaluation of women's industrial labour in the post-socialist era. Visual sources are also being used in the volume as a complement to written sources. Whenever possible, I collected old photographs of the socialist era from bankrupted factories, museums and existing archives and compared such images with contemporary photographs of empty factory spaces, as a way to underline the transformations of the factory as a social space. I also collected and analysed two documentary films and a television series that directly address the position of textile workers during socialism.

In terms of methodology, a few additional words are needed here in relation to the usage of oral history sources, and particularly on the usage of recollections of the socialist era. Seeing my project as rooted in the tradition of feminist oral history,[44] I did not aim to achieve a representative sociological sample across the region, which was beyond my research possibilities. I aimed instead to collect working-class women's voices in a variety of local settings, and to uncover different localized narratives of industrialization and deindustrialization across the post-Yugoslav space in a comparative perspective. The geographical scope taken by this project was often determined by the pre-existing connections I could mobilize in the region to get access to former industrial settings and their inhabitants. Unlike my previous research work, for which I interviewed feminists and communist activists who were more or less known public figures, the research for this book required access to ordinary and anonymous textile workers, especially those living outside the main regional urban centres, thus necessitating the presence of a local network. Besides Pula, where I created such a network over the course of two years, the other research settings required the help of friends and activists from the region as gatekeepers and intermediaries. I could also count on a wide activist network dealing with women's and

---

[44] For a multivocal definition of feminist oral history, see Sherna B. Gluck and Daphne Patai, *Women's Words: The Feminist Practice of Oral History* (New York, 1991), as well as Katrina Srigley, Stacey Zembrzycki and Franca Iacovetta, *Beyond Women's Words, Feminisms and Practices of Oral History in the Twenty-First Century* (London and New York, 2018).

workers' rights, having conducted research on the post-Yugoslav region for the past ten years.

Speaking the local language obviously helped in getting access to narrators and their memories. Despite the fact that my name pointed at my Italian origin, the language I used and the fact of being based in Pula meant that I could 'pass' as bilingual or as a member of the Italian minority in Istria, until I explicitly identified myself as an Italian from Bologna, Italy. Still, even when knowing that I was Italian, narrators did not censor their complaints towards 'Italians' in general. Working-class Istrian ladies told me they resented the behaviour of Italian tourists in Istria and of Italian employers in the elderly-care sector in neighbouring Italian cities, while narrators in Slavonia and Dalmatia told me of their suffering at the hands of Italian entrepreneurs who had brought their factories to bankruptcy, or of factory owners known for their mobbing practices. Local white-collar workers, on the contrary, generally expressed positive memories of past exchanges with Italian colleagues within the framework of the fashion industry. Therefore, narrators seemed to relate to my Italian nationality more on the basis of their class position and generation than on the basis of their national belonging.

Class and generation are indeed very salient elements in the construction of blue-collar and white-collar textile workers' narratives. While the book provides a comparative, polyphonic assemblage of many voices across post-Yugoslav ethnic and national borders, workers' narratives are very much shaped by a common generational and class belonging and reflect the socialist structure of feeling shaped by everyday factory work. Since factory closures are very recent or happening as we speak, workers were often very keen to denounce the present state of affairs. At the same time, it should also be noted that some of the workers who were contacted declined to take part in the interviews, particularly workers who lost their jobs during the latest bankruptcies, but also retired workers who explicitly stated that the recent closure of their factory was too painful a subject to dwell upon. Moreover, even if I could conduct interviews with a few workers currently employed in private firms through the help of acquaintances and thanks to the guarantee of anonymity, it is well known that many current workers – especially those employed in local chapters of big multinational companies – are reluctant to speak of their labour conditions as they fear retaliation from factory owners. In this sense, former and current workers' silence speaks as much as the interviews, and points to the fact that the collected voices only document a fraction of the collective trauma experienced during post-socialist deindustrialization and in the current context of widespread exploitation of industrial labour.

Structure

The book is organized in two main parts: Chapters 1 and 2 mainly deal with the history of garment factories and of textile workers in the socialist era, while Chapters 3, 4 and 5 address the current circumstances of garment workers in post-socialist states, looking at the ways in which the industrial structure of feeling that developed within socialist factories lingers on in their voices and memories after the end of Yugoslavia and after deindustrialization. All five chapters make use of oral history narratives in combination with other sources, but the second part of the book relies more extensively on oral history sources and on their complexity in the post-socialist context.

The first chapter, 'Industrializing Yugoslavia: Market socialism and textile workers' structure of feeling', traces the history of garment factories in the Balkans since the interwar period and the Second World War, and highlights the expansion of the sector during the process of industrialization in the early socialist period. It also examines the formation of the specific structure of feeling typical of socialist factories, which functioned as a microcosm of socialist values, and the inclusion of women in the industrial labour force in a prevailingly rural and patriarchal context. The chapter establishes a dialogue with the existing literature on self-management and class and proposes a gendered approach to social history in the post-Yugoslav region.

The second chapter, 'Being a seamstress in Yugoslav times: The "working mother" gender contract', investigates the figure of the seamstress in official discourse and popular culture through the analysis of archives, workplace periodicals and visual documents which had garment workers as protagonists. The chapter also addresses the 'working mother' gender contract proper of socialist times, and historicizes women's 'double burden' of productive and reproductive work, a theme that has been at the centre of feminist literature on socialist regimes. The chapter considers how women's labour in the productive and reproductive spheres was simultaneously valorized and naturalized in socialist popular culture, and how the gendered norm of women's endless resilience became part of garment workers' industrial structure of feeling, together with intersubjective factory relations and welfare entitlements.

The third chapter, 'Labour after Yugoslavia: Post-socialism and deindustrialization in the textile sector', deals with the specificities of post-socialist and post-conflict deindustrialization in the Balkans, detailing how deindustrialization affected workers in the garment sector in post-Yugoslav successor states, and how workers' social and labour rights worsened during post-socialist transformations. It also addresses the precarization and intensification of labour in the private textile sector, and the ways in which new capitalist relations challenged workers' previous structure of feeling, particularly when workers maintained their positions in a recently restructured socialist factory, and were thus able to directly compare working conditions during and after socialism.

The fourth chapter, 'Workers' structure of feeling after deindustrialization: Loss, nostalgia and belonging', analyses the reconfigurations of urban landscapes and social communities caused by deindustrialization across the post-Yugoslav space, as well as workers' complex attachment to the space of the socialist factory after the end of Yugoslavia. The chapter considers how workers' industrial structure of feeling emerges in present-day narratives, particularly through their memories of lost symbolic recognition, welfare rights and multi-ethnic coexistence in the workplace. At the same time, the ambivalences and contradictions in current and former workers' memories are also discussed, particularly in relation to workers' naturalized double burden and in relation to class hierarchies within the factory.

The fifth and final chapter 'Beyond nostalgia: Workers' struggles for social justice and everyday resilience', addresses garment workers' demands for social justice and everyday resilience, in relation to wider social movements against privatization and corruption in the post-Yugoslav region. It considers in particular workers' strikes and political initiatives, such as the Kamensko workers' strike of 2010, but also various cultural projects initiated by activists of younger generations who feel emotionally connected to the textile industrial heritage, as well as individual workers' everyday resilience taking the form of cross-border work migration, informal work and handcrafting. The conclusion of the book, finally, assesses the implications of the book for gender history and social history in the post-Yugoslav region, arguing for the need for further cross-border, comparative research on industrial workers' structure of feeling in socialist Yugoslavia and in post-Yugoslav states.

1

Industrializing Yugoslavia: Market socialism and textile workers' structure of feeling

We were nine children in the family and we all lived off our father's wage as a Tivar worker. That's why we, my brothers and I, had to start working as soon as we were strong enough. So I started working at 13 years old. But in order to be accepted for work, I had to lie and say that I was born in 1932 rather than in 1934, which was the truth. In the beginning we walked to the factory because there was no other choice. The work was divided into three or four shifts. The first shift started at 5.00 am and ended at 1.00 pm. In order to 'warm up', we sang the whole way from Trnovac to Varaždin. We had no proper footwear, so we wrapped our legs in nylon bags, and those who had shoes carried them in their hands until the city, and wore them only then. We were poor, but united and cheerful. And yes, I immediately had to hand in my wage to my daddy, as we affectionately called him. And that continued for a long time, until I got married.

Anka Ž., Varteks worker since 1947.[1]

Difficult living and working conditions were common among textile workers in the interwar era, and they were further aggravated by the devastation caused by the Second World War in Yugoslavia. After the war, when previously private textile factories were nationalized by socialist authorities, most textile workers across the country lived in dire poverty and deprivation. This chapter retraces the beginning of the textile industry in the interwar Kingdom of Yugoslavia. It also describes the numerous workers' strikes that occurred in the 1920s and 1930s, which later became embedded in the socialist narrative about workers' resistance against capitalist exploitation.

---

[1] The extract is published in the commemorative album published by the Varteks factory in 2008, *90 priča za 90. Rođendan Varteksa* (Varaždin, 2008), priča 15.

The rest of the chapter deals with the transformations of garment factories in the period after the Second World War. Workers' experiences in textile factories were marked first by Soviet-style industrialization, and then, after 1948, by the new self-management system coined by Yugoslav leaders after the Soviet–Yugoslav split of 1948. Throughout this time, the textile sector also played a significant role in the socialist politics of women's emancipation. According to socialist ideals, backward village girls had to be turned into modern, active self-managers. In many villages, young women entered the factory and started working outside the home for the very first time, challenging patriarchal norms and traditions, and developing the specific industrial structure of feeling that is analysed throughout this book. Despite fast industrial growth and redistributive efforts, workers' living standards remained critical throughout the 1950s. It is only in the 1960s that the country could be considered industrialized, and well-being across social strata significantly increased.

Textile factories in the interwar era

Textiles emerged as a global product from the beginning of industrialization, especially after textile production became increasingly mechanized in the nineteenth century.[2] Global textile industries generally employed a predominantly female, young and rural workforce, which could provide cheap labour, 'nimble fingers' as well as political 'docility'. Each national and regional context, however, presented different articulations of gender, class and labour.[3] The first textile factories in the South-East European region date from the late nineteenth century, when Slovenia, Croatia, Bosnia-Herzegovina and Vojvodina were part of the Austro-Hungarian Empire. Croatia's oldest factory, the cotton mill in the town of Duga Resa, was founded in 1884. The majority of textiles, however, was produced in Bohemia, Moravia and Czech Silesia, and consequently in the newly independent Czechoslovakia after the fall of the empire in 1918.[4] As a result, in the newly created Kingdom

---

[2] Lex Heerma van Voss, Els Hiemstra-Kuperus and Elise van Nederveen Meerkerk (eds), *The Ashgate Companion to the History of Textile Workers, 1650–2000* (London, 2010).
[3] Janet Hunter and Helen Macnaughtan, 'Gender and the global textile industry', in Heerma van Voss, Hiemstra-Kuperus and van Nederveen Meerkerk (eds), *The Ashgate Companion to the History of Textile Workers*.
[4] Andrea Komlosy, 'Austria and Czechoslovakia: The Habsburg Monarchy and its successor states', in Heerma van Voss, Hiemstra-Kuperus and van Nederveen Meerkerk (eds), *The Ashgate Companion to the History of Textile Workers*.

of Serbs, Croats and Slovenes in 1918, local textile production took time to develop. The Kingdom's heavy and light industry was dominated by foreign companies, which also opened new textile plants.[5]

As reconstructed by the late Zdenka Simončić-Bobetko, 49 per cent of overall imports in 1920 Yugoslavia consisted of textile. From 1925, however, a new regime of custom protections favoured the expansion of the local industry, heavily taxing finished products from outside while allowing the cheap import of raw materials. Except for hemp production, which was widely exported, making Yugoslavia the third hemp exporter in the world, the other yarns (wool, cotton, linen, jute, silk) were produced only for the internal market, or imported from abroad, so that spinning plants remained limited, while weaving and knitting mills boomed in the interwar era. New interwar factories were the result of local or foreign entrepreneurs' investments, and of monopolistic concentrations of capital, which included foreign banks.[6] Cheap and outdated machinery was usually imported from neighbouring countries, and low-paid workers were easily available, especially in rural areas. Due to the fact that Yugoslavia was mainly rural and 80 per cent of local inhabitants produced their own garments in their farms, the internal textile market remained limited to the main urban centres. Yugoslavia had 14.5 million inhabitants in 1931, but only 4 to 5 million citizens could be described as having consumer power.[7]

Between 1932 and 1939, the overall labour force in textiles grew from 31,461 workers to 60,908 for the whole of Yugoslavia. Women made 57.43 per cent of all textile employees in 1939. In Slovenia, Kranj and Maribor became the main centres of the cotton industry, with Maribor totalling 7,000 workers in local textile factories, usually owned by local entrepreneurs in joint ventures with Czech and Austrian investors.[8] In Croatia, the case study of Simončić-Bobetko, 60 per cent of textile workers were so-called 'workers-farmers', and 78.38 per cent of all workers were concentrated in Zagreb and in the north-western part of the country, in the cities of Duga Resa, Varaždin, Donja Stubica and Čakovec.[9] The working conditions in the industry were

---

[5] Carl Ulrik Schierup, *Migration, Socialism and the International Division of Labour: The Yugoslavian Experience* (Aldershot, 1990), pp. 38–9.
[6] Zdenka Šimončić-Bobetko, 'Razvoj tekstilne industrije u Hrvatskoj u razdoblju između dva svjetska rata (1918-1941)', *Povijesni Prilozi* 1 (Zagreb, 1982), pp. 101–203, see English summary pp. 202–3.
[7] Ibid., p. 121.
[8] Marjan Matjašić, *Jugoslovanski Manchester: mariborska tekstilna industrija – The Manchester of Yugoslavia: Maribor textile industry* (Maribor, 2016).
[9] Ibid., p. 131.

known to be very exploitative. Simončić-Bobetko wrote for instance that, in interwar Croatia,

> workers in the textile industry often worked longer than the agreed working time. People worked mostly in very bad hygienic conditions. Working rooms were cramped, without enough air and poorly lit. The consequences of working and living in bad conditions, and the low wages affected the health of the workers. Even if it was the first generation of workers, many were sick and unable to work. An important number of workers suffered from tuberculosis.[10]

These statements can be generalized to the rest of the Kingdom of Yugoslavia if we look at the volume written by Jovanka Kečman on women's participation to workers' struggles in the interwar era.[11] A wide array of strikes and protests reportedly happened in the textile industry, and Kečman is listing many textile workers' grievances across Yugoslavia. Kečman noted that of the 57.5 per cent of female employees in the garment industry, which approximately meant 24,000 workers depending on yearly fluctuations, 41 per cent were below nineteen years old. Even if labour was forbidden below fourteen years of age, cases of younger children and teenagers working in the industry were common.[12] In Serbia, working conditions were reportedly very exploitative in Belgrade, Leskovac and other smaller centres, which frequently employed children. All across the Kingdom, the level of exploitation in garment factories was very high, with working days lasting up to 16 hours a day, and unpaid overtime and night work. The average wage was not close to a living wage, and women were paid much less than men. In the textile factory Stipe Šare in Šibenik, for instance, men were paid 10 to 15 dinars, while women received 4 to 7 for the same work.[13] At the Tivar factory in Varaždin, men received an hourly rate of 3.5 to 6 dinars, whereas women got 1.50 to 2.5 dinars, leading the management to employ more and more women to save on labour costs.[14]

Textile workers, women especially, were active against difficult working conditions and state repression, joining trade unions, women's organizations of different orientations and political parties, including the newly founded Communist Party of Yugoslavia (KPJ). In 1924, twenty-two-year-old textile

---

[10] Ibid., pp. 136–7.
[11] Jovanka Kečman, *Žene Jugoslavije u radničkom pokretu i ženskim organizacijama 1918-1941* (Belgrade, 1978).
[12] Ibid., p. 29; p. 33.
[13] Ibid., p. 51.
[14] Ibid., p. 52.

worker Ljubica Ljubičić was killed in custody in a police station after being accused of stealing on the shopfloor of a Belgrade canvas factory, generating a protest in front of the factory.[15] Textile workers' strikes for higher wages and better living conditions were reported in the following locations in the early 1920s: Duga Resa, Zagreb, Pančevo, Novi Sad, Split, Sarajevo, Subotica, Kumanovo, Belgrade, Šabac, Zemun, Sombor, Užice, Kraljevo and Kragujevac. Important strikes in Duga Resa and Belgrade were recorded also in the late 1920s. The 1930s were also characterized by important strikes in textile, particularly in Croatia. In January 1935, a mass strike of 900 workers was organized in the cotton mill Hermann Pollak and sons in Zagreb.[16] In 1936, the most known interwar workers' strike took place in Varaždin, in the textile industry known as Tivar, founded in 1918, which employed 2,300 workers, of which more than half were women. Workers demanded a minimal hourly wage and the equality between men's and women's wages. After six weeks, the strike was won and a new collective agreement was signed.[17] In this same year, a common trade union for textile workers across Yugoslavia was founded (*Ujedinjeni savez tekstilno-odevnih radnika i radnica Jugoslavije*). Only 5 per cent of workers across the country, however, were organized in trade unions. Strikes also occurred in Slovenia and Serbia in 1936–7. In 1937, workers striked in different firms in the Leskovac area, South of Serbia, to ask for a 8-hour working day. Workers toiled for 10 to 16 hours, and children below ten years of age were also included in production.[18] The first significant textile strike in Bosnia-Herzegovina was organized in 1938 at the Ključ stockings factory in Sarajevo, involving 180 workers.[19] In the Macedonian city of Bitola, a textile strike was also organized in 1938. Also in Macedonia, a strike was organized in 1940 in the Vardar garment factory in Skopje. In the same year, strikes took place in Mostar, Herzegovina, and in Novi Sad, Vojvodina.

In the 1930s the Yugoslav communist party attempted to expand its membership among working women. A few young communist garment workers became radicalized, and further looked for employment in garment factories with the goal of organizing workers in unions, as in the case of partisan heroines Vukica Mitrović (1912–41), from Montenegro,

---

[15] Ibid., p. 136. On this specific case, see also Gordana Stojaković, 'Povodom međunarodnog praznika rada. Po drugi put o slučaju tekstilne radnice Ljubice Ljubičić i nešto malo o Klari Cetkin', 27 April 2016. Available at: http://pravonarad.info/?p=909 (accessed 20 January 2018).
[16] Kečman, *Žene Jugoslavije u radničkom pokretu*, p. 220.
[17] Ibid., pp. 225–6.
[18] Ibid., p. 239.
[19] Ibid., p. 243.

who organized textile workers in the Belgrade suburb of Karaburma, and Anka Butorac (1906–41), a worker of peasant origin who was among the organizers of the Tivar strike in Varaždin in 1936.[20] Other textile workers who later died in the partisan struggles were: Marijana (Marija) Gregoran (1921–41)[21], from Čakovec, organizer of the Karaburma strikes in 1939–40; Leposava Stamenković (1915–43), born in a well-known antifascist family in Leskovac, also active in Karaburma; the sisters Jelena (1923–43) and Mara Đorđević – Ćućulika (1919–42), garment workers and strike organizers from Leskovac; Đurđelina Đuka Dinić (1913–43), a worker and organizer at the leather factory in Niš.[22]

Since textile workers strongly contributed to the interwar left-wing workers' movements, and as many of them lost their lives in the antifascist resistance during the Second World War, it is not surprising that they were made into heroes and martyrs during the socialist era, with factories and streets renamed after them. Most importantly, the conditions of severe exploitation which existed in the textile sector before the Second World War came to be used as the symbol and benchmark of an unwanted capitalist past, which the socialist system was meant to overcome.

'Factories to the workers': From shock-work to self-management

In 1945, the Yugoslav communists came to power after a successful antifascist resistance against foreign occupation and local collaborationist forces. By spreading a message of 'brotherhood and unity' between different ethnicities and nationalities, and by combining this message with a hopeful vision of social change, they managed to gain grassroots supports across ethnic groups. The country they inherited, however, was devastated by war, plagued by immense human losses and by the destruction of pre-war material infrastructure. Following the Soviet model, Yugoslav authorities thus embarked upon an overly ambitious plan of fast industrialization, which served both economic and ideological purposes. Existing industries and properties belonging to upper class citizens and political opponents, notably, were confiscated and nationalized, in order to support the newly

---

[20] Ibid., p. 329; p. 226.
[21] Ibid., p. 258.
[22] See the biographies included in the publication edited by Women in Black, Belgrade, *Leskovac iz ženskog ugla* (Belgrade, 2012). Available at: http://zeneucrnom.org/pdf/Leskovac.pdf (accessed 20 January 2018).

established popular powers. Also, the Yugoslavs nationalized many mines and factories, including textile factories, that had already been expropriated by Nazi Germany during the occupation: 'The lead and zinc mines at Trepča (formerly British), the Allatini chrome mine (formerly British), the Bor copper mine (formerly French), the Zenica steel plant, the Bata leather works (formerly Czech), and many textile and cotton mills – a total of 55 per cent of Yugoslav industry.'[23] To Yugoslav authorities, industrialization seemed to be the best guarantee for economic independence from foreign powers, which had dominated the local industry in the interwar period. In its first post-war years, the industrialization effort was overwhelmingly focused on infrastructure and heavy industry: hydro-plants, electrification, metal factories, chemical factories and the mining industry were at the centre of state investment. This focus on heavy industry meant, however, that resources from the agricultural sector were overwhelmingly transferred to the industrial sector, causing a wide array of damage also due to the politics of collectivization of the land.[24] The light industry of immediate consumer goods was also neglected. Existing textile industry, in particular, produced consumer goods of low quality, with very old machines and with a constant shortage of necessary raw materials. This resulted in shortages of food and basic consumption items across the country.[25]

The Yugoslav authorities strove to remedy to the lack of resources and raw material by mobilizing a cheap, largely peasant and illiterate workforce. Next to the inclusion of workers in all the emerging factories, masses of men and women were also mobilized to join the reconstruction effort through voluntary work (which sometimes bordered on forced labour). Special 'work actions' of male and female youth were organized, particularly to construct new railroads and highways such as the so-called Brotherhood and Unity Highway between Slovenia and Macedonia, or the Brčko-Banovići railway in Bosnia and the Lupoglav-Štalije in Istria.[26] Young antifascists and communists from abroad also took part in some of these actions before 1948.[27]

---

[23] Susan L. Woodward, *Socialist Unemployment: The Political Economy of Yugoslavia, 1945–1990* (Princeton, 1995), p. 57.
[24] Melissa Bokovoy, *Peasants and Communists: Politics and Ideology in the Yugoslav Countryside, 1941–1953* (Pittsburgh, 1998).
[25] Ivana Dobrivojević, 'Industrijalizacija kao imperativ. Ekonomska politika Partije 1945–1955', in L. Duraković and A. Matošević (eds), *Socijalizam na klupi. Jugoslavensko društvo očima nove postjugoslavenske humanistike* (Pula-Zagreb, 2013), pp. 19–45.
[26] Andrea Matošević, 'Omladinske radne akcije: kontinuiteti i odmaci iz iskustva *akcijaša*', *Traditiones*, 44/3 (2015), pp. 93–111.
[27] See for instance the work actions' account contained in the biography of Italian communist Luciana Castellina, *Discovery of the World: A Political Awakening in the Shadow of Mussolini* (London, 2014).

The situation further worsened with the economic blockade that followed the Soviet–Yugoslav split in 1948, which caused Yugoslavia's economic isolation and cessation of exchanges with the countries belonging to the socialist bloc. Workers' ideological and material mobilization became even more stringent in this period of international isolation and reduced capital flows. Work brigades were encouraged to engage in competitions in fulfilling the quotas required by the Five Year Plan (1947–52). *Udarništvo*, or shock-work, which had already started in 1946–7, became an important symbol of Yugoslavia's self-reliance after 1948. Yugoslav shock-work was modelled after Soviet Stakhanovism, but after the Soviet–Yugoslav split it was aimed to challenge Stakhanovism by showing that Yugoslav workers could easily overcome past Soviet work records. Those selected as best workers, the male *udarnik* or the female *udarnica,* would receive material prizes, but especially countrywide recognition in the press.[28]

Textile workers were also part of the so-called 'Movement for high productivity'. The Nada Dimić textile factory in Zagreb originated from the merging of different pre-war textile firms, and was named after a young partisan heroine, a Serbian student from Lika, who was murdered by the Ustasha forces at age nineteen. At Nada Dimić, a notable *udarnica* was Sonja Erbežnik, who carried out her five-year plan in 'two years, 8 months and 21 days', and received a 10,000 dinars prize. Another heroine of labour was Slavica Travkikar, a twenty-one years old textile worker in the Ivančića factory in Ivanec, near Varaždin, who simultaneously worked at twenty different looms. Obviously such workers were supposed to be giving an example in raising the productivity of socialist factories. Of Slavica, for instance, it was said that 'her colleagues are proud of her and are seeking to emulate her working achievements'.[29] A female shockworker in textile was also the protagonist of *Story of a Factory* (1949), a socialist realist movie set in a Zagreb textile factory, in which the young heroine strove to augment productivity and work simultaneously on different looms, but was injured by a bomb placed by the pre-war factory owner, who attempted to sabotage the new collectively owned socialist factory.[30]

---

[28] Andrea Matošević, *Socijalizam s udarničkim licem. Etnografija radnog pregalaštva* (Zagreb, 2015).
[29] The vignette from *Glas Rada* (9 January 1948) is contained in Matoševic, *Socijalizam s udarničkim licem,* p. 148. On Sonja Erbežnik, see ibid., p. 63.
[30] Nebojša Jovanović, *Gender and Sexuality in the Classic Yugoslav Cinema,* PhD dissertation (CEU Budapest, 2014), p. 138.

Labour shortages and low productivity, however, persisted despite such symbolical and material mobilizations of shock-work.[31] In order to find new forms of revolutionary legitimation that could counter the excommunication from the socialist bloc, but also in order to find ways to increase the productivity and the discipline of the labour force, Yugoslav leaders turned to the idea of workers' self-management, which derived from Marx's early writings on free association of producers. The new self-management doctrine, developed from the early 1950s, opposed the Soviet model of state control over the planned economy, and led to a decentralization of state power and to the proclamation of workers as decision makers within their own factory. A new law in June 1950 'rendered the workers' collective of a single enterprise a sovereign body, able to debate and vote upon fundamental factory matters through the workers' council, elected among its members'.[32] Even more importantly for the 'self-perception of the working class' was the definition of the factory as social property, with each worker de facto becoming 'a property-owning producer receiving a share of the company's income'.[33] Another relevant element to workers' social property was the fact that most social services were paid through income taxation, so that part of workers' wages were used for the establishment and funding of welfare services.[34]

Workers' social property of their own factories, as I will show in this book, was indeed an important component of the industrial structure of feeling developed during Yugoslav socialism. This structure of feeling, however, was equally influenced by the gap between workers' formal entitlement in decision-making and the reality on the ground. Critics of self-management have underlined the excessively bureaucratic character of the system,[35] as well as managers' privileged position in decision-making deriving from their party affiliation and educational status, which resulted in blue-collar workers' low participation to self-management institutions. As concrete examples will later make clear, indeed 'the workers did not feel they had the necessary time, competence or information to make increasingly

---

[31] Woodward, *Socialist Unemployment*.
[32] Goran Musić, 'Yugoslavia: Workers' self-management as state paradigm', in Dario Azzellini (ed.), *Ours to Master and to Own: Workers' Control from the Commune to the Present* (Chicago, 2011), p. 175.
[33] Ibid., p. 177.
[34] Ellen Turkish Comisso, *Workers' Control under Plan and Market: Implications of Yugoslav Self-management* (New Haven, 1979), p. 79.
[35] Ichak Adizes, *Industrial Democracy: Yugoslav Style* (Los Angeles, 1977).

complex market decisions, so they let management formulate the options and present them to the workers' council'.[36] This was especially the case for low-skilled female workers in industries such as textiles. The decentralization of economic decision-making at the municipal and republican level, moreover, favoured competition among the different republics and fragmentation in the redistribution of resources. From the beginning of industrialization, local party functionaries strove to direct industrial investments to their own village, town or region, without much concern for the development of the Federation as a whole.[37] This extremely decentralized economic structure – and the emphasis on workers' ownership of *their own* factory – meant that workers' interests and loyalties were framed as coinciding with the ones of the firm they worked in. The self-managed system ultimately, as noted by Goran Musić, 'discouraged the formation of an all-Yugoslav working class with a sense of common interest'.[38]

The self-management system had also a specific depoliticizing effect on trade unions, which had been at the forefront of workers' struggles in the interwar era. While in the late 1940s the unions were seen as pedagogic instruments or 'schools of socialism' for workers, whom they mobilized following the Soviet model, thus 'imposing the party's or management's control over the working class', after the establishment of self-management they became part of the internal functioning of the factory, and thus their role consisted in 'inducing self-control within the working class', in the words of Sharon Zukin.[39] Within socialist factories, trade unions were mostly in charge of social welfare functions (allocating apartments, scholarships, organizing holidays, excursions and other fringe benefits), and of different form of legal aid to workers. Indeed, in textile workers' memories trade unions are prevailingly associated with the organization of social rights and leisure within the factory. It is not surprising, thus, that workers were also deeply aware of the ambivalence of trade unions' role in the system, and that strikes mainly happened outside unions' control – the first strike in the federation was led by Slovenian miners in Trbovlje in 1958.[40]

The need to improve living standards for workers was finally acknowledged by the 1958 Seventh Congress of the League of Communists,

---

[36] Musić, 'Yugoslavia', p. 178.
[37] Dobrivojević, 'Industrializacija kao imperativ', pp. 32–3.
[38] Musić, 'Yugoslavia', p. 177.
[39] Sharon Zukin, 'The representation of working-class interests in socialist society: Yugoslav labor unions', *Politics & Society* 10/3 (1981), pp. 281–316, p. 293. From the same author, see also *Between Marx and Tito: Theory and Practice in Yugoslav Socialism* (London and New York, 1975).
[40] Ibid.

which emphasized the need for a rise in workers' living standards and led to new investments in light industry.[41] By the mid-1960s, Yugoslavia itself had turned into an industrialized country, and socialist consumer culture had greatly expanded across republics and social strata.[42] The socialist economy, however, had grown increasingly dependent on Western loans and foreign markets after the split with the Soviet Union, and economic competition between most developed and least developed republics had increased.[43] After the 1965 economic reforms, which further liberalized market socialism in a decentralized direction, intra-federal redistribution was halted and unemployment emerged as a specific paradox of the socialist system in Yugoslavia, with Yugoslav foreign workers looking for fortune and better living standards abroad.[44]

All these elements – the difficult post-war industrial beginnings, the ambivalences of self-management, the ideological and material mobilization of the new labour force and the periodical fluctuations of the Yugoslav economy – contributed to create the industrial structure of feeling that was typical of socialist factories. The existing literature on self-management provides precious insights into the overarching historical, political and economic mechanisms of the Yugoslav system, and on its pitfalls. It tells us less, however, about the social impact of industrialization on ordinary working class and peasant citizens, particularly women. The significance of the self-management experiment needs to be understood in parallel to another important process, namely, the access of masses of women to education and labour after 1945, as a result of the new ideology of women's emancipation through productive work propagated by the communist party and by socialist women's organizations. With a specific attention to intersection of gender and class, the rest of the chapter will highlight the trajectory of socialist garment factories from their post-war beginnings until the mid-1960s, mapping the parallel implementation of self-management and the emergence of a new, young female labour force that moved from the

---

[41] Igor Stanić, 'Društveno-ekonomski položaj radničke klase u Hrvatskoj 1950-ih', in I. Duda, A. Buhin and I. Stanić (eds), *Radionica za suvremenu povijest* (Pula-Zagreb, 2013), pp. 27–47.
[42] Marie-Janine Calic, 'The beginning of the end – The 1970s as a historical turning point in Yugoslavia', in M. Calic, D. Neutatz and J. Obertreis (eds), *The Crisis of Socialist Modernity: The Soviet Union and Yugoslavia in the 1970s* (Göttingen, 2011); Patrick Hyder Patterson, *Bought & Sold: Living and Losing the Good Life in Socialist Yugoslavia* (Ithaca, 2011).
[43] Vladimir Unkovski-Korica, *The Economic Struggle for Power in Tito's Yugoslavia: From World War II to Non-Alignment* (London, 2016).
[44] Woodward, *Socialist Unemployment*.

villages to the cities in search of a better life, as a result of the Yugoslav politics of women's emancipation through productive labour.

Biking to the night shift: Women's emancipation through labour

In order to understand the industrial structure of feeling created in socialist garment factories, another important historical element needs to be added to the picture, namely, the socialist politics of women's emancipation promoted by the Antifascist Women's Front (*Antifašistički front žena*), or AFŽ. The organization – led by a generation of urban and educated prewar female communists – was founded during the Second World War in an effort to mobilize women of all backgrounds, and especially illiterate peasant women, in support of the antifascist resistance led by the Yugoslav communist party. During the war, over 100,000 women fought as partisans, and the organization reached over a million women in its activities. Women's participation in the antifascist resistance proved crucial for the victory of the National Front led by the Communist Party. The AFŽ – transformed after 1945 into a hierarchical, federal organization – continued its activities in the post-war era, focusing notably on eradicating illiteracy and infant mortality, and mobilizing women in support of the socialist government. The activities of this organization have been the object of a wide array of studies and debates among feminist scholars.[45] As I have argued elsewhere, even if the AFŽ could never properly be considered as an autonomous women's organization, it nonetheless opened up a space for women's different degrees of political agency at different moments in time.[46]

The AFŽ as a women-only political organization was dissolved in 1953, and replaced with another loose network of women's associations called the Union of Women's Societies (*Savez ženskih društava*, or SŽD). This event has often been read by feminist scholars in the region as the reinstatement of patriarchal control over women's autonomous organizing, and as the end of all women's organizations in socialist Yugoslavia. Yet, the creation of the SŽD

---

[45] See notably Lydia Sklevicky, *Konji, Žene, Ratovi* (Zagreb, 1996); Barbara Jancar-Webster, *Women & Revolution in Yugoslavia – 1941–1945* (Denver, 1990); Jelena Batinić, *Women and Yugoslav Partisans: A History of World War II Resistance* (Cambridge, 2015); Andreja Dugandžić and Tijana Okić (eds), *Izgubljena revolucija: AFŽ između mita i zaborava* (Sarajevo, 2016).
[46] Bonfiglioli, 'Women's political and social activism'.

constituted an attempt to integrate – or better decentralize – women's issues and interests within the newly founded self-management system. In the view of communist female leaders, decentralized women's societies were to appear in each locality, in order to solve the specific issues related to women's participation to self-management in each specific commune or republic. The dissolution of a federal, hierarchical organization like the AFŽ, whose orders ran from its Belgrade main office to the republican councils, until the local councils, meant that women were supposed to become engaged and 'self-manage' their specific interests in cooperation with local institutions and authorities. This, however, did not always happen, often because of many women's lack of time and interest in politics, but mostly due to the reluctance of local party officers, trade unions, workers' councils and local institutions in supporting women's organizing and women's rights. A number of women's organizations, sections and initiatives, however, continued to be present at the local level and within factories, so that it would be erroneous to state that the 'women's question' was closed once and for all with the dissolution of the AFŽ in 1953.[47]

The socialist revolution certainly did not solve the issue of patriarchal domination, but it nonetheless challenged traditional patriarchal views that were rooted in rural life and its gendered division of labour. Even within interwar Yugoslavia, patriarchal practices greatly differed according to the various regional traditions and historical legacies. Women's subordination and exploitation in rural areas, however, was widespread and generally tied to the hierarchies based on gender and age that were typical of the extended household, the *zadruga*.[48] Peasant women's grassroots participation to the antifascist struggle partially subverted traditional gender roles.[49] Women's equality as citizens and workers was inscribed in the 1946 Yugoslav Constitution, and so was welfare protection for mothers and children, particularly in the case of working mothers. Civil marriage also became obligatory, replacing the different family codes which existed in each region before the Second World War.

This new modernizing message was at odds with rural patriarchal practices, and for the first time treated women as legally autonomous individuals and productive subjects. In the view of socialist elites, it was necessary to transform not only women's role in the productive sphere, but also family relations, which were supposed to become more 'modern', 'egalitarian' and

---

[47] Ibid.
[48] Vera Stein Erlich, *Family in Transition: A Study of 300 Yugoslav Villages* (Princeton, 1966).
[49] Batinić, *Women and Yugoslav Partisans*.

compatible with the gendered norms and customs which were typical of the educated middle class. As Woodward noted, this family model 'was foreign to much of the population, although closer perhaps to the small, urban, nuclear family of many policymakers or to the marriages of political and revolutionary comrades during the war or the radical days immediately preceding it'.[50] Such new model undoubtedly presented patriarchal elements when it came to gender norms and the gendered division of labour inside the home, and reinforced women's role as main caretakers in the family. At the same time, the socialist model significantly departed from patriarchal rural traditions, and recognized that women's reproductive tasks needed to be socialized in order for women to enter the workforce. It would be reductive, therefore, to consider the socialist politics of women's emancipation as an imposed, homogenous form of 'state patriarchy', without recognizing that a major shift in gender norms had happened during the Second World War and in its aftermath, as a result of women's mass participation to antifascist politics, and as a result of the new legislative and cultural changes that followed.[51]

In line with Marxist ideology, female communist leaders attempted to spread the message of women's emancipation across the country, even if they rarely received sufficient support from their surroundings, and even if they often had to start from scratch, so to say, due to the big social differences existing between them and the women they had set to emancipate.[52] Educating illiterate women to reading and writing, and to hygienic norms, was often the first step adopted by this generation of antifascist pedagogists. Mobilizing women to work outside the home was the consequent second step. During the Second World War, besides literacy and sanitation classes, AFŽ leaders had organized sewing, knitting and weaving workshops. The resistance movement was in dire need of clothing, and many peasant women already possessed such feminized skills, which were valorized and mobilized by antifascist leaders.[53] Even after the dissolution of the AFŽ, its former leaders continued to propagate their socialist gendered pedagogies.

In the early 1950s, a teacher and partisan from Herzegovina, Rajka Borojević, who took shelter with her husband and two children in rural

---

[50] Susan L. Woodward, 'The rights of women: Ideology, policy and social change in Yugoslavia', in S. L. Wolchik and A. G. Meyer (eds), *Women, State and Party in Eastern Europe* (Durham, 1985), p. 241.

[51] Bonfiglioli, 'Women's political and social activism'. See also Franciska de Haan (ed.), 'Forum: Ten years after, communism and feminism revisited', *Aspasia*, 10 (2016), pp. 102–68.

[52] Ibid.

[53] Batinić, *Women and Yugoslav Partisans*.

Serbia during the war, and who felt indebted to the local peasant population, moved to the village of Donji Dubac, where she started her first pedagogic workshops with peasant women in 1954.[54] A member of the plenum of the Central Committee of the AFŽ in the late 1940s, Rajka Borojević had already led cultural-political courses for peasant women in Banja Luka. Peasant women in Banja Luka, notably, had been introduced to factories and met 'many female shock-workers about whom they had heard previously, but without believing their stories when they were told at conferences'. The villagers also saw how books and newspapers were printed, and were taken to the theatre, the cinema and various political events. They were also 'placed in the different homes of the best activists, so that they could see how to cook, how to raise children, and could learn everything that villages still lack'.[55]

In Donji Dubac, Borojević managed to set up a variety of workshops, after winning the resistance of local male peasants, who finally agreed to let their wives attend the classes. Borojević's classes included a theoretical part (hygiene of the home, women's hygiene and sexual education, first aid, childcare, alcoholism, food, etiquette) and a practical part (cooking, serving, preparing preserves, making soap, dying textiles, knitting and sewing, collecting aromatic and medicinal plants, beekeeping, cultivation of raspberry, handwork, singing).[56] Women walked several miles from various surrounding villages to attend. Later, villagers were taken to study visits in Belgrade, where they went to the cinema for the first time in their lives, and later to Sarajevo, Banja Luka, Kumrovec (Tito's birthplace) and Zagreb. In the early 1960s, the Dragačevo weaving cooperative was launched, to increase women's economic independence in the community. Women's position in the village gradually improved, and in 1967, the newly founded House of Culture even hosted the finals of 'The Best Husband' competition, during which women openly assessed the most respectable prospective mate.[57]

---

[54] Rajka Borojević, *Iz Dubca u svet* (Belgrade, 2006), first edition 1964. See also Natalja Herbst, 'Women in socialist Yugoslavia in the 1950s: The example of Rajka Borojević and the Dragačevo Women's Cooperative', in R. Kersten-Pejanić, S. Rajilić and C. Voß (eds), *Doing Gender-Doing the Balkans* (München, Berlin, Washington DC, 2012). See also the recent artistic project on Rajka Borojević curated by her granddaughter Ana Džokić, *Taking Common Matter into Your Own Hands*. Available at: http://www.stealth.ultd.net/25_taking.common.matter.into.your.own.hands.html (accessed 3 December 2016).

[55] Zapisnik IV Plenuma Glavnog Odbora AFŽ-a, Sarajevo, 13 March 1948. The Archives of Bosnia-Herzegovina, Sarajevo, box 5, 2912/32, p. 7.

[56] Borojević, *Iz Dubca u svet*, p. 39.

[57] *Najbolji Muž* (Vera Jocić, 1967). Available at: https://vimeo.com/134070626 (accessed 20 January 2018).

The weaving cooperative, renamed after Rajka Borojević, employed up to 300 women in different neighbouring villages, and functioned until 2010.

As shown by this example, socialist gendered pedagogies were based on an holistic view of social transformation, which aimed to reshape both women's productive and reproductive spheres, turning peasant women into self-managers, but also making sure that they would be conscious wives and mothers in their family life.[58] Gendered pedagogies were implemented within socialist factories, through various educational courses and through the presence of women's societies or women's 'actives' (*aktiv žena*) within each factory (from 1961 onwards, the main women's organization was called, in fact, the Conference for the Social Activity of Women, *Konferencija za Društvenu Aktivnost Žena*, or KDAŽ). As I will show in the next chapter, such organizations within the factory were usually active around Women's Day celebrations, or voiced female workers' various demands for additional welfare services.

Specific suggestions targeting women were present in factory newspapers, which also detailed a wide array of classes and workshop targeting female workers. In the town of Duga Resa, some 60 kilometres south-west of Zagreb, whose daily life was dominated by the spinning mill founded in 1884, a new People's University had been created in 1948, offering a variety of courses and screening movies on the most disparate political and practical subjects. In 1955, the factory newspaper, after a survey among workers, reported that the following proposed themes were the ones that had received most votes:

1) Causes and consequences of divorce, 152 votes;
2) Dalmatian national songs, 121 votes;
3) Can the H-bomb destroy the world, 110 votes;
4) Alcoholism and curing alcoholics, 102 votes;
5) Does the world go towards peace or towards war, 101 votes;
6) Rheumatisms and how to cure them, 96 votes.

Interestingly, the newspaper commented, women were the most interested in learning more about divorce, Dalmatian songs and alcoholism.[59] In 1955, Duga Resa women's society, called *Aktivnost Društva Naprednih Žena*

---

[58] See also Blanka Tivadar and Andreja Vezovnik, 'Cooking in socialist Slovenia: Housewives on the road from a bright future to an idyllic past', in Luthar and Pušnik (eds), *Remembering Utopia*; Wendy Bracewell, 'Eating up Yugoslavia: Cookbooks and consumption in socialist Yugoslavia', in Paulina Bren and Mary Neuburger (eds), *Communism Unwrapped: Consumption in Cold War Eastern Europe* (Oxford, 2012).

[59] Duga Resa workplace periodical, 11 (1955), p. 5.

(The Activity Society of Progressive Women) organized workshops in the surrounding villages, on the subjects of cooking and preserving food. The society also distributed People's University's lecture tickets among women, and made sure that there were themes of women's interests among the teachings. Next to this report, the factory newspaper published a special column titled 'Advice for women'.[60] The column admonished parents – but especially mothers – who pampered children too much, and thus limited their autonomy and ability to relate with others. The column continued in the following number, advising parents on how raise children using reasonable rules instead than fear, with a variety of practical examples.

The socialist gendered pedagogies enacted within garment factories aimed to counter existing models of femininity, especially in rural areas, where women mainly worked at home and in the fields and were subjected to the hierarchies of the extended household, or *zadruga*.[61] In the rural area around the small town of Sinj, 30 kilometres from the coastal city of Split, the Dalmatinka (Dalmatian woman) spinning mill was founded in 1951 (Figure 2). The foundation of the factory in Sinj is attributed to the will and perseverance of Vice Buljan (1905–78), a communist from an upper class family who managed to become town mayor already in 1940 during the Kingdom of Yugoslavia, and who was later a partisan and politician. The factory originally had to be placed in the nearby town of Livno in Bosnia-Herzegovina, but Vice Buljan managed to redirect the project to Sinj. At the entrance of the factory, a commemorative plaque stated:

> Through the struggle of the working class of Yugoslavia, and under the direction of the League of Communists and of comrade Tito, it was realized Marx's and Engels' principle, 'Factory to the workers', and this factory on the 4th of November 1951 for the first time came under the management of the workers' collective.[62]

Workers, however, and particularly female workers, were far from being conscious self-managers in charge of production in the early 1950s. At the very beginning of Dalmatinka, only very poor village girls accepted to work in the factory, while most of the community and local families rejected young women's possibility to work outside the home, which was seen as something immoral. People in the villages would talk of the factory as a whorehouse

---

[60] Duga Resa workplace periodical, 16 (1955), p. 4.
[61] On changes in traditional family patterns in rural Yugoslavia, see Erlich, *Family in Transition*.
[62] Vedrana Premuž Đipalo, 'Žene u Doba Socijalizma: Slučaj "Dalmatinka"', *Ethnologica Dalmatica*, 23/1 (2016), pp. 159–92.

Figure 2 Work at the Dalmatinka spinning mill, Sinj, 1950s. Courtesy of Muzej Jugoslavije, Belgrade, and Dalmatinka Project, Sinj.

(*kurvanjska tvornica*), where girls went prostituting themselves ('*ona se kurva u Dalmatinki*').[63] The night shift was seen in particular as a cause of moral panic, especially due to the fact that at the time, since there was no bus available, the only mean of transportation for working women who lived in the neighbouring villages was walking or cycling. Young women who cycled to the factory were often despised by the local community, as a former worker recalled within the factory newspaper:

> People avoided us, the mothers of those girls who did not work in the factory told to their children: don't hang out with them, they work in the factory, and that meant being disreputable in our region. As for the excursions, there was no way, we had to lie that it was compulsory to go, that it was a working trip, otherwise we could not go. Travelling to work with the only available mean of transportation, the bicycle, was seen as something very immoral, and not rarely there were cases of old women who crossed themselves and closed their eyes when they saw our workers hurrying to the factory on the bike.[64]

---

[63] Ibid.
[64] Dalmatinka workplace periodical, 8 (1981), p. 5.

This testimony was published in the factory newspaper thirty years after the creation of the factory, in the early 1980s, when young workers found these stories extremely funny and hard to believe, due to the fact that women's work outside the home had become by then taken for granted. It took at least ten years, however, before the opening of the factory led to a change in mentalities. As related by a former Dalmatinka worker, it is only when it became apparent that young workers were bringing money home, and improving theirs and their families' lives, that everyone started to long for factory jobs ('many people did not want to give their girls to the factory, but later begged [for their employment]').[65] In the early years of Dalmatinka, anyhow, women from rural areas often combined work in the factory with work in the fields in summer, often falling asleep at the machine. Some workers also never got used to wearing trousers, and quickly went back to their traditional long skirt (*šotana*, from the Italian *sottana*) after factory work.[66] Initially, it was also common for women to hand their wages to their husband, or mother-in-law.[67]

Within factory newspapers published across Yugoslavia during late socialism, such stories were often part of the myth of foundation of each socialist factory. They stood as the proof of socialist factories' modernizing influence when it came to workers' living standards, including female workers.[68] Narratives of gendered modernization, however, somehow remained in the background, and were often limited to a reinstatement of women's achieved equality as workers and citizens on Women's Day (8 March). Most prominent were female workers' narratives that emphasized material progress and economic growth, as well as individual sacrifices for collective well-being. As I show in the following chapter, such narratives appeared in the countless testimonies of pensioners, often former partisans or shock-workers, who recounted their difficult post-war beginnings and the extraordinary material progress they had witnessed during their working lives, as well as their inevitable hardships as workers, wives and mothers. In the rest of this chapter, I will continue my exploration of the formation of workers' structure of feeling within socialist factories, by looking at how work discipline, welfare rights and community values were fostered within each firm, and by considering how local and world politics entered the walls of the factory.

---

[65] Premuž Đipalo, 'Žene u Doba Socijalizma', p. 169.
[66] Ibid.
[67] Rebeka Mesarić Žabčić and Marina Perić Kaselj, 'Žene i Industrijska Baština: primjer "Dalmatinke" Sinj', in A. Černelić Krošelj and H. Rožman (eds), *Kulturna dediščina industrijskih panog i industrijska kulturna baština* (Ljubljana, 2011), pp. 286–300.
[68] Vodopivec, 'On the road to modernity', pp. 621–2.

The factory as a socialist microcosm: Work, welfare and leisure

Garment factories built after 1945 functioned as socialist microcosms, in which everyday work coexisted with a variety of political, social, educational and cultural activities. As Rory Archer and Goran Musić have argued:

> The socialist factory, not only as the site of employment and production, but also as an important institution of political activity, daily routine and leisure practices, is a fruitful entry point for the exploration of multifaceted aspects of socialist modernization, its contradictions and demise.[69]

Factories were a crucial site of redistribution of welfare services (canteens, health services, childcare facilities, subsidized housing and holidays) and other fringe benefits (scholarships and trainings, solidarity funds, banking), which were organized and administered by the trade unions in cooperation with workers' council and management. Yugoslav factories also hosted sport associations, safety organizations such as the firefighter brigades, women's organizations and cultural clubs of various kinds. Such arrangements were typical not only of Yugoslavia, but of socialist factories more generally, and of their strong integration between the realm of production and the realm of social reproduction. In the Polish town of Nowa Huta studied by Kinga Pozniak, similarly,

> Lenin Steelworks provided subsidized meals at work, day care for the workers' children, medical care, company-funded holidays, and other cultural and recreational programs for the entire family. The steelworks also owned and operated a vocational school, a cultural center, a sports club and stadium, movie theaters, and a local newspaper, and it assisted in the construction of a significant share of the town's housing.[70]

Socialist factories, thus, were a space in which a variety of socialist pedagogies were applied in the field of work, welfare, leisure and culture, and interiorized by workers themselves.[71] Socialist pedagogies – which, as I have showed in the previous section, were also gendered pedagogies – aimed to turn male and female villagers into conscious industrial workers and self-managers.

---

[69] Archer and Musić, 'Approaching the socialist factory', p. 44.
[70] Pozniak, *Nowa Huta*, p. 34.
[71] On the 'making' of socialist citizens, see also Igor Duda (ed.), *Stvaranje socijalističkoga čovjeka. Hrvatsko društvo i ideologija jugoslavenskog socijalizma* (Zagreb and Pula, 2017).

As Adizes noted in his study of industrial democracy in socialist Yugoslavia published in 1971,

> Self-management is, and still appears to be, a major national educational project. If they are compelled to manage, workers have to learn to read, to compute, to account, to forecast – in other words, to acquire a certain amount of sophistication. The peasant of yesterday has to learn for a good reason: his paycheck will grow as he shares the results of the company's effort.[72]

Not every worker, however, benefited from socialist pedagogies and socialist modernization in the same way, as scholars of self-management have shown. Within factories, social differentiations between skilled and unskilled workers, blue-collar and white-collar workers, men and women, urban workers and 'workers-peasants', party members and non-party members were created and reproduced in the course of time.[73] Social mobility through education appeared to be very significant in the early socialist phase, but was practically inexistent in the late socialist period.[74]

Within garment factories, the majority of blue-collar workers were female and unskilled. As soon as they arrived in the factory, often as trainees from vocational schools in their teenage years, they had to grow accustomed to the discipline of the *norma*, that is, piece-rate production. Each worker had to reach a certain *norma* everyday, meaning a certain amount of produced pieces, which was calculated by the so-called *normirac* or *normirka*, a staff member who would chronometer each work action and determine how many pieces a worker could produce per minute and per hour. Blue-collar workers in the spinning, weaving, knitting and sewing phases generally alternated on three shifts, either during the same week or during consecutive weeks: a morning shift, an afternoon shift and a night shift, with breaks of half hour for a meal. Workers in certain phases, such as cleaning or controlling the final production, were not subjected to the *norma*. If women had managed to achieve a technical education beyond basic schooling, either before or, more rarely, during their time within the factory, they could aspire to career progression as middle managers or white-collar staff, particularly in the early socialist period when qualified managing personnel was missing and workers were encouraged to achieve further education. Getting to such positions meant to escape the *norma*, and thus to have a less restricting working

---

[72] Adizes, *Industrial Democracy*, p. 233.
[73] Archer and Musić, 'Approaching the socialist factory'.
[74] Ibid.; see also Archer, Duda and Stubbs (eds), *Social Inequalities*.

rhythm. Older workers or workers with disabilities were also regularly assigned to tasks which were not 'normed' (*normirane*), such as controlling and cleaning phases. Men in garment factories were either technicians (*majstori*) or directors. During the socialist era, factory directors in the garment industry were inevitably male, even though many women reached white-collar status in secretarial, trade union and other middle management jobs. Factory directors and management staff had significant autonomy and decision-making powers in the socialist era, and often established corporatist and paternalist relations with their workers.[75]

Management's autonomy grew significantly after the economic reforms of 1965, which increased the independence of firms from the state, and their competitive stance on the world market, by reducing taxes and diminishing price controls. Firms' autonomy, then, 'meant not only that enterprises made their own decisions regarding prices, wages, investment, and other business matters, but also that they bore the consequences of these decisions'.[76] Workers' income depended directly from factory's profits, as well as on one's individual performance. It consisted of different components: 'individual basic salary, bonuses based on personal achievement, shares in the Economic Units' profits, and shares in the profits of the company'.[77] Workers did not know their final salary for a certain month until they saw the check, whose variable part could amount to a maximum of 60 per cent. According to Adizes, this made it difficult for the low-qualified worker to plan his or her expenses, especially if credit repayments were taken out of the salary each month. In the unnamed Belgrade textile factories where he conducted fieldwork in the late 1960s, on payday Adizes noted 'many pale, tearful faces; people stood with a paycheck in one hand, with faces lifted and eyes glassy'.[78]

Undoubtedly market socialism meant that the factory's productivity was often put before workers' needs, especially in labour intensive and feminized sectors such as textiles. All textile workers I interviewed complained that wages in textile were always very low compared to other industrial sectors. Yet, they also added that wages were always on time, and that they allowed a much greater purchasing power than today's post-socialist wages. A wide array of welfare benefits partially compensated for workers' low wages, since workers made use of free health services and housing, subsidized canteens and holiday facilities, and received yearly summer holiday allowance or *regres*. Factory jobs provided a symbolical and material access to the Fordist

[75] See Adizes, *Industrial Democracy*. See also Musić, 'Yugoslavia'.
[76] Comisso, *Workers' Control under Plan and Market*, p. 74.
[77] Adizes, *Industrial Democracy*, p. 49.
[78] Ibid., p. 182.

promise of increasing living standards, consumption and well-being. Such promise was a constituent element of socialist industrialization in Yugoslavia, and appealed to so many of its citizens due to the widespread hardships that they had experienced during the Second World War and in the immediate post-war era. Even in the republic of Slovenia, traditionally considered the most developed of Yugoslavia, the post-war daily life of the working classes was characterized by sheer material deprivation. Factory jobs, thus, often embodied the possibility of economic growth and material progress, even if achieved through hard work and sacrifice. This is best exemplified by the life story of Majda (born 1944), a Slovenian seamstress from Celje, whom I could reach through her niece, an art curator.

The industrial Slovenian town of Celje hosted the textile factory named Metka (from *Mehanička Tkalnica*, weaving mill), founded in 1929 by a Czech Jewish owner. During the socialist period, the new nationalized Metka came to employ up to 1,000 workers, who mainly produced bed linen and underwear (Figure 3). Majda started to work at Metka when she was fifteen years old, in 1959. Her father was a bricklayer, travelling all over the country, and her mother a housewife. With five children at home, there was no money to continue studying and work had to be found as quickly as possible. Her mum often cried, she recalled, because she could not buy what she needed for her children. Once, she told me, a neighbour offered her mum to buy a pair of trousers for Majda, since they were too small for her daughter. Her mum took them and said she would pay upon the return of her husband. Majda wore the pants in church only. Still, as her father would not be back with money after two-three weeks, she had to give the trousers back to the neighbour.

Majda told me that everything had to be recuperated, mended, used and reused. The laundry was washed in the river with ashes, and they came out unbelievably white and clean, better than in a washing machine, she said. Shortly after she started working at Metka, in 1961, Majda received a special retreat paid for by the factory for young workers below 50 kilograms of weight. She was supposed to stay ten days, but when the staff saw that she was benefiting from the retreat, they let her stay for a month. The food was good, she said, and she ended up gaining eight kilos:

> When I came back to the factory everyone looked at me, how much weight I gained (*she laughs*). I went with 47 kilos and came back with 55. At 17, you know, it was hard to wake up at 4.00 am, you wanted to sleep so much.[79]

---

[79] Majda, Celje, January 2016.

Figure 3 The Metka factory in post-war Celje. Courtesy of Zgodovinski Arhiv Celje.

The walk to the factory took half an hour, since there were no buses at the time. There was also no canteen at the beginning, so food had to be brought from home. The story of Majda's teenage retreat sheds light on the social aspects of the factory, and on authorities' propensity to provide welfare services, leisure and holidays for workers as a way to keep the workforce healthy and productive – even if economic resources were scarce. Since 1945, socialist authorities promoted social tourism for ordinary citizens and workers through the construction of subsidized holiday centres (*odmarališta*) and through the establishment of paid summer leaves. Most factories had a subsidized holiday facility, often on the Adriatic Sea, or in mountain and lake resorts. Trade unions had an important role in managing such facilities, and in providing different holiday options for workers. White-collar families, however, were more likely to take holidays and to benefit from such facilities, while working-class families were often lacking time and money for travelling, or were not accustomed to the idea of leisure travel itself.[80]

In 1964, Majda married Adin, a Bosnian worker who came to live and work in Celje as a mechanic in a factory. That is when she arranged to have running

---

[80] Igor Duda, 'Adriatic for all: Summer holidays in Croatia', in Luthar and Pušnik (eds), *Remembering Utopia*. See also Grandits and Taylor (eds), *Yugoslavia's Sunny Side*.

water installed inside the home. Shortly afterwards, when her first daughter was born, they decided to travel to Trieste to buy a washing machine. When her second daughter was born, and when a football tournament was about to start, two years later, they bought a television. Majda and her husband received an apartment from the factory, which was 'small but cozy'. Taking advantage of the normalization of foreign relations with Italy and of open borders since the late 1950s, the majority of Yugoslav citizens headed to Trieste for shopping, where they could find items that were either unavailable or too expensive in their home country. In 1965, more than 11 million motor vehicles crossed the border, and by the mid-1970s, 'the journey to Trieste had become a monthly, or at least seasonal, event for the majority of the Yugoslav population.'[81] In the eyes of Yugoslav citizens, Trieste symbolized Western capitalism, modernity, variety and opulence. Paradoxically, socialist modernization had brought levels of economic growth that allowed such mass consumption, but could not fulfil new consumers' demands and expectations due to the limits of the socialist economy. Majda smiles when she recalls the joys of her trip across the border:

> For us Italy was incredible, here there was socialism as in Russia, nothing was available, in Italy there was everything, modern. I looked at all the shop windows. It was also cheaper. And we bought coffee. Going to Italy was the greatest celebration, we were so happy, I bought everything for the kids, it was much cheaper. In Trieste everything was beautiful, interesting. Shop windows were not the same here, you could not see everything you wanted. Everything was better in Italy. For us, Italy was worth gold (*zlatna vredna*). Shopkeepers were really nice, they earned a lot with us. They let us buy even if they had to close. ... There was so much people. On the Riva [Trieste's main walkway by the sea] you would only see Yugoslavia (*Na rivi samo Jugoslaviju si vidio*). I was happy, I bought everything, even if I could not buy much. I liked to have something special. Today girls have all sorts of things. I remember when I bought some shoes, some *opanke*, with a bit of heel, I felt so good, so well dressed. [Products from] Yugoslav factories were expensive. At 23 I already had two daughters, I could not buy things for me but I bought things for them, so my mum gave me something, she said: 'Buy something for yourself.'[82]

---

[81] Breda Luthar, 'Shame, desire and longing for the west: A case study of consumption', in Luthar and Pušnik (eds), *Remembering Utopia*, p. 342.
[82] Majda, Celje, January 2016.

Majda's testimony highlights the structure of feeling created not just by industrialization and economic growth, but also by Yugoslavia's open borders and new possibilities of consumption in neighbouring Italy which came about in the mid-1960s, after the immediate post-war experiences of material deprivation. It also shows how, for women, patterns of consumption were inevitably interrelated with individual habits of self-sacrifice that sustained the family budget. The apparent contradictions in Majda's narrative testify working-class women's constant battle between what they desired, what they could afford, and what had to be sacrificed for the sake of the children. ('I bought everything, even if I could not buy much'; 'I could not buy things for me but I bought things for them'; 'Buy something for yourself.') In the following section, I highlight how white-collar workers in garment factories also oriented women's lives and choices through discourses and practices of welfare paternalism.

Balancing welfare and productivity: Paternalist management in socialism

State socialist regimes' reliance on welfare redistribution as a source of legitimacy has been conceptualized through the concept of 'socialist paternalism', or of a 'parent-state' which imagined itself as a family, with the Communist Party at its head.[83] Even if paternalism was undoubtedly a feature of socialist rhetoric, in the Yugoslav case paternalism can be best described as a diffused phenomenon, particularly when it came to technocrats, white-collar workers and the ruling classes in charge of politics and the economy. The first generation of managers and white-collar workers, who were often of communist convictions, thought of themselves both as entrepreneurs who had to maximize the factory's profits on the market, but also, simultaneously, as enlightened chiefs who had to take care of workers' well-being and living standards within the limits of their factories' budget. Another oral history interview, this time with a white-collar worker who started her career in the 1950s, well illustrates the mix of work discipline and welfare paternalism that characterized workers' structure of feeling within the factories. The Istrian town of Pula, which was assigned to Yugoslavia in 1947 after two years under Allied military government, saw the exodus of the majority of its Italian population in the immediate post-war years. In a formerly Italian-owned tobacco factory on the seashore across the harbour, a knitwear factory was

---

[83] Verdery, 'From parent-state to family patriarchs', pp. 225–55.

founded in 1947 and named after Olga Ban (1926–43), a young local partisan heroine killed by the occupation forces. The factory started as a workshop to provide supplies to the army, and continued thanks to the hiring of qualified staff, who had completed textile schools in Belgrade and Zagreb. Together with the Astra shoe factory nearby, the Olga Ban knitwear factory employed most women from the town and from the surrounding villages. In the early 1960s, after the merging of the factory with two other firms in Novigrad and Pazin,[84] the factory took the name of Arena, due to the Roman amphitheatre that dominates the city of Pula. Since then, the firm was known as the Arena knitwear factory (*Arena Trikotaža*). The local inhabitants often just call it Trikotaža, being it Olga Ban or Arena.[85]

The secretary of the Arena factory from 1961 until 1981 was Bruna, a brisk eighty-eight-year-old woman who is still an authoritative figure in town, and is now in charge of the pensioners' trade union. After her economic high school diploma, Bruna came to Pula with her husband, who had been in the partisans and was a state officer, and took up clerical work in the factory in 1956, until she was promoted secretary in 1961. Then, a great effort was placed in qualifying the existing clerical staff and the blue-collar labour force at Arena. Clerical staff had to follow adult education in economics, even if many spoke little Croatian due to the previous politics of Italianization of the region, which meant that primary school was in Italian. A knitting school was organized for regular workers since the mid-1950s, so that they could reach the status of qualified workers and increase their monthly wages. Women constituted 96 per cent of the labour force, including both blue-collar and white-collar workers (Bruna herself, a head of accounting, and a chief of production), while the leading director, the technical director and commercial director were male. The factory employed many village women who were very poor, widowed, or single mothers (*samohrane majke*). This term, which indicates the mother as the sole breadwinner (lit. the only one that feeds), is still commonly used, and it conveys a sense of legal welfare entitlement, together with the indication of a difficult social position, which

---

[84] The Pazin factory affiliated to Arena was previously named Istranka. From 1958 onwards, Pazin also hosted an important chemical and textile factory that produced synthetic threads, named Pazinka, which employed up to 1800 workers. See Nikolina Rusac, *Pazinka. Kulturnoantropološki i muzeološki pristupi tematizaciji industrijsko nasljeđa socijalizma*, MA dissertation (University of Zagreb, 2014).

[85] The factory started with around 400 workers in 1948, and employed over a thousand workers in the late 1960s. These numbers gradually diminished, with over 700 employees in the 1970s and around 650 employees on average in the 1980s. In the 1990s, employees were in the 350–400 range. Arena, 'Naših Prvih 50 Godina', commemorative catalogue (Pula, 1998). When it closed in 2014, sixty-two workers were left.

should be protected and respected. Bruna is particularly proud of the social role of the factory towards single mothers. Her sensitivity on this matter was probably enhanced by the fact that her late sister was also a single mother. As in every garment factory, sick leaves (*bolovanje*) were frequent, due to women's caretaking responsibilities, but factory management attempted to improve the situation, according to Bruna:

> So there was this problem with sick leaves, but we helped many women to get their children accepted in crèches and kindergartens. That helped. At a certain time we had a very good canteen so that workers, not many of them, but those who lived alone, they could always bring a meal home for the child and so on. We helped as much as we could. At a time there were stories about the knitwear factory employing 'social cases'. And that's how it was.[86]

Bruna recalled that many young women who came to Pula from the surrounding villages ended up marrying young men from the local navy base, who had migrated from all over Yugoslavia.[87] Every Saturday in the canteen there were parties organized in cooperation with the army and its orchestra, and at least a hundred Arena workers married local army officers. At least twenty factory workers gave birth outside of wedlock, so that the factory had to help them to raise their children. In Yugoslavia, children born out of wedlock had the same rights as other children, but the popular stigma around 'illegitimate' births was very high, especially in rural areas. Abortion was legal from 1951, but only in limited health-related cases and after approval of a specific medical commission. Only from 1960 onwards it was also allowed for social reasons after commission's approval, until 1969, when the interruption of pregnancy became completely liberalized.[88] Many women looking for an abortion in the early socialist period, thus, fell into the hands of what Bruna calls *false babice*, fake midwives who adopted 'primitive' methods, and ended up risking their lives. Bruna's sister also wanted to see

---

[86] Bruna, Pula, June 2015.
[87] Marriages with male workers employed in the Uljanik shipyard were also very frequent. As Maja Maksić writes in her MA dissertation on the history of the Arena knitwear factory, 'Uljanik and [Arena] Trikotaža were the standard combination of typical working class families in Pula – the dad employed at Uljanik, the mum at [Arena] Trikotaža'. Maja Maksić, *Trikotaža Arena Pula. Etnologija Ženskog Rada*, MA dissertation (University of Pula, 2016).
[88] Mirka Merunka-Golubić, 'Reprodukcijska Prava', in D. Dijanić, M. Merunka-Golubović, I. Nijemčić and D. Stanić (eds), *Ženski biografski leksikon. Sjećanje žena na život u socijalizmu* (Zagreb, 2004), pp. 342–4.

the doctor to have an abortion, but Bruna convinced her that she could perfectly raise a child on her own.

As the secretary of Arena, Bruna paid special attention to single mothers when the factory's collective holiday came, which was generally spent in an *odmaralište* (holiday resort) in Slovenia. Bruna herself spent ten days of holidays with the workers, sometimes bringing her son, and twenty days of holidays with her husband. She sometimes encouraged the most destitute female workers to take a holiday:

> Bruna: Those who were on their own, and poor ... by all means. I even had to oblige some to come. [I said:] 'At home you have nothing decent to eat, take a rest, if you take a rest even the production will be different.'
> C.B.: Why didn't they want to go?
> Bruna: You know, some were saying: 'poor me, what shall I wear, how can I.' Yes, yes, there were women that we had to persuade to take a rest. And afterwards they were happy they came.[89]

Female workers' reluctance to take advantage of subsidized holidays was not an isolated case, as made clear by a report documenting similar cases among the employees of the Slovenian knitwear factory of Rašica – Arena's direct competitor – in the 1970s.[90] Bruna's position illustrates the enlightened paternalism that was typical of socialist factories, which were supposed to educate peasants into becoming disciplined workers, and conscious citizens. Discipline, however, went hand in hand with human understanding based on socialist principles, as in the case of a poor worker who was caught stealing a shirt for her daughter at the exit of the factory. Usually, a traffic light installed at the exit of the factory would go green or red, and randomly establish which worker had to undergo a check. In this case, however, other workers had phoned the concierge and had suggested the management to carry out a check, so that the woman was found guilty and got sacked. After a month, however, Bruna went to the director and told him: 'Come on, director, let's

---

[89] Bruna, Pula, June 2015.
[90] Vuteks workplace periodical, 198 (1977), p. 2. The report explicitly mentions that female workers from the less developed parts of Slovenia had to be convinced of the usefulness of paid annual leave. A similar case is reported by Igor Duda for the Varteks resort held on the island of Rab in the late 1950s, whose ninety beds could not be filled, even if Varteks employed over five thousand workers. Many workers, especially those of peasant origin, were not used to the idea of travelling for holiday, and preferred to stay home. Igor Duda, *U potrazi za blagostanjem. O povijesti dokolice i potrošačkog društva u Hrvatskoj 1950-ih I 1960-ih* (Zagreb, 2005).

take her back, she is a good worker, she won't do it again, she is poor, she did it for her daughter.' The worker was hired once again after Bruna's intervention.

Arena's factory director from 1966 to 1989, Ivan Škrinjarić, shared a similar paternalist ethic, which combined productivism and economic entrepreneurship with an attention to the modernization of workers' living standards. In 2015 the former director, now a retired economist in his late eighties, gave a long interview to the main Istrian newspaper, *Glas Istre*, titled 'We were producers, bankers and traders – the factory was our home' (*Bili smo proizvođači, bankari i trgovci – tvornica je bila naša kuća*).[91] As he retold in the interview, at the beginning of his career in the late 1940s, Škrinjarić started to work at the Umberto Gorjan factory in Novigrad, which had modern Swiss machinery, since it was part of the Free Territory of Trieste until 1954. The Olga Ban factory in Pula, instead, worked with old machinery imported from nationalized mills in Slavonia, which made it uncompetitive and led to the sacking of 400 workers in the early 1960s. In 1963, after the merging of the Novigrad, Pula and Pazin garment factories due to market reforms, all the cadres moved to Pula, with Škrinjarić becoming commercial director. Three years later, in 1966, the economy was again in crisis and the Novigrad complex had to be liquidated, while workers from another garment factory in the nearby island of Cres had to be integrated into the company. Škrinjarić, then, was appointed general director of Arena by the Party, and lobbied for the possibility to modernize the entire machinery park in order to save production from bankruptcy. New Swiss knitting machines were bought on credit, and in order for the factory to access liquidity, an internal bank was created, so that most workers deposited their wages in the internal factory bank, and received a 12 per cent credit for their savings, which were used to fund new investments, particularly shops across Yugoslavia, where production was sold without having to pay intermediary fees. As Škrinjarić himself summarized in 2015:

> We concluded that if we wanted to survive, we had to enrich ourselves and save ourselves in three ways: to be producers and to make money from our work, to be bankers – we were laughing at that! – and from that make some interest, become ourselves creditors and live off the interest; and, finally, to be sellers, selling our own products in our own stores and save that part of the income.[92]

---

[91] Duška Palibrk, 'Bili smo proizvođači, bankari i trgovci – tvornica je bila naša kuća', *Glas Istre*, 24 April 2015.
[92] Ibid.

These new economic arrangements brought to the booming of the factory from the late 1960s onwards, and to a wide array of investments in workers' living standards, which Škrinjarić defines as the 'humanisation of work' (*humanizacija rada*) (Figure 4).

In 1972-3, Arena was equipped with an air conditioning system, before all major Pula hotels. The old canteen was turned into a modern restaurant, also 'at hotel standard' (*na nivou hotelskih*). The bathrooms for workers were also equipped with towels, soap and shampoo, so that women could wash themselves before leaving, at a time in which not all of them had a bathroom at home. A factory clinic was also added in the 1970s, which included a doctor and a nurse, as well as gynaecologists, orthopaedics, dentists and oculists visiting the factory periodically. A florist was even in charge of displaying fresh flowers within the factory. As Škrinjarić further recalls, female workers went to have systematic controls at the specialized hospital Thalassotherapia in Opatija and there were frequent trips organized across Yugoslavia. All workers received special prizes for their fifteen years of work (a golden necklace), their twenty-five years of work (a golden ring) and for their thirty-five years of work and retirement (a golden broche). Prizes were distributed during special celebrations held on the 1st of May (International Workers' Day) at the Home of the Yugoslav National Army, *Dom JNA* (now renamed Home of Croatian Veterans, *Dom Hrvatskih Branitelja*), a beautiful 1913 palace built in the centre of Pula as a recreational site for the Austro-Hungarian Navy,

Figure 4 The canteen in the Arena factory, Pula. Reproduced with permission from the Arena factory archive in 2015.

which is still used today as the main hall for various events, including Pula's local book fair. Škrinjarić expressed his pride for the factory's modernization and social impact on workers' lives, which he greatly attributes to his own initiative and to the collaboration of the managing staff. He made sure to stress that decision-making was a prerogative of the qualified management: 'We said, self-management, yes. But the representatives of workers are only half of the self-management process, the other half are the qualified cadres (*stručni kadar*). ... Even in capitalism there should be a constant connection between owner, manager and worker' (Figure 5).[93]

In garment factories like Arena, self-management practices remained strongly in the hands of white-collar workers, while blue-collar workers were the beneficiaries of what was defined as the increasing 'humanization of working conditions'. Male factory directors enjoyed a specific gendered prestige as well as strong discretionary powers in the self-managed Yugoslav economy. Their personality, decision-making and authority were an integral part of the industrial structure of feeling developed within socialist factories. They had to balance between party directives, entrepreneurship

Figure 5 Arena's director Ivan Škrinjarić with leading communist politician Milka Planinc. Reproduced with permission from the Arena factory archive in 2015.

[93] Ibid.

and social concerns, and had to find creative ways of coping with the fluctuating socialist market economy and world economy. This competitive atmosphere of market socialism was recalled by two of my narrators, blue-collar workers at Arena, who described the skills of a former technical director and joked that 'each of his moustache was worth a thousand dinars!' Thanks to Yugoslavia's Non-Aligned foreign policies, garment factories exported to Western Europe and North America, but also to the Soviet Union and to Non-Aligned countries in the Middle East, especially Iran, Iraq, Kuwait, Libya and other emerging markets. Raw material, on the other hand, was often imported from other Non-Aligned partners, such as India or Egypt. From the 1960s onwards, socialist factories had frequent commercial exchanges with Asia, Africa and the Middle East. As I will show later in the book, such transnational exchanges, together with Yugoslav factories' competition on the internal and on the international market, contributed to reinforce workers' attachment to the prestige of their factory, and to the quality of its production at an international level.

2
Being a seamstress in Yugoslav times: The 'working mother' gender contract

When my mum gave birth to me it was 1962. Then maternity leave only lasted a month and a half. ... Do you know how it is for women after giving birth? Breastfeeding, milk and all that. My mum says it was terribly hard. She worked three shifts, and left me to a neighbour who would take care of me while she worked. She did not do four hours, she worked the full eight hours. And at night as well, no one asked if she had a small baby at home.

Leda, white-collar worker, Varaždin, April 2016.

The widespread entry of women in industrial jobs after 1945 posed new issues for the socialist state, particularly when it came to guaranteeing the protection of working mothers, which was inscribed in the 1946 Yugoslav Constitution. This chapter deals with the specific position of women working in the garment industry during the socialist period, discussing in particular the ambivalences of the 'working mother' gender contract established during the socialist era. I propose to historicize the phenomenon of the 'double burden' of productive and reproductive work throughout the different decades of socialist Yugoslavia, from the early to the late socialist period, rather than simply using the term as a shorthand for the pitfalls of socialist gender politics. As I will show, discussions of women's work within and outside the home simultaneously valorized and naturalized women's multiple obligations between society and the family. This simultaneous valorization and naturalization of women's double burden, which informed the socialist welfare system, also shaped female workers' specific structure of feeling within garment factories. Through archive material and through the analysis of two documentaries and a television series, the chapter aims to highlight women's different forms of agency in the midst of conflicting societal messages and constraints, with a specific focus on the late socialist era.

Re-conceptualizing the double burden in the Yugoslav context

The theme of women's double burden during the socialist era has been widely addressed within feminist literature on state socialist regimes, particularly in the 1990s.[1] Socialist regimes have been faulted for conceptualizing 'women as workers *and* mothers without any parallel conceptualization of men's role', as well as for additionally pressuring women to be politically active on the top of it, a phenomenon defined as the 'triple burden'.[2] With time, these insightful earlier analyses crystallized into (post-)Cold War 'common knowledge' about gender regimes in Eastern Europe,[3] and into a ritualistic denunciation of women's victimhood under state socialism, despite the fact that the phenomenon of the double burden is common to advanced industrial economies across the world, and despite the fact that socialist regimes often provided more gender equality in the sphere of labour than capitalist democracies, which were largely following the male breadwinner model.[4]

Within scholarly discussions about socialist Yugoslavia, women's double burden – together with the abolition of the Antifascist Women's Front in 1953 and the lack of autonomous women's organizations – has become a shorthand formula for the failure of the socialist state in achieving the women's emancipation it had promised. Working-class women's agency and the ways in which female workers appropriated labour and welfare entitlements have been often silenced.[5] Studies of gender, class and welfare

---

[1] See notably Chris Corrin (ed.), *Superwomen and the Double Burden: Women's Experiences of Change in Central and Eastern Europe and the Former Soviet Union* (Great Britain/Canada, 1992); Barbara Einhorn, 'Where have all the women gone? Women and the women's movement in East Central Europe', *Feminist Review*, 39 (1991), pp. 16–36; Barbara Einhorn, *Cinderella Goes to Market: Citizenship, Gender, and Women's Movements in East Central Europe* (London, 1993); Maxine Molyneux, 'Gendered transitions in Eastern Europe', *Feminist Studies*, 21/3 (1995), pp. 637–45.
[2] Einhorn, 'Where have all the women gone?', p. 19.
[3] Ghodsee and Liskova, 'Bumbling idiots or evil masterminds?'
[4] For a comparison of women's position in the labour markets of Austria and Hungary in the twentieth century, see Fodor, *Working Difference*, p. 65.
[5] See, for instance, Renata Jambrešić-Kirin and Marina Blagaić, 'The ambivalence of socialist working women's heritage: A case study of the jugoplastika factory', *Narodna Umjetnost*, 50/1 (2003), pp. 40–73. Even if the article is extremely well researched and well argued, the voices of former Jugoplastika workers are practically absent from the analysis, since they do not fit with the authors' views on the socialist era: 'Their narratives reveal a selective view and evaluation of their lives in socialism; a lack of critical reflection on their own ideological position within the local and national context, a nostalgic look back at the economic empowerment they experienced and pride in the

are available for other post-socialist contexts[6], but in the Yugoslav case, little is known about how female workers differently coped with conflicting obligations at home and outside the home, and how class differences influenced labour, welfare and consumption. As Malgorzata Fidelis has shown in her study of industrialization and gender in post-war Poland, women interacted with socialist industrialization processes and with the authorities' conceptualizations of the double burden in many different ways. That is why it is important to historicize the concept of the double burden, as Fidelis suggests, and to look at how it ultimately reproduced women's subordination, without, however, assuming that women had no agency in the process.[7] Backlashes in gender equality, moreover, also have to be read in connection to de-Stalinization processes and increased openness to the Western markets and models of consumption and femininity.[8]

When it comes to the Yugoslav case, as mentioned earlier, a wide array of welfare services was put in place within factories across the country to favour women's participation to the labour market, configuring the 'working mother' gender contract typical of the socialist bloc. After the model of the Soviet Constitution of 1936, the 1946 Yugoslav Constitution recognized women's equal role as citizens and workers and their right to equal pay. At the same time, it also recognized women's role as mothers, and their entitlement to increased social rights when combining paid work and domestic work. Article 24 stated: 'Women have the right to the same pay as that received by men for the same work, and as workers or employees they enjoy special protection. The state especially protects the interests of mothers and children by the establishment of maternity hospitals, children's homes and day nurseries and by the right of mothers to a leave with pay before and after childbirth.' Together with the vision of work as a source of human emancipation, and as the main source of emancipation for women, the Yugoslav state after 1945 promoted the socialization of domestic work and social reproduction, namely, the so-called 'social motherhood' that was ingrained in the Soviet model after Marxist theory.[9]

---

skill with which they performed their working tasks.' As an example, see also Drakulić, 'How women s (post-) communism (and didn't laugh)'.

[6] See, for instance, on the Hungarian case: Lynne Haney, *Inventing the Needy: Gender and the Politics of Welfare in Hungary* (Oakland, 2002); Susan Zimmermann, 'Gender regime and gender struggle in Hungarian state socialism', *Aspasia*, 4 (2010), pp. 1–24.

[7] Fidelis, *Women, Communism, and Industrialization in Postwar Poland*, pp. 11–12.

[8] Ibid., pp. 214; 244.

[9] Bonfiglioli, 'Women's political and social activism'.

This 'working mother' gender contract was maintained after the break with the Soviet Union in 1948, when the resolution of women's welfare protection was delegated to every single factory and municipality, following the decentralized self-management system. Because of decentralization, and because of a developing economy, however, welfare services could not always keep up with the fast pace of industrialization, especially in smaller towns and villages. Each factory decided upon the construction of workers' canteens, health clinics, factory housing and subsidized holiday centres, and federalized regulations on welfare provisions gradually subsided, which meant that women's access to welfare services was highly uneven, and that women's paid and unpaid labour in the household provided a buffer to the frequent crises and reforms of the socialist economy. Maternity leaves, for instance, were federally regulated in the early socialist era, providing six weeks from 1946 onwards, which were subsequently extended to 105 days of paid leave in 1957. Since the mid-1960s, each republic had the right to allow additional days of leave. In Slovenia, 141 additional paid days (shareable between both parents) were allowed since 1974, while in Croatia from 1973 it was possible to claim 180 additional paid days. It is only between the late 1970s and the mid-1980s that each republic extended paid maternity leave up to a year. Women were also protected from night shift and from dismissal during pregnancy and in the first year of life of their child.[10] In the field of childcare, however, there was no federal regulation as to the extent of welfare provisions in each republic or factory.

Moreover, as scholars of socialist economy have pointed out, due to a labour surplus women in Yugoslavia, unlike in the rest of Eastern Europe, were not pressured to enter the labour force (except for some sporadic cases during immediate post-war mobilizations). Women's employment rates reached a maximum average of 33–40 per cent in the 1970s and 1980s, making Yugoslavia more similar to Western Europe than to Eastern European socialist regimes.[11] As I will show in this chapter, the so-called 'triple burden'

---

[10] Federally regulated maternity leaves went from 6 weeks of paid before and after childbirth in 1946, to a total of 105 days from 1957 onwards. See Mira Alinčić, 'Law and the status of women in Yugoslavia', *The Columbia Human Rights Law Review*, 8 (1976–7), pp. 345–72; Marta Korintus and Nada Stropnik, 'Hungary and Slovenia: Long leave or short?', in S. B.Kamerman and P. Moss (eds), *The Politics of Parental Leave Policies: Children, Parenting, Gender and the Labour Market* (Bristol, 2009).

[11] According to Woodward, the share of women in the social sector labour force was of 33 per cent in the late 1970s. Woodward, 'The rights of women', p. 245. Milić reports that women made up 39.6 per cent of total employment in 1990. Anđelka Milić, 'Women and work in former Yugoslavia and their present situation', in Barbara Łobodzińska (ed.), *Family, Women, and Employment in Central-Eastern Europe* (Westport, CT, 1995), p. 238. Milica Antić, after Pesić, reports the following rates for the different Yugoslav republics

of political participation could also be easily avoided by invoking the 'double burden' itself, so that we cannot talk of state enforcement in that sphere either. In this context dominated by uneven economic development, decentralization and rural/urban divides, women's social position was largely determined by intersections of gender, class, education and geographical location. As Woodward aptly noted, 'the autonomy given to domestic relations by the new government and an economy founded on market principles have tended to reinforce the importance of social origin ... in defining the set of opportunities and constraints within which most Yugoslav women operate.'[12] As other authors have noted, social stratifications, including gender, were also crucial in determining who could benefit from the 'Yugoslav dream' of consumption and rising living standards.[13] The openness of Yugoslavia to the West, in addition, led to a fascination towards urban and bourgeois femininity in popular culture and advertisement, so much so that working-class readers complained of not being equally represented in women's magazines.[14]

Besides social origins, women's opportunities in socialist Yugoslavia were also constrained by the gendered segregation of jobs in the labour market, as in other socialist countries, a widespread phenomenon which resulted in gendered pay gaps across the region.[15] Since most women of working class or peasant origin were employed as unskilled workers in feminized, low-paid professions, such as agriculture, education, social services, and in labour-intensive sectors such as the textile industry, garment factories are a very significant site of investigation when it comes to the 'working mother' gender contract during Yugoslav socialism and its lived experience on the ground. Throughout the socialist period, but especially in the 1970s and 1980s, seamstresses' hard work at the machine – and particularly their night shifts – allowed export-oriented garment production to flourish. As Milić wrote, 'the textile industry (highly feminized) had the highest rate of productivity growth, the highest rate of export to the Western markets, and the most significant development in managerial organization. The textile

---

in 1990: BiH 36.7, Montenegro 39.2, Croatia 42.9, Slovenia 46.7, Macedonia 37.4, Serbia 38.2 (with Kosovo averaging 23.7 and Vojvodina 40.2). Milica Antić, 'Yugoslavia: The transitional spirit of the age', in Corrin (ed.), *Superwomen and the Double Burden*, p. 163.
[12] Woodward, 'The rights of women', p. 252.
[13] Bracewell, 'Eating up Yugoslavia', p. 184. See also Hyder Patterson, *Bought & Sold*.
[14] Patterson, *Bought & Sold*, p. 271.
[15] See notably Silva Mežnarić, 'Theory and reality: the status of employed women in Yugoslavia', in S.L. Wolchik and A.G. Meyer (eds), *Women, State and Party in Eastern Europe* (Durham, 1985). On Central and Eastern Europe, see Fidelis, *Women, Communism and Industrialization in Poland*, as well as Rozsa Kulcsar, 'The socioeconomic condition of women in Hungary', and Ivan Volgyes, 'Blue-collar working women and poverty in Hungary', in S. L. Wolchik and A. G. Meyer (eds), *Women, State and Party in Eastern Europe* (Durham, 1985).

workers, however, receive the lowest earnings.'[16] Next to Yugoslavia's exports of finished collections, the late socialist period saw an increase in the amount of subcontracting agreements, the so-called *lon poslovi* (from the German word *Lohn*, which means payment or wage), in which workers assembled pre-designed models and materials received from Western clients. The profitability of such agreements was largely based on cheap labour, and was the consequence of Yugoslavia's increasing dependency from foreign loans, exports and hard currencies.[17]

Even if textile workers' exploitation within factories and their double burden of productive and reproductive work clearly emerge in the archival material and in oral history interviews, such condition is apparently at odds with post-socialist narratives of attachment and belonging to the factory as a 'second home'. To explain this apparent contradiction, it is important to understand that women's double burden was both valorized symbolically through protective legislation, but also simultaneously naturalized as an inevitable societal phenomenon. On the one hand, following the 'working mother' gender contract, and the idea that some social costs should be provided for by the state, factory management usually provided flexible solutions for workers through a variety of welfare arrangements (part-time work, maternity leaves, sick leaves, canteens, health clinics, sometimes housing). On the other hand, it was also generally assumed that working women would design their own private solutions when balancing between productive and reproductive work, notably concerning choices related to childcare. It was not uncommon for garment workers to leave their children at home alone during their shift, or to bring them to the shop floor when they had no alternative. Mostly, however, female workers could count on grandmothers, female relatives or neighbours whenever there was no childcare facility available.

Such fundamental ambivalence, as I will argue later in the book, explains why former workers' memories of the double burden are as much naturalized as they are privatized. In my narrators' narratives, the double burden is seen mostly as a 'natural' fact of women's life, while at the same time each woman found a personal and specific way of balancing productive and reproductive work, depending on family size, household income, partner's and relatives' support, etc. The fatigue of the double day, therefore, is less susceptible to be remembered in collective terms, as it happens instead for the factory space and for the social services and social connections it

---

[16] Milić, 'Women and work in former Yugoslavia', p. 240.
[17] Schierup, *Migration, Socialism and the International Division of Labour*, p. 261.

provided. The 'working mother' gender contract, at the same time, is often evoked as a term of comparison, especially when former workers point at ways in which post-socialist precarity is affecting the stability and security of their household, as opposed to socialist times, when the combination of work and family obligations was made possible by the socialist welfare state. The 1970s and 1980s, especially, were times in which maternity leaves were extended up to one year, and in which social services were more widespread than in the early socialist phase, something which is also likely to affect workers' memories. In the following section, I will look at the ways in which industrial workers' productive and reproductive work, as well as their (lack of) political participation was represented and discussed in the public sphere during socialism.

From 3.00 am to 10.00 pm: The seamstresses' endless working day

The woman portrayed on the cover of this book is the protagonist of the movie *Od 3 do 22* (From 3.00 am to 10.00 pm), filmed by Croatian director Krešimir Golik in 1966, which is considered a classic of documentary film in the post-Yugoslav region.[18] The short film in black and white, lasting less than 15 minutes, portrays a day in the life of Smilja G., a twenty-two-year-old female factory worker, married with a small child, who lives in the suburb of Dubrava and is employed in the Pobjeda (Victory) textile factory in the city of Zagreb. Smilja had migrated to Zagreb from a village near Osijek, and was a trade union and communist party member.[19] The director followed the protagonist in her daily activities, exposing the reality of women's endless working day. In the movie, the young worker wakes up at 3.00 am, lightens up the wood-burning stove, and prepares a breakfast of hot milk and bread for her husband and baby girl, whom she feeds while eating. She and her husband then leave the home to work, while the toddler remains in her bed, locked inside the little wooden house. After crossing the muddy road that leads to the house, Smilja proceeds to her work by bus, while her husband goes to work on his bike. At 5.00 am, she then switches to a tram to reach her destination. She hurriedly does some grocery shopping at the local market before entering the factory. At 6.00 am, she starts her shift within the factory,

---

[18] *Od 3 do 22* (Krešimir Golik, 1966). Available at: https://www.youtube.com/watch?v=ava as3e37T4 (accessed 20 January 2018).

[19] Maja Đilas, *Prostori reprezentacije moći alternativnih kulturnih praksi u Jugoslaviji:1945–1980*, PhD dissertation (University of Novi Sad, 2014), p. 19.

where she works deftly at the spinning machines. The director follows her during her working shift and during her break, when she eats again some bread and milk, sitting alone and looking pensive. At 2.00 pm, when her shift ends, Smilja briskly walks back towards the tram stop, buying a loaf of fresh bread on the way. She barely manages to get into the overcrowded tram on the way home. She finally returns to her house a bit later than 3.00 pm, where she immediately takes care of her child and starts cooking lunch (in socialist Yugoslavia, the main meal was consumed in the early afternoon upon returning from work). Her husband then comes back from work and they have their meal. The woman is first feeding her child and then eating her soup afterwards. Her husband plays for a short time with the child and then has a nap, while the wife fetches water at a water pump, does the dishes, scrubs the floor and washes clothing by hand, trying to keep her toddler away from the water. The husband then wakes up and goes out, probably to see some friends, but Smilja continues her household chores and childcare. She even finds the time to mend some clothes and to iron them, as well as for writing down the daily expenses, until she goes to sleep at 10.00 pm.

Probably in order to emphasize feelings of alienation, throughout the movie there is no dialogue or human interaction between the protagonist and her husband or colleagues. What we hear are ambient sounds (the noise of the city and of spinning machines), as well as few words and sounds pronounced by the baby girl, who appears to be very well taken care of, despite spending time at home unattended. The practice of leaving young children at home alone was not uncommon among women working in garment factories, who, like Smilja, were often migrants from the countryside to the city, or from the less developed Yugoslav republics to the most industrialized ones, and thus had no opportunity to rely on other female family members for domestic help. The factory newspaper of the Pobjeda mill, where the protagonist worked, testified that this problem was widespread. The Pobjeda factory employed at the time around 1,700 workers, of which 1,100 were women. A 1965 report of the women's political organization within the factory, the *aktiv žena*, discussed the results of an inquiry which showed that 'only a small number of children of employed women is cared for in a nursery or kindergarten, and that the majority of children is left at home alone or is left to the neighbours'.[20] The organization recommended that the factory management open a nursery and a kindergarten, in collaboration with local authorities. That would allow women, it argued, to avoid taking sick leave from work, as 80 per cent of sick leave was for childcare reasons.

---

[20] Pobjeda workplace periodical, April 1965, p. 5.

Female industrial workers' plight was often discussed in factory newspapers and in the meetings of official women's organizations. During a 1954 governing board meeting of the Union of Women's Societies (SŽD), which was supposed to replace the Antifascist Women's Front (AFŽ), Judita Alargić, a former partisan and communist activist, who became radicalized as a textile worker during the strikes of the interwar period, portrayed an alarming state of working conditions in garment factories in Belgrade, Yugoslavia's capital. Workers were indebted, amassed in unhealthy housing conditions, insufficiently fed and often struck by tuberculosis. Women were working for very long hours, adding second jobs to factory work, and had no place where to leave their children to be taken care of. The trade unions did not seem to care about women's status as workers, and all over the country women's equality was undergoing a political and economic backlash.[21] Alargić summarized the gravity of the situation by stating: 'In any other system these workers would strike, but this is a socialist country and people understand the situation. We are however indebted to help them as much as we can.' Such a situation was a far cry from the provisions of the 1946 Yugoslav Constitution, which recognized working mothers' equal rights and protection. In fact, a patriarchal backlash had occurred since the 1950s after the initial post-war mobilization of the female labour force: the numbers of women elected to republican and district committees rapidly decreased, as did the number of women employed in the industry. Women became a characteristic 'reserve army' of labour, whose work was seen as less productive and valuable, also due to the social costs associated with female workers (frequent sick leaves due to childcare, maternity leaves, etc.).[22]

Reports about women's 'double burden' abounded in Yugoslavia not only as a result of the relatively open character of the social sciences, but also due to the fact that institutional reform was a constant feature of the system.[23] As in other socialist regimes, 'constructive criticism' was accepted and widespread.[24] Even if socialist authorities extensively discussed the problem, however, women's double burden was also naturalized, since it was treated as a by-product of industrialization, which was going to be solved through socialized welfare services and the increase in living standards.

---

[21] Zapisnik sa sastanka Upravnog odbora Ženskih društava Jugoslavije, Belgrade, 6 March 1954. The Archives of Yugoslavia, Belgrade, collection 354, SŽDJ, box 1: Zapisnici i stenografske sa sastanaka upravnog odbora i sekretariata SŽDJ i sa savetovanja SŽDJ 1954–1961, p.X/3.
[22] Woodward, *Socialist Unemployment*.
[23] Archer, Duda and Stubbs (eds), *Social Inequalities*.
[24] Paulina Bren and Mary Neuburger, 'Constructive criticism', in Bren and Neuburger (eds), *Communism Unwrapped*, pp. 321–4.

Yet these changes were slow to materialize, and largely left to the whims of local administrations and market forces. When it came to garment workers, difficulties in combining productive and reproductive labour remained a constant, from early to late socialism. In 1961, Vaska Duganova, secretary of labour and president of the Chamber for Social Affairs and Health of the Assembly of the People's Republic of Macedonia, wrote a report titled 'Problems of female workers in the new industrial settlements of the processing industry in Macedonia', in which she discussed the situation in the newly created textile factories in Titov Veles, Štip and Tetovo.[25] The Republic of Macedonia was the one of the most underdeveloped of the Federation, and since the early 1950s it had been the object of state investments in light industry, notably textile. These investments, however, were limited by a lack of raw materials, out-dated technologies and poor infrastructure. Moreover, the authorities' will to create new socialist workers, and particularly female workers, clashed with local gendered values and traditions. In the towns of Titov Veles, Štip, and Tetovo, 80 per cent of the workers were entering paid labour for the first time. New female workers, according to Duganova, were displaying 'a lack of discipline and a lack of understanding towards the problems of the factory, as well as a lack of understanding about their rights and their responsibilities'.[26]

In order to increase women's participation within the factory, the author recommended an increase in women's qualifications, adequate childcare facilities and women's 'liberation from superfluous tasks' in the home.[27] Welfare services, however, took time to develop: for instance, in Tetovo all the workers' meals were taken care of through the factory canteen, and workers could also bring food home for their families, whereas this did not happen in the other two cities.[28] Female workers' low qualifications were also limiting the effects of investments in the textile industry. A number of technical training and vocational schools had been created, and some women were interested in the possibility of higher qualification (and increased earnings), but many others did not attend the courses 'for reasons of an objective nature: they worry too much about the problems of the family and of the household'.[29] Duganova frequently noted how women's domestic obligations limited both

---

[25] Vaska Duganova, 'Problemi zaposlene žene u novim industrijskim naseljima preradjivačke industrije u Makedoniji', Titov Veles, 25 March 1961. The Archives of the Republic of Slovenia, Ljubljana, Vida Tomšič collection, AS 1413, box 193, pp. 1–14.
[26] Ibid., p. 3.
[27] Ibid., p. 1.
[28] Ibid., p. 5.
[29] Ibid., p. 8.

their possibility of qualification and their activism in the workers' councils. In the three cities, on average 68–75 per cent of female workers carried out all domestic work alone, while 20–25 per cent could benefit from the help of other family members (most probably female relatives). Ninety per cent of these households, moreover, did not dispose of any domestic appliance.

Women's unpaid labour had no end: according to a survey carried out by the workers' council in the Makedonka factory in Štip, of thirty female workers performing the night shift, *only one* had some rest afterwards, whereas others took care of the laundry, of cooking, of cleaning the house, and so on. Many women, moreover, could not properly concentrate on work since they used to leave their children at home alone, or under the supervision of older children. The workers' councils had attempted to provide some solutions and had organized childcare at the factory level. However, the factory management was not keen to use its funds for that and demanded that childcare be funded by municipal authorities, which in turn did not have sufficient funds.

Vaska Duganova, in her conclusion, expressed both her 'constructive criticism' towards the system and her solidarity towards female workers:

> For years already we have been talking of the problems of the female worker, particularly in the workplace. We expect her to develop her creative initiative to the maximum degree within the workers' collective, to become a managing expert of the machine on which she works, to often increase her qualifications, to understands all the changes imposed by social development, to understand economic problems, to be active in the self-managing organs and in other social organisations, to be an exemplary mother and a good housewife, etc. *We demand a lot from our female workers.* We should also ask the question, considering the social and economic development of our country, of *what can be done by society in its entirety to help her.* It is a fact that the Constitution and other legal provisions gave a number of rights to the Yugoslav woman, particularly to the woman in the workplace, and that such rights rarely exist for women in other countries. Still, the question remains as to *how much is the female worker in the position to make use of her equality, and if women alone should fight with these problems.*[30]

Duganova appealed for workers' councils and municipal authorities to jointly create sustainable welfare services and to guarantee childcare facilities to female workers. Female workers undoubtedly had to understand

---

[30] Ibid., p. 13. Emphasis added.

their responsibilities and to turn into active socialist citizens, but the factory management and local authorities also needed to help them in this endeavour. This passage highlights the contradictory processes that were at stake during Yugoslavia's industrialization. Female workers fell under the pressure of conflicting discourses and expectations: they had to cope with the unevenness of social services which were supposed to replace women's domestic work, and had to perform such work in very labour-intensive ways, since household appliances such as washing machines and fridges were not widespread outside the country's urban centres or in less developed republics.[31]

Another 1959 survey published by the Makedonka factory newspaper in Štip highlighted that women needed on average 1.5 hours for shopping, 2 for cleaning, 1.5 for washing, 1.5 for cooking, and 3 hours for childcare every day. The authors ended up wondering how women managed to show up for work at all.[32] Makedonka employed 2,000 workers in its early phase, and childcare facilities were established in the early 1960s. Their quality, however, did not satisfy many workers. The crèche was allegedly too far from the factory, and it was cold and dirty. Childcare facilities were also understaffed, with one crèche employee taking care of twenty children. Some workers found crèche employees to be arrogant; an upset worker was reported to have hit out at a crèche employee: 'You have to serve me as I am the one who pays you, otherwise you can be the one who works at the machine.' Crèches were generally paid through individual contributions, and workers felt entitled to receive a better service. The factory social workers, in turn, tried to hush the complaints and told workers: 'If it suits you, bring the child – otherwise leave the child home.'[33]

The issue of childcare was still a burning one in 1976, when the factory had expanded to 4,500 employees, of which 2,300 were women. Among the 1,700 workers' children, only 160 were of preschool age and could attend the crèche. The others remained alone, or were not properly taken care for. Women were in serious difficulties with childcare during their night shift and during the public holidays, when the crèche did not work. When the children were sick, they had to take them to the doctor, where the waiting time was endless. So, even if interested in entering the self-management

---

[31] Patterson, *Bought & Sold*; Isabel Ströhle, 'Of social inequalities in a socialist society: The creation of a rural underclass in Yugoslav Kosovo', in Archer, Duda and Stubbs (eds), *Social Inequalities*.
[32] Makedonka workplace periodical, 20–1 (September 1959), p. 4.
[33] Makedonka workplace periodical, 114 (November 1966), p. 6. The report on childcare facilities continues in 115, p. 4.

organs, many women could not make it. Only eight women were part of the management, out of seventy to eighty posts.[34] Several suggestions were made to solve these issues, such as improving childcare facilities and exonerating women from working during the night shift and during public holidays. As reported in the newspaper in the following years, and as testified by former Makedonka workers, however, adequate childcare facilities were never built for the factory, and many preferred to leave children with family members rather than in the factory crèche.

The usage of public childcare remained uneven throughout Yugoslavia, with social differences playing a role when it came to accessing welfare services. A 1975 survey across Yugoslavia reported 62 per cent of women did not make use of public childcare facilities, which could indicate a lack of material services, but also strong traditional values. Women with higher incomes, however, were twice more likely to make use of such facilities, because they were often residing in bigger cities with more facilities available.[35] As I will show in the next section, women's double burden of productive and reproductive work, as well as class and educational differences among women, were also connected to the issue of women's (lack of) political participation, the so-called 'triple burden', an issue that was also frequently discussed in public settings.

'What do you get from being a party member?': On the 'triple burden'

Discussions over women's difficulties in combining paid work, unpaid work and political participation were frequent both in factory newspapers and in official publications. Generally, workers' political participation was very much dependent on class and education, as well as on gender. Together with men, skilled female workers and white-collar female workers, in fact, were more likely to be part of management structures and party structures in the factory, while unskilled female workers with low education were the least likely to take part in self-management organs. Women's voluntary

---

[34] Makedonka workplace periodical, 180 (April 1976) p. 2.
[35] Miro A. Mihovilović i suradnici, *Žena između rada i porodice: utjecaj zaposlenosti žene na strukturu i funkciju porodice* (Zagreb, 1975), p. 69; p. 76. The sample included 1,544 female workers, living in urban centres as well as in smaller towns, from different educational background, professions, religion and nationality. The narrators were even asked to fill in a survey with different questions, to keep a 24-hour diary that calculated their time budget, and to go through a qualitative interview.

associations within textile factories (such as sport associations and voluntary firefighter brigades), as testified by different factory newspapers, were mainly attended by unmarried young women, while women with a family generally expressed their lack of time for leisure, voluntary meetings or for political engagement. While leisure time was almost non-existent for many women with lower qualifications and skills, middle-class women were more likely to afford the luxury of having some free time. Only a minority of urban, middle-class women took part in concerts, art exhibitions and regularly attended movie screenings and theatre shows, as reported by the 1975 cross-Yugoslav survey mentioned earlier.[36] Overall, only 15–20 per cent of women were engaged in self-management organs and local associations or in other activities within cultural, sport or women's associations.[37] In 1978, of the 825,000 women who were part of the League of Communists, only 45,000 were ordinary workers, and barely 892 were women working in the agricultural sector.[38]

The magazine *Žena* (Woman), published by the Conference for the Social Activity of Women (KDAŽ), which replaced the Union of Women's Societies (SŽD) in 1961, also dedicated several reports to the issue. In 1972, the magazine published the edited minutes of a round table with the employees of the cotton mill of Duga Resa, a small town in the Republic of Croatia.[39] As many as 2,113 women were employed in the mill, which had a total of 3,600 workers. The round table focused in particular on the issue of women's political participation. Difficult working conditions in the factory (high temperature, noise, night shifts), long commutes from the surrounding villages and insufficient welfare services were mentioned as objective reasons for women's limited participation in self-management activities. Lack of schooling was also mentioned as an important factor that prevented workers from being more active. A female engineer who was part of the management, Ljubica V., argued: 'In my opinion, a woman with low education and many obligations in the family, and with many other unsolved issues, cannot think of the development of self-management. That is an illusion.'[40] Blue-collar workers seemed to agree with this position, and emphasized their lack of education and consequently their inability to follow what was being discussed.

---

[36] Ibid., p. 144; pp. 172–4.
[37] Ibid., pp. 113–20.
[38] Vuteks workplace periodical, 214 (March 1978), p. 1.
[39] *Žena*, 5 (1972), p. 2.
[40] Ibid., p. 18.

The discussion at Duga Resa made clear that women's 'triple burden' – the expectation for women to take part in self-management organs – was more of a general programmatic orientation than a state imposition towards female workers. The expectation that female workers would participate in political meetings and activities was often put aside due to the existing social and economic limitations. Due to the state's recognition of women's domestic tasks, it was relatively easy for women to avoid taking part in such meetings, particularly in the late socialist period. Next to a lack of time, interest, and or next to the feelings of not being sufficiently competent to take part in decision-making, however, there were also other subjective reasons for not taking part in factory politics. One of them was disillusionment. During the round table at Duga Resa, in fact, the strongest complaint came from weaver Zora R., who lamented that female workers' political participation in self-management organs made little difference:

> I would like to speak, and to say that it's not correct to say that women are not interested. That hurts me and disturbs me very much. *Women are interested, only nobody listens to women. They, so to say, have no right to vote (pravo glasa).* No one listens to what they say. I have been working for 10 years already in the weaving mill, and for 6 years I have been in the self-managing organs and in different commissions. From my first day at the weaving mill, I am a member of the League of Communists. This year we even revived the work of the Conference for the Social Activity of Women, which so far had reached a deadlock. The same we did with the League of Communists. People have lost trust. I tried to influence the young women, suggesting that they become members of the League of Communists. Some replied: 'Comrade, what do you get from being a member of the League of Communists, and who listens to you at all?' (*Što ti drugarice, imaš od toga što si član Savez komunista, i tko tebe uopšte sluša*).[41]

Due to the dominance of male cadres, including in feminized sectors such as the garment industry, many blue-collar workers felt disillusioned with the processes of decision-making. The lack of interest in women's issues in self-management organs was partially countered by the local *aktiv žena*, the women's political organization within the factory, but the work of women's organizations could not counter the overall resignation of many ordinary workers. A 1972 survey among female workers published by the newspaper

---

[41] Ibid., p. 29. Emphasis added.

of the RIO factory, located in Rijeka, was significantly titled 'Women are the best workers, and men are the best leaders?' and voiced female workers' discontent about men's privilege in the workplace.[42] Men, it was said, were immediately looking for possibilities of career advancement, and they were seen as more capable of leadership, while women were perceived as naturally unable to assume important responsibilities, even if this wasn't the case and even if women had proven that they could excel as leaders, too. A female leader in the sales department, Anica M., stated that most women avoided additional obligations because they still saw the family as the centre of their lives. Anica herself had to leave her child to her mother, while her husband had 'to wait for lunch' while she was attending meetings. The only man interviewed in the survey, in charge of human resources, blamed women for underestimating themselves and for avoiding to invest time in factory activism.[43]

Similar complaints were voiced in 1980 by a female trade union activist in the Kamensko garment factory in Zagreb, on Women's Day (8 March), a date of official celebration which was often used in factory newspapers to host discussions on the position of women within the factory and across Yugoslavia more generally. Pavica O., a former partisan and shock worker and president of the trade union in one of the local Organisations of Associated Labour, declared then that she did not feel unequal to men (*neravnopravna*), despite the fact that she carried a 'big burden' (*veliki teret*) as mother, housewife and worker. Still, she complained openly about women's discrimination in decision-making processes, arguing that women's inferiority in self-management institutions was a direct consequence of women's oppression in the domestic sphere, and of men's privilege when it came to education and social mobility:

> In general, I think that in our collective there is little trust in women, when it comes to managerial positions. Maybe it's because men are able to achieve qualifications before women. See our male colleagues, many of them got educated in the course of work. Fewer women had that luck. Despite the good climate, which is conducive to make men and women more equal, men are in a better position than us. They are the leaders,

---

[42] RIO workplace periodical, 50/51 (1972), p. 5.
[43] Ibid. Women's difficulty in participating in self-management was quite understandable due to the conditions of the workforce in the factory. Another survey from the previous year, in fact, related that of 660 female workers at RIO Rijeka, 48 were single mothers, and 338 were in a difficult housing situation. Only 46 children were going to kindergarten while 114 children remained at home alone. RIO workplace periodical 36 (1971), p. 6.

they are the experts, because we make it possible. We, the housewives, the wives. We cook for them, we iron, we raise children while they are studying. We can practically say that many men receive a scholarship from their wives (*Gotovo da se kaže da su mnogi muževi stipendisti svojih žena*). It makes me angry. There should be more confidence in women and less flowers.[44]

As this quote demonstrates, issues of male privilege were sometimes openly addressed in factory newspapers. Within socialist factories, education and access to decision-making were highly differentiated by gender, with women mostly excluded from positions of authority and responsibility. At times, gender and class domination went too far, spurring protest among blue-collar female workers, as in the case of the textile workers' strike in the Trudbenik (Worker) textile factory in Banja Luka in 1969. After they complained of excessively low wages, unlawful procedures, corruption and harassment by the male factory director and his collaborators, the 220 mainly female workers were successful in having all the management removed from the factory. The workers' assembly, in this case, could make use of self-management provisions and reclaim workers' rights against power abuse on the part of the management, and against patriarchal practices within the factory.[45]

Generally, however, strikes were rare among female textile workers, who were perceived as less combative and more docile than male workers in heavy industry. Among my narrators, only a Metka worker recalled a strike against shortages and mishaps in production in early 1960s Celje, and an Arena worker in Pula mentioned another short strike to get better wages, without being able to recall the exact date.[46] Scholars also report strikes by female textile workers in 1980s Mostar and Zrenjanin, but overall the late socialist period was marked by male workers' strikes in heavy industry.[47] While gender differences were obviously crucial in determining workers' degree of participation to self-management and work protests, one should also not underestimate the generalized, universal disillusionment of male and female blue-collar workers towards the increasingly bureaucratized decisional

---

[44] Kamensko workplace periodical, 15 (1980), p. 7.
[45] Vladan Vukliš, 'Štrajk tekstilnih radnica 1969. u retrospektivi', *Glas Srpske*, 28 February 2015.
[46] This is probably the same strike recalled by another Arena worker interviewed by Maja Maksić. The strike likely happened in the mid-1970s and aimed to obtain a better redistribution of factory profits. See Maksić, *Trikotaža Arena Pula*, p. 53.
[47] Jake Lowinger, *Economic Reform and the 'Double Movement' in Yugoslavia: An Analysis of Labor Unrest and Ethno-nationalism in the 1980s*, PhD dissertation (John Hopkins University, Baltimore, Maryland, 2009).

mechanisms typical of self-management, which often lasted for entire days without delivering the expected results, as reported by Ichak Adizes in his witness account of two unnamed textile factories in the city of Belgrade.[48] A satirical vignette from the Sana factory newspaper in the early 1980s, for instance, made fun of the length of factory meetings, exposing both the limits of the self-management system and women's gendered negotiations within it. The vignette went as follows: during an interminable meeting, two women left, using their children as an excuse for not staying longer. A third woman, then, also wanted to leave. When she was asked why, since she had no children, she replied that if she kept spending all her time at meetings, she would never manage to get any![49]

Women's wariness towards joining the communist party emerged in some of my interviews with former workers, whether they were blue collar or white collar. Ines, for instance, a former blue-collar worker at the Arena knitting factory in Pula, told me that she was once elected in the workers' council as representative, but that she never got involved in politics. Since she was a good worker, she was often asked to join the communist party, but, she states, 'I was never interested.' I asked her if it was ok for her to refuse, and she said:

> Yes, yes, I don't want that, I am not interested in politics. I like to work and I pray God that there is peace at home and around the home and all the rest does not interest me, politics doesn't interest me. That's it.[50]

She also told me that it was stupid for her to pay for a party membership, and that she would rather use the money to buy something at home.[51] During our interview, Ines also added that 'you have to be born for it [politics], you know, you cannot be forced to go. You must be interested, and if you aren't, better not.' During another meeting with Ines and two of her colleagues at Arena, they recalled the story of a woman who refused to join the party as 'she did not want to sell herself'. They all agreed that 'politics is always politics', and that staying out of the party allowed to have more freedom and live better,

---

[48] Adizes, *Industrial Democracy*.
[49] Sana workplace periodical, 20 (1983), p. 8.
[50] Ines, Pula, October 2015.
[51] A similar reason was presented by Sana workers in Bosnia-Herzegovina in the mid-1980s, who complained that the necessary quota to join the party was too high. Sana list 41 (1985), p. 3. Workers also mentioned family obligations and disillusionment with managers' privileges as reasons for abandoning, or not joining, the League of Communists.

even if joining the party could bring some advantages in terms of flats and credits distribution, since 'close to the fire one gets warmer'.[52]

Besides class and educational differences, personal freedom – and particularly religious faith – was indeed something that was an obstacle when deciding to join or not the communist party. Party members were not supposed to attend masses and take part in other religious celebrations, such as the baptism of their children. Pavlica, a white-collar worker at Arena born in 1938, took part in the youth association as well as in the voluntary firefighter brigade in the early 1960s. She was asked to join the communist party earlier on, but she only entered it in 1973. She could not marry in the church given that her future husband was an officer in the Yugoslav National Army (JNA), but she still insisted to get her daughter baptized, even if it meant that for a while she would be seen as a 'backward witch' (*baba vještica*). One of Pavlica's sisters was a nun, so she was not willing to completely give up her religious upbringing. Moreover, while we were looking at old pictures of workers in the Arena factory during our interview, Pavlica recognized one female worker who was prevented from entering the party because she was regularly attending mass. Pavlica recalled that this specific worker cried a lot when she was refused party membership.[53]

These different examples make clear that there were both subjective and structural elements which limited women's political participation to self-managing organs, and that these were often interrelated. Blue-collar workers generally felt the least entitled and the least likely to benefit from political activism, and thus preferred to concentrate on their daily work in the factory and at home without taking up further engagements. Nonetheless, workers were not forced to take part in politics if they did not wish to – thus, various degrees of agency and various spaces of negotiation existed when it came to political participation. Kinga Pozniak makes a similar point when she discusses everyday life in socialist Poland, challenging the representation of socialism as a time in which ideology permeated every aspect of life. As she notes, Nowa Huta inhabitants were conscious of the restrictions posed by the system, and 'exercised agency within this framework, balancing their own needs and beliefs against practical considerations, requirements, and constraints'.[54]

In the following chapters, I will discuss how oral history narrators often highlight the multiple contradictions and negotiations typical of daily life

---

[52] Ines and colleagues, Pula, January 2016.
[53] Pavlica, Pula, May 2015.
[54] Pozniak, *Nowa Huta*, p. 144.

under socialism. Former workers, for instance, retrospectively express their scepticism towards self-management bureaucratic procedures, and power hierarchies on the shop floor, while at the same time they positively recall the welfare benefits and working-class sociability they experienced within these same factories. In the next section I will look at the ways in which women's daily hard work and sacrifice were both naturalized and valorized in factory newspapers and popular representations of seamstresses.

Women 'made of granite': Workers' portraits in the factory press

After having highlighted the limitations and constraints experienced by garment workers who combined factory work and household responsibilities, I further address in this section how women's everyday problems were represented and commented upon in garment factory newspapers, which provide very significant insights into the gendered imaginaries, values and structures of feeling that were circulated and reproduced within socialist factories.[55] As I mentioned earlier in the chapter, the position of women was frequently discussed in socialism in a way that provided recognition and value to women's work, while at the same time naturalizing women's double burden as workers and mothers. Nowhere is this phenomenon more visible than in the frequent portraits (long interviews accompanied by photographs) of ordinary workers published by workplace periodicals.

While hailing women's ordinary heroism, hard-working spirit and sacrifice for the factory collective, these portraits reinforced the gender norms according to which women were expected to continue their working day at home after factory work. Besides their double burden, female workers often listed sewing, knitting and cooking as their main hobbies, emphasizing their selfless dedication to family life. In turn, their husbands were generally represented through satirical cartoons as jealous, inept and barely able to carry out the so-called 'male jobs', that is, small house repairs and tasks that were not seen as 'feminized'. In the numerous satirical cartoons published by the RIO factory newspaper in Rijeka, for instance, men's reluctance to deal with anything related to reproductive work was often made fun of. In a vignette, one husband asks his wife if she would like to 'amuse herself with the patching of his shirts, since the television was broken'; in another, one wife was seen telling her friend that her sleeping husband was helping a lot at home: 'Today, for instance, he took away a page from the wall calendar.'

---

[55] Archer and Musić, 'Approaching the socialist factory and its workforce'.

Another cartoon showed a father with his children sitting around the table waiting for food. Then the realization came: it was the morning of Women's Day and 'no one thought of waking up mum!' As much as ordinary workers' portraits, these satirical representations of working class family life contributed to normalize the traditional gendered division of labour inside the home.

Ordinary workers' testimonies also highlighted specific socialist values, such as antifascism and collective solidarity between workers of different ethnicities. Growing living standards were also emphasized by pointing at the availability of welfare services such as subsidized holidays and housing, as well as at the creation of hospitals and new factory facilities (notably new subcontracting workshops of the main firm built in surrounding villages or in other peripheral towns). The sense of progress in relation to the difficult post-war years was conveyed, in particular, through the various portraits of pensioners and shock workers (men and women) who had witnessed extreme poverty and deprivation during the Second World War and in its aftermath, and who could testify about material progress on the basis of their lived experience, while inciting the new generations to be as productive as them, and to reach and overcome working norms.

Stories of workers entering the factory at fourteen or fifteen years old, with no shoes, and working in terrible conditions with old machines in the post-war era were extremely common. As I will show in the next chapters, this aspect of intergenerational sacrifice remained very much present within garment workers' memories and structures of feeling. At the same time, workers also openly testified of wrenching poverty, material deprivation and lack of necessary welfare facilities during late socialism, especially when it came to long-standing housing problems and to the fall in living standards caused by the economic crisis and austerity measures of the 1980s. They also frequently complained of the low level of retirement pensions they received after spending their entire lives in the working collective.

I will now proceed to give a few examples of the language and style of such portraits, focusing in particular on the Vuteks factory newspaper, which paid special attention to women's social problems as a result of its tradition of women's political organizing within the factory. The Vuteks mill, located in Vukovar in Croatia, near the Eastern border with Serbia, was founded in 1930 by foreign owners and nationalized after the Second World War. In the late socialist phase, it employed approximately 1,500 workers. Vuteks was well known for its production of bed linen and wool blankets, which were exported in millions to Western countries but also to the Soviet Union and the Middle East. As the employees' portraits make clear, Vuteks employed workers of different ethnicities, many of whom had migrated to the city from other parts of Yugoslavia to escape poverty. Many had also experienced family losses during the Second World War. In the early 1970s, Vuteks employed 1,300 workers, of which 63 per cent were women.

The employee with the longest service (*radni staž*) was Anica S., who started when she was fifteen years old in 1941 in the stockings department, which was later dismantled, forcing her to adjust to a new role in the car upholstery section. The title of her portrait was 'Anica, are you tired?' It retraced Anica's thirty years of faultless service in the firm through a narrative account of her interview with the author. The article contained three pictures, a close up of Anica, another picture of her working in the kitchen, and a portrait of Anica with her son. Anica was presumably a single mother, since no husband was mentioned in the portrait. Her own mother dealt with domestic tasks, while she focused on work and on providing an education for her son. Her daughter, instead, was already employed as a teacher. Anica explained: 'I had no possibility to study, that's why I do not want to deny this to my children. I work and live for them,' she said, 'that's why I do not think of my age, because my children still need me'. (Figure 6). [56]

Figure 6 Anica's portrait in the newspaper of the Vuteks factory, Vukovar.

[56] Vuteks workplace periodical, 110 (1971), p. 4.

Together with women's self-sacrifice for children and family, the theme of unfulfilled life dreams was also a common one in the Vuteks newspaper. Female workers often had lost family members during the war, or came from large impoverished families, and mostly started to work when they were still teenagers. Another portrait, for instance, was dedicated to weaver Zdenka K., born in Mostar in 1943, married with two children, who had worked at Vuteks for the past ten years. Zdenka was born in a very poor family, and could not fulfil her dream of becoming a hairdresser, so she kept arranging friends' hair in her spare time. While working at a knitwear factory in Cerna when she was eighteen years old, she took advantage of the possibility of completing textile schooling in Vukovar against her parents' advice, and later moved to Vuteks, where she met her husband, with whom she alternated work shifts and domestic obligations. Zdenka was overall happy with her working life, but nonetheless complained that it was impossible to rest after the night shift due to her small children:

> That work on three shifts … represents the heaviest load for a mother. When the night shift has to be carried out, very few of us manage to rest during the day, since there is so much work at home that I don't manage to finish it even if the day has 24 hours. The children do not realize that I need rest.[57]

Complaints about the night shift were a constant subject of garment factories' newspapers, not just at Vuteks but across Yugoslavia. Despite many discussions on ending night work at the federal level, the 'third shift' remained an integral part of life at Vuteks and at other factories. Although Yugoslavia had ratified the 1948 ILO Convention on the overall prohibition of women's night work in industry, which became controversial later on grounds of gender discrimination, night work was common in Yugoslav garment factories, and restricted only for pregnant workers or workers with children up to one year of age. Often, workers did not want to give up night work because of increased compensation and in order not to lose their specific place at the machine after each shift. Night shift, however, made it very strenuous for women due to the fact that after the night shift there was work to be done at home, and female workers could not rest in view of the next day's shift.

Yet, workers' portraits indicated that women's domestic work was not negotiable. As another Vuteks worker, Elza T., noted matter-of-factly,

---

[57] Vuteks workplace periodical, 125 (1972), p. 7.

'every woman, next to be a good worker, should also be a good mother and housewife'. She also added: 'it is not said for nothing that a woman holds three corners of the house, while a man only one', as the traditional proverb went. Elza herself attempted to cook in advance before each shift, so that the family would not feel her absence.[58] Another worker, Ivka S., from Split, complained about night work and also noted grudgingly that there was no difference between working women and housewives when it came to family expectations: 'Like every housewife I am expected to take care of all domestic tasks, plus the children, and today a woman is perceived as complete if she can be at the same time a mother, a housewife and a worker' (*a smatra se danas da je žena kompletna ako u isto vrijeme može da bude i majka i domaćica i radnica*).[59] The impersonal form 'smatra se' indicates wide societal consensus over such gendered norms and expectations.

The simultaneous valorization and naturalization of hard work, self-sacrifice and resilience was not only a matter of traditional gender norms but also a class phenomenon, shared between working-class women and men. Working-class families were often employed in the same factory, as in the case of Vuteks, and shared a class-based daily struggle for survival, especially when it came to the scarcest and most desirable resource: housing. The distribution of available flats at Vuteks was made according to a variety of social criteria (including years of service, number of family members and current housing situation). Many workers also made use of factory credits for private house-building, using the free labour force of male relatives and neighbours.[60] As it has been noted by different scholars, housing distribution in socialist Yugoslavia did not always benefit the poorest or most needy, but rather privileged white-collar workers and the most educated, reinforcing class differences and social stratification. Unskilled migrant workers, in particular, were especially discriminated against, particularly in less profitable industries such as the textile sector, in which 40 per cent of the workforce had no access to social housing.[61]

Life for those without social housing was harsh, especially when it came to old pensioners and former migrant workers. A Vuteks pensioner, Anđa B.,

---

[58] Vuteks workplace periodical, 128 (1973), p. 6.
[59] Vuteks workplace periodical, 154 (1974), p. 6.
[60] On home building in socialist Yugoslavia, see Rory Archer, 'The moral economy of home construction in late socialist Yugoslavia', *History and Anthropology*, 29/2(2018), pp. 141–62.
[61] Rory Archer, '"Paid by the workers, occupied by the bureaucrats": Housing inequalities in 1980s Belgrade', in Archer, Duda and Stubbs (eds), *Social Inequalities*; see also Brigitte Le Normand, 'The house that socialism built: Reform, consumption and inequality in postwar Yugoslavia', in Bren and Neuburger (eds), *Socialism Unwrapped*.

born in 1909, who had migrated from Dalmatia, was interviewed in a small house which she shared with her unemployed sick husband and daughter, and which had no electricity. This little house, however, which they built in 1968, was far better than her previous accommodation of fifteen years, which consisted of an abandoned wagon placed among the corn fields.[62] A similar complaint was voiced by a pensioner couple born in 1907 and 1918, migrants from Lika and from Serbia, who had met at the factory. They had received accommodation, but without a bathroom, and generally felt that the factory had forgotten them and their past efforts.[63] Another pensioner, Jelena M., started to work at fourteen years old and retired after thirty years, and also had seventeen awards as shock-worker. She complained of not having received a flat from the factory collective, and that flats 'were given to those who needed them less'. A widow, she lived in a dilapidated old house with her mother.[64]

While many were perpetually waiting for their housing situation to be resolved, some did in fact receive flats through the factory system of redistribution. This often happened, however, after decades of waiting, as the reports in the Vuteks newspaper make clear. Obtaining a flat after decades of material deprivation and poor housing arrangements was experienced as a life-changing event, reinforcing the socialist progress narrative which promised better living standards at the price of long-lasting selfless work and sacrifice. Similarly to the 'Yugoslav dream' of consumption described by Patterson, social housing was within reach for enough of the population, feeding the hope of those who could not attain it yet.[65] A 1976 report titled 'Happy and satisfied in their own flat' collected some workers' voices after they had received a new flat.[66] A male worker, Franko F., stated that he had been waiting for a flat since he started working in 1957, and that he felt 'reborn'. Another male worker, Mićo K., lived for fourteen years in a privately rented, damp room with his wife, also a Vuteks employee, and their three children, before getting a flat. Another worker, Anica, worked for thirty years and did not dare to retire until she was assigned a flat. Heartbreaking stories related to workers' long-standing lack of proper housing were common. Women with children suffered especially when they had to be *podstanari*, that is, tenants in privately rented rooms located in someone's else home. Ljubica M., for instance, waited for over twenty years to receive a flat, moving

[62] Vuteks workplace periodical, 131 (1973), p. 9.
[63] Vuteks workplace periodical, 144 (1974), p. 7.
[64] Vuteks workplace periodical, 171 (1975), p. 9.
[65] Patterson, *Bought & Sold*, xvii.
[66] Vuteks workplace periodical, 187 (1976), p. 4.

from place to place with her old mother. Finally, the women's association in the factory intervened in her favour. It is only in the new flat, she said, that she dared to finally place some flowers, and to invite her nephew to visit without fear of getting into trouble with the landlord.[67] Within private lodgings, in fact, which often consisted of a highly priced room within someone's else flat or house, children were not well accepted. Social housing, thus, signified the start of a new life with fewer worries and limitations.

The reports and portraits contained in workplace periodicals were highly personalized, and yet they all emphasized how working-class women possessed an almost endless and inexhaustible resilience. Female workers themselves openly spoke of their work and fatigue, sometimes in a critical note. They were mostly conscious of their social entitlements as working mothers, but they also interiorized their multiple and conflicting obligations. In a way, the valorization of women's endless labour was simultaneously a form of naturalization of women's innumerable tasks, and of men's privilege in society and at home. The idea of women's resilience as a societal norm is best summarized by the opening passage of another newspaper report at Vuteks:

> Someone once said: 'A woman is like a granite stone', and next to it we should add that *she can do it all, she wants it all, and always remains unbreakable, strong, and bears everything in a stoic way*.[68]

This report was published on Women's Day (8 March 1972) and detailed the activities of the women's organization within the factory and its struggle for the obtainment of better working conditions for female workers, including a kindergarten. The representation of women as granite-like, repeated countless times in official discourse and publications, was interiorized by women themselves and expressed through their selfless dedication to their work for the factory and the family. As I will show in the rest of the book, factory work – together with reproductive work – became an integral part of textile workers' structure of feeling and horizon of possibility, giving meaning and value to their lives in the public and private sphere. The representation of working women as endlessly resilient was also common in movies and documentaries that had garment workers as protagonists, as I will show in the next section. Visual representations of garment workers in their workplace, moreover, highlight the importance of the factory as a space of

---

[67] Vuteks workplace periodical, 188 (1976), p. 5.
[68] Vuteks workplace periodical, 112 (1972), p. 3. Emphasis added.

working-class sociability, intersubjectivity and solidarity, often summarized in the definition of the factory as a 'second home'. Such visual documents also testify to the relative modernity and normality conveyed by socialist industrialization and its working rhythms, especially in comparison to the dire conditions of deindustrialized garment factories in the contemporary post-Yugoslav region. These elements played and still play an important role in workers' structures of feeling and memories of factory work.

Seamstresses on screen: Workers' representations in popular culture

After the death in 1980 of its president and symbolic father figure, Josip Broz Tito, socialist Yugoslavia appeared as a country full of political, social and economic contradictions, particularly as a result of foreign debt and the application of austerity measures, which resulted in inflation, increased unemployment, falling living standards and shortages. In recent years, scholars have been investigating late socialism and its specificities, with an accent on social stratifications and differences across the country.[69] When it comes to industrial production, however, the crisis of the 1980s appears less severe, especially if compared to the decades of deindustrialization and destruction of industrial production that followed the Yugoslav break-up and the Yugoslav Wars, as I will argue in the following chapters.

In the textile sector, notably, the 1980s represent a moment of growing exports for all Yugoslav factories, with workers following their regular working rhythm, and even working extra hours to respond to the increase in subcontracting. Garment factories became an emblem of local industrial production and of the successes of socialist modernity, so much so that in 1985 Radio Television Sarajevo took the Sana textile factory in the picturesque Bosnian town of Bosanski Novi, at the border with Croatia and at the confluence of the Una and Sana rivers, as the setting of a fictionalized television series titled *Priče iz Fabrike* (Factory Tales). Sana mainly produced light garments for women and children, as well as underwear and swim-wear. A well-known 1980s advertisement from Sana showed a young seamstress at the machine, sewing fashionable women's garments, with images of folds of clothes alternating with pictures of waves and waterfalls in the Sana river, from which the factory took its name. The advertisement recited: 'all rivers go

---

[69] Archer, Duda and Stubbs (eds), *Social Inequalities*.

from the source to their delta, only Sana goes towards you.' In the series, the Sana factory was renamed as Zvijezda (Star), from the red star that was the symbol of socialist revolution.

According to the director of the 1985 series, Vojislav Milašević (1932–2012), the series aimed to portray workers' everyday lives through an accessible language. Workers even took part in the series as extras and greatly appreciated the series, according to the factory newspaper.[70] The opening song of the series was called '800 women', and the series is often remembered by this name today, even if the factory employed over 3,000 workers as a whole in the mid-1980s. The song main theme is a homage to all that could be considered feminine, as it states: 'All that is of female gender / soul, life, everything / under the firmament / that's all of us together; all that is of female gender / mother, sister, daughter / fire, earth and water / that's all of us together.' The song also contains references to the romantic subplot of the series, and perhaps to women's circumscribed circle of affects and acquaintances ('We just know a few people / but always someone dear / crosses the path in our direction / and there leaves a trace').[71] In parallel with the song, the opening scenes show the flow of real workers entering the factory on a summer day.

The plot of the series revolves around the new factory director, Ivan Đaković, a young ambitious man who is the son of one of the female workers, who comes back to his hometown after his studies in Belgrade. He is represented as an idealist who strives to fight for social justice against endemic corruption, for instance by refusing to give an expensive dress for free to a local politician's wife. He ends up falling in love with Jasna, a young worker who previously spent some time in jail and is thus ostracized by the factory collective, including Ivan's mother. The series does not refrain from sensitive topics, such as women's hard work, domestic abuse, alcoholism and socialist elites' corruption. In the series, however, the factory functions as a community centre and as a 'big family', on which workers can always count to solve their daily problems. Feelings of community and belonging are symbolized by the figure of the factory doctor, nicknamed Doctor Pjevalica, impersonated by popular Yugoslav actor Zoran Radmilović, who decides to hide his illness and to die in his little home-clinic within the factory (Radmilović died of a cancer like his character, soon after the series was completed). Doctor Pjevalica is not just a doctor but also a social worker, who frequently consults with women about their daily problems, and for

---

[70] *Sana* workplace periodical, 36 (April 1985), p. 4 and 40 (September 1985), p. 5.
[71] *Priče iz Fabrike* (Vojislav Milašević, 1985). First episode available at: https://www.youtube.com/watch?v=Ukm9bKwC2oc (accessed 20 January 2018).

whom a kind word is more important than prescribing medicines. Pjevalica's figure reflects the important role of medical personnel and social workers in garment factories.[72]

The character symbolizing women's hardship in the series is the one of Tereza, a seamstress who suffers daily psychological abuse from her alcoholic partner, a former sportsman who ended up in a wheelchair after an accident, with whom she has a daughter. Thanks to the help of the factory staff, Tereza finally decides to leave her abusive partner, while her teenage daughter also gains employment at Zvijezda. Besides the romanticized plot revolving around the different characters, the most successful scenes of the series are the collective ones on the shop floor and in the canteen, which portray friendly interactions among colleagues, as well as gossiping, solidarity, fights, singing at the machine and complaints about daily work. The series also shows common occurrences in the factory, such as the collective ceremonies held when workers retired, or the parties with music and singing organized in the factory courtyard for 1st of May celebrations. In the next chapter, I will investigate former Sana workers' memories of the factory, which also include memories of the televised series, perceived as a truthful representation of factory life.

Another visual document that testifies seamstresses' simultaneous hardships and attachment to the workplace is Želimir Žilnik's documentary *Vera i Eržika* (1981). Vera and Eržika are two textile workers employed in the Trudbenik factory in Pančevo, an industrial town in Vojvodina, close to Yugoslavia's capital city, Belgrade. Vera is Serbian and Eržika (Erzsébet) is Hungarian. Both started to work very early after the Second World War, and almost reached retirement age in the early 1980s. With its characteristic realist style, Žilnik's documentary manages to portray on the one hand elderly women's hardships with factory work, especially long-term industrial work's damaging consequences for health. On the other hand, the movie conveys workers' awareness of their social entitlements and their attachment to the working collective. Vera, born in 1927, is a sturdy, chatty woman, who has been working in textile for thirty-four years. She is married with two sons who are serving the obligatory service in the army. The movie follows Vera as she is asking for a transfer to an easier job because she feels that she cannot hold anymore the rhythm on the shop floor. She has hearing and lung

---

[72] An interview with the nurse of the Vuteks clinic, for instance, underlined the connection between medical and psychological issues when it came to female workers. The nurse related that many women came to her to talk about their unhappy family relations, husbands' drinking habits, etc. and that she worked in close cooperation with the doctor and the social worker stationed in the factory. Vuteks workplace periodical, 145 (1974), p. 6.

impairment due to the noise and dust of the factory, together with problems with her legs. Vera goes through several medical examinations before obtaining a disability certification that allows her to move to a less strenuous job in the canteen of the factory. Before working in textile, Vera was working in a farm. Together with her husband, she bought a plot of farmland where she built a weekend house and where she keeps pigs. Vera's passion is casting horoscopes and fortune telling for her friends and acquaintances, which adds a note of humour to filmic interactions.

The other protagonist of the movie, Eržika, born in 1937, has also been working for thirty-two years, ever since she was thirteen years old. More reserved than Vera, she lives with her husband and has two daughters, married with children. She has sight problems and sleeping troubles due to the night shifts. She also undergoes medical examinations to be able to ask for a less strenuous job position. After various examinations, she is also assigned an easier job for invalid workers in the cleaning section, which pays less than work at the shop floor. Even though she started to work when she was thirteen years old, in 1948, her work service (*radni staž*) is recognized only from her fifteenth year onwards. This means that she still needs to work four more years to achieve a full pension, something which she defines as 'unfair' since the early post-war period was the hardest in terms of working conditions. Despite her multiple attempts with the union, she fails to receive recognition of her first two years of service, since the Yugoslav law only recognizes employment from age fifteen. Vera also tries to get recognition for six months of work performed during the Second World War under occupation, but to no avail.

Both protagonists show their awareness of social entitlements as they discuss wage calculations, social contributions and existing legislation. Besides these two personal stories, we see them shopping and complaining about rising prices for primary items such as coffee and sugar, as well as interacting with daughters, nephews and older colleagues close to retirement. The significance of intergenerational and intersubjective relations and of the factory as a community centre, fully emerges throughout the movie in various scenes and interactions. One worker, for instance, started to work in the mill before the war, when her mother and father also worked there. She remembers how she became used to cleaning her mother's machine as a teenager. After thirty-eight years in the factory she had trouble accepting that it was time to leave. In another collective scene, workers were reminiscing about receiving their first apartments from the factory management and about having to accommodate in-laws who wished to wash themselves since they had no bathroom in their homes. In the final scene of the movie, workers joined a collective boat excursion on the Danube, followed by a picnic on the

Danube river bank, to celebrate the women who were about to retire. Vera, Eržika and their colleagues shared homemade food, as well as personal and collective stories about their struggles with night shifts and work discipline, while new pensioners received poems and small presents. (Figure 7).

Other moving intergenerational scenes are the ones in which Eržika discusses her early work experience first with her small nieces and then with her mother and her daughter. Eržika's daughter asks: 'Granny, were you ok with mum going to work when she was 13?', to which the grandmother replied that she regretted it, but she had no choice at that time of extreme poverty, when the coupons obtained through factory work were the only way to access some basic items of consumption. 'The fact that she came back home happy somehow consoled me,' she states. The women in the movie not only show a sense of resignation and acceptance on the necessity of hard work for survival, but also testify to a high degree of existing social protection and social security that is somehow interiorized and taken for granted, especially in their interaction with doctors and factory administration. Even more than *Priče iz Fabrike*, *Vera i Eržika* manages to convey all the ambivalence of factory workers' structure of feeling and of the 'working mother' gender contract typical of the socialist era.

Garment workers undoubtedly faced exhaustion and hardships at work and at home during socialism, but at the same time gained significant

Figure 7 A photograph from the shooting of *Vera i Eržika*, Pančevo. Courtesy of Želimir Žilnik.

economic and social rights, gradually improving their position in comparison to the post-war era and to the older generation. They also developed a strong attachment to the textile factory as a community centre and as a source of welfare redistribution and intergenerational sociability. All these elements contributed to form workers' structure of feeling, and later became a powerful frame of reference through which the social and economic changes that invested Yugoslavia in the 1990s were interpreted and evaluated.

3

Labour after Yugoslavia: Post-socialism and deindustrialization in the textile sector

> *With the sale of the factory we did not sell the dignity of these workers. We ask the inhabitants of Kragujevac to join the protest that we will soon organize in front of the factory, to defend the dignity of these workers – their sisters, daughters and wives.*
> Union of Independent Trade Union of Kragujevac, 29 March 2016.

Industrial workers' protests are a common occurrence in post-socialist, post-Yugoslav states. In the case of the Slovenian firm Fori textile, whose production was delocalized in Kragujevac, Serbia, 400 female workers accused the management of disrespecting working hours and of imposing a working day of twelve hours. Seamstresses also complained of exhausted colleagues fainting, unpaid night work, faulty redistribution of working hours so that overtime doesn't get paid, working targets that almost no one can reach, manipulated earning calculations, and of managers' rough behaviour towards workers, including a worker being hit with a piece of equipment.[1] Such complaints – of strenuous working hours, low wages, unsafe working conditions and mobbing practices – are an intrinsic part of contemporary textile workers' narratives across the post-Yugoslav space. This chapter addresses the deterioration of workers' rights in textile production, focusing on the case studies of Štip (Macedonia) and Osijek (Croatia), as well as on the dilemmas faced by trade unionists in Varaždin (Croatia) and the rest of the region in the current context of extreme labour exploitation.

As a result of post-socialist and post-conflict transformations, and partly also as a result of the global economic crisis of 2008, many former socialist textile factories underwent bankruptcy and closure, while local privatized firms and foreign companies took over existing premises and unemployed

---

[1] Savez samostalnih sindikata Kragujevca, 'Saopštenje za javnost' (2016). Available at: http://www.sindikat-kragujevac.org.rs/novi/wp-content/uploads/2017/03/Pobuna-rad nica-u-Fori-Textile.pdf (accessed 20 January 2018).

workforce, but often ended up violating labour laws and workers' rights. Deindustrialization and job losses, thus, went hand in hand with processes of labour intensification, informalization and precarization for the remaining textile workforce across the post-Yugoslav region.[2] While all industrial sectors were severely affected by privatization and labour intensification, the post-Yugoslav textile industry was even more exposed to the transformations occurring in the global garment industry, characterized by a worldwide 'race to the bottom' for production costs in order to respond to the requirements of 'fast fashion'.[3] The outsourced processing of garments (the so-called OPT – outward processing trade – or *Lohn* work), in which Western partners are sending the textile material and the local factories carry out the sewing and finishing phases, before shipping back the final products, gradually became the dominant type of production in the region.[4] Yugoslav workers already performed outsourced work in exchange for hard currency for Western countries before 1989, taking part in 'processes of global class formation'.[5] The existence of the Yugoslav state and its prestige on a world scale, however, together with the self-management system, meant that workers were sheltered, up to a certain extent, from the extremes of global competition that became the norm in the 1990s and 2000s in new private firms. As this chapter shows, therefore, socialist experiences of work and welfare often serve as a benchmark of dignified life and labour, as opposed to the current precarious and exploited condition of textile workers in post-Yugoslav states. The value of dignified work, rooted in the socialist structure of feeling, is mobilized in textile workers' narratives about present industrial production.

Post-socialist transformations in the textile sector

In the post-Yugoslav space, post-socialist transformations occurred in parallel and interrelated ways with the demise of the multinational Yugoslav Federation, and with the creation of new nation states, which were immediately enmeshed

---

[2] About the connection between deindustrialization and labour intensification, see High, MacKinnon and Perchard (eds), *The Deindustrialized World*.
[3] Lucy Siegle and Jason Burke, *We Are What We Wear: Unravelling Fast Fashion and the Collapse of Rana Plaza* (London, 2014).
[4] Bettina Musiolek, 'Tools for enforcing labour rights and ensuring corporate social responsibility in the garment sector: The South-East European context', *South-East Europe Review for Labour and Social Affairs*, 3/3 (October 2000), pp. 123–35.
[5] Don Kalb, 'Introduction: Class and the new anthropological holism', in James G. Carrier and Don Kalb (eds), *Anthropologies of Class. Power, Practice and Inequality* (Cambridge, 2015), p. 19.

in the violent Yugoslav Wars (1991–9). If 1960s Yugoslavia could be described as a country aspiring to entry into the category of 'core' industrial countries, the economic crisis of the 1980s and the transition to market capitalism that followed in the 1990s brought a new 're-peripheralization' of the region vis-à-vis the European Union and global geopolitics.[6] Yugoslavia's standing on the world market – largely funded through international loans and export growth – suddenly turned into decline in the 1980s, when inflation and unemployment skyrocketed as a result of the austerity measures imposed by the International Monetary Fund (IMF) structural adjustment programmes to repay foreign debt.[7] During the Yugoslav Wars, and throughout the early and later phases of privatization, economic decline, inflation and unemployment rose even further, leading to an overall destruction of jobs and of industrial development, a process that has been defined also as 'de-development'.[8] In comparison to 1989, in 2003 real gross industrial output had fallen by 87 per cent in Bosnia-Herzegovina (excluding Republika Srpska), 48 per cent in Croatia, 61 per cent in Serbia and Montenegro, and 55 per cent in Macedonia.[9] It took almost two decades for post-Yugoslav states to reach their pre-existing 1990 GDP level, and Bosnia-Herzegovina, Montenegro and Serbia are still far from that target. Unemployment rates are among the highest in Europe, and social inequalities have risen sharply since the Yugoslav break-up.[10] In addition, the external debt of post-Yugoslav states is five times greater than that of Yugoslavia in 1990, and post-Yugoslav states' economies are highly dependent on loans and trade with core EU countries.[11] The re-peripheralization of the region vis-à-vis of the European Union also led to a devaluation of local industrial production (Slovenian and Croatian industrial production, for instance, was highly prized on the Yugoslav market, but is now less valued within the EU common market, despite both countries' accession to the EU in 2004 and 2013).

---

[6] Carl-Urik Schierup, 'Quasi-proletarians and a patriarchal bureaucracy: Aspects of Yugoslavia's re-peripheralisation', *Soviet Studies*, 44/1 (1992), pp. 79–99.
[7] Woodward, 'The political economy of ethno-nationalism in Yugoslavia', pp. 73–92. See also Andreja Živković, 'From the market … to the market: The debt economy after Yugoslavia' in Horvat and Štiks, *Welcome to the Desert of Post-Socialism*.
[8] Mieke Meurs and Rasika Ranasinghe, 'De-development in post-socialism: Conceptual and measurement issues', *Politics & Society*, 31 (2003), pp. 31–53.
[9] Martin Upchurch and Darko Marinković, 'Serbia from the October 2000 revolution to the crash', in G. Dale (ed.) *First the Transition, Then the Crash – Eastern Europe in the 2000s* (London, 2011), p. 234.
[10] Marija Stambolieva and Stefan Dehnert (eds), *Welfare States in Transition: 20 Years after the Yugoslav Welfare Model* (Sofia, 2011). See also Marija Stambolieva, *Welfare State Transformation in the Yugoslav Successor States: From Social to Unequal* (London, 2016).
[11] Živković, 'From the market'.

The negative impact of such transformations on industry and labour are wide-ranging, more so due to the uneven development of different areas of Yugoslavia during socialist times. While a comparison of economic data goes beyond the scope of this book, there are similar societal patterns and trends that can be observed through the shifting position of industrial workers across the region. The marginalization of workers and the general devaluation of labour and welfare rights in the region, in parallel with processes of privatization and deindustrialization, notably, can be observed in all post-Yugoslav states to varying degrees. Overall, post-socialist transformations led to a deterioration of social citizenship and to a rise in class and gender inequalities in the field of labour and welfare, alongside to the ethnic and gendered warfare and to the targeting of ethnic minorities that was characteristic of the Yugoslav Wars of the 1990s.[12] In recent years, new scholarly and activist publications have been highlighting workers' exploitation in free export zones and in foreign direct investment (FDI) companies subsidized by the state, as in the case of Serbia, as well as clientelist networks' dispossession of social property and real estate speculations at the expenses of industrial workers, as in the case of Croatia.[13] The transformation of discourses surrounding class in the transition from socialism to post-socialism has also been analysed, particularly in relation to the instrumental mobilization of workers by the Milošević regime in Serbia.[14]

Scholars of labour and deindustrialization in other post-socialist contexts have underlined how post-socialist transformations and industrial workers' symbolic marginalization go hand in hand, as a way to legitimize the new

[12] See Chiara Bonfiglioli, 'Gendering social citizenship: Textile workers in post-Yugoslav states', *CITSEE Working Papers Series*, School of Law, University of Edinburgh, 2013/30.
[13] See for instance the following recent publications on post-socialist transition, neoliberalism and privatization processes in the region: Horvat and Štiks, *Welcome to the Desert of Post-Socialism*; Ivan Radenković, *Foreign Direct Investments in Serbia* (Belgrade, 2016); Milenko Srećković, *Corporate Imperialism: The Zones of Exploitation in Serbia* (Belgrade, 2015); Marina Ivandić and Igor Livada, *Lines of (Dis)Continuity: Forms and Methods of Labour Struggle in Croatia 1990-2014* (Belgrade, 2015).
[14] On class and politics in Serbia see: Upchurch and Marinković, 'Serbia from the October 2000 revolution to the crash'; Goran Musić, *Serbia's Working Class in Transition, 1988-2013* (Belgrade, 2013); see also Tibor T. Meszmann, 'The lingering constituency: Discourses of class in postsocialist Serbia', *East European Politics and Society* 29/3, pp. 672–84. On Croatia, see: Tea Škokić and Sanja Potkonjak,'"Working class gone to heaven": From working class to middle class and back', *Narodna Umjetnost*, 53/1 (2016), pp. 117–32. On socialist Yugoslavia and its aftermath, see Darko Suvin, 'On class relationships in Yugoslavia 1945–1974, with a hypothesis about the ruling class', *Journal of Contemporary Central and Eastern Europe (Debatte)*, 20/1 (2012), pp. 37–71; Inga Tomić-Koludrović and Marko Petrić, 'Class in Yugoslav socialism and in the post-Yugoslav societies: Toward a bourdieuan repositioning of the issue (Part 1)', *Revija za sociologiju*, 44/2 (2014), pp. 107–37.

social and economic transformations and redistribution of wealth and resources. As Kinga Pozniak argued in the context of Poland:

> Industrial workers ... are popularly depicted as spoiled by socialist-era privileges, entitled, lazy, and unwilling to work hard and reinvent themselves in the new economy. This demonization of people who voice alternate memories is a very effective strategy for preventing the emergence of alternative discourses that might seek to challenge the present political or economic arrangements.[15]

While workers' symbolic marginalization is part and parcel of the problem, it should not divert our attention to simultaneous material phenomena of precarization, labour intensification and increased exploitation in post-socialism. As Kideckel argues, the temporary aspects associated with the terms 'post-socialism' and 'transition' might obscure the relevance of 'neo-capitalism' for East-Central Europe, namely, of a 'social system that reworks basic capitalist principles in new, even more inegalitarian ways than the Western model from which it derives'.[16] While Central and Eastern Europe are turned into a 'dependent hinterland' of Western capitalism, the working classes are placed at the bottom of the social scale, as 'neo-capitalism manufactures social structures with which workers engage either as degraded supplicants or as alienated antagonists'.[17]

As I will show in the rest of the chapter, the elements that Kideckel singles out as characteristic of the 'subalternization of labour' in post-1989 Romania can as well be applied to the post-Yugoslav context, particularly when it comes to the limited access to knowledge and information on the labour market and on the privatization process. In the post-Yugoslav space, the process of privatization of the previously socially owned industrial plants was very often characterized by corruption and clientelist arrangements. Thanks to privatization agreements through shareholders' quotas or through tender, the managers of previously socially owned companies, who already possessed the necessary social and cultural capital, often appropriated the assets of their enterprises to establish private firms. This is the case, for instance, of the Arena factory in Pula. Alternatively, managers without no experience whatsoever in a specific industrial sector were appointed 'politically' with devastating consequences, as in the case of the Dalmatinka factory in Sinj before privatization. As Živković notes, 'Privatisation was

---

[15] Pozniak, *Nowa Huta*, p. 186.
[16] Kideckel, 'The unmaking', p.115.
[17] Ibid., p. 116.

simply a link in the chain of the debt economy, allowing the insider class of state and firm managers to secure property rights, or for criminals to launder illegal earnings, at the expense of the destruction of industry.'[18] Workers have often been working without receiving a wage for months, while new factory owners could 'strip assets, resell company plant, equipment and land, or take out loans against these, using the money to speculate in real estate transactions', until bankruptcy was declared and workers were left with nothing, while factory owners walked away with massive profits without being held accountable by the state.[19] During these transformations, many workers found that they could not claim back decades of social contributions, savings or unpaid wages. Workers also often missed the legal and political resources to oppose such processes, so that disempowerment in relation to the privatization process became a common phenomenon across the former Yugoslav space and across industrial sectors.

As a traditionally feminized and labour-intensive industry, the textile and garment industry in post-Yugoslav states was greatly affected by processes of post-socialist transformation and privatization. Another element that greatly impacted the industry was the break-up of the Yugoslav Federation and the loss of the common Yugoslav market, which provided a trade outlet for local firms during socialism. Together with the end of Yugoslavia, the trade links established with the socialist bloc and with Non-Aligned countries in the global South that existed during the Cold War disappeared after 1989. The terms of exchange with Western clients in the European Economic Community (EEC) and then with the European Union also changed in the course of time: Western European neighbouring countries, particularly Germany and Italy, were preferential trade partners, but, since the global recession of 1974–5, the EEC raised trade barriers in export area where Yugoslavia had competitive advantages, including textiles.[20] In the 1990s, after the collapse of the socialist bloc and of the Yugoslav Federation, these unfair terms of exchange were further strengthened, since the tariff and custom protection put in place by the European Union towards Eastern European and South-Eastern European countries reinforced the power of EU core countries towards candidates and non-candidates to EU accession.[21] The WTO trade agreement on textile and clothing of 2005, additionally, abolished tariffs and liberalized the textile trade from the global South to the global North, leading to the booming of

---

[18] Živković, 'From the market'.
[19] Ibid.
[20] Ibid.
[21] Dorothee Bohle, 'Neoliberal Hegemony, transnational capital and the terms of EU's eastward expansion', *Capital & Class*, 30/1 (2006), pp. 57–86.

textile sweatshops in Asia, with the introduction of new cheap products on the European market.

The booming of garments produced in Asia put increased competitive pressures on producers located in Eastern and South-Eastern Europe, whose competitive advantage is represented by the proximity to Western markets and by the availability of a qualified workforce previously employed in the socialist sector. The only way to withstand this pressure and to avoid delocalization in cheaper locations is to keep labour costs as low as possible.[22] While Western European producers invest in know-how, design and technology, and are able to profit from the creation of brands and collections, the labour intensive, sewing phases are outsourced to Eastern Europe, North Africa and Asia in order to benefit from the lower labour costs and the lack of protective workers legislation in the global South and the European peripheries. What this means, de facto, is that the post-Yugoslav garment industry is affected both by the global 'race to the bottom' in production costs and by trade dependency from core EU countries, leading to an increase in low-paid subcontracting and to the weakening or disappearance of local brands and know-how. In the case of FDI and free export zones, there is also a regional 'race to the bottom' among local municipalities, who compete in extending special privileges to multinational companies, as in the case of Serbia and Macedonia.[23] Intra-regional processes of delocalization, particularly of Slovenian companies to Serbia, are also common.[24]

In the 1980s, Yugoslavia was 'among the world's leading producers of textile and wearing apparel'.[25] Several textile complexes employed thousands of workers, such as the Mura factory in Murska Sobota, Slovenia, which employed 6,200 workers, or the MTT textile kombinat in Maribor, Slovenia, which included various textile branches and employed over 6,500 workers. The Makedonka kombinat in Štip, Macedonia, employed over 5,700 workers in the 1970s, while the Varteks kombinat in Varaždin, Croatia, employed almost 10,000 workers between the main factory complex and the annexes in the surroundings. Textile factories were spread both in bigger cities and in smaller towns, and successful firms often subcontracted work to other smaller workshops in their surroundings, or in peripheral areas. During

---

[22] Adrian Smith, et al., 'Outward processing, EU enlargement and regional relocation in the European textile and clothing industry: Reflections on the European Commission's communication on "The future of the textiles and clothing sector in the enlarged European Union"', *European Urban and Regional Studies*, 12/1 (2005), pp. 83–91.
[23] Srećković, *Corporate Imperialism*.
[24] Živković, 'From the market'.
[25] Doris Hanzl-Weiss, 'Enlargement and the textiles, clothing and footwear industry', *World Economy*, 27/6 (2004), pp. 923–45.

socialist times, textile factories in Yugoslavia were both producing so-called 'full package' collections for the internal and international markets and outsourced production in partnership with foreign firms, particularly in the 1970s and 1980s. Between the 1990s and the 2010s, many formerly successful factories underwent privatization and restructuring, and subcontracting for Western clients became the norm, while local brands and collections gradually disappeared. Bankruptcies and factory closures pushed thousands of workers into unemployment, leading to what is commonly described as the 'collapse' (*propad*) of the local textile industry.

To get an idea of the extent of this collapse, it is worth recalling that in the late 1980s, the industry employed approximately 474,000 workers, amounting to 17 per cent of all industrial workers, according to official reports.[26] Post-Yugoslav media, following local chambers of commerce and trade unions, report slightly higher numbers, with a total of around 487,000 workers employed in the late 1980s and early 1990s, as opposed to approximately 128,000 workers currently employed in the sector across the post-Yugoslav region.[27] On the basis of such data, it can be gathered that around 350,000 jobs were lost in the textile and garment industry in the past thirty years. At the same time, alongside job losses in the formal sector, the rise of employment in the informal sector should also be taken into account.[28] Job losses and

---

[26] Ilija Draganić, 'Neki problemi i pravci razvoja tekstilne industrije Jugoslavije', *Ekonomika preduzeća*, 39/7–8 (1991), pp. 391–404. These data are consistent with a 1991 World Bank report, which lists 470.000 workers in the sector. World Bank, 'Yugoslavia – industrial restructuring study: Overview, issues and strategy for restructuring' (1991), Available at http://documents.worldbank.org/curated/en/839571468304234506/Yugoslavia-Industrial-restructuring-study-overview-issues-and-strategy-for-restructuring (last accessed 20 January 2018).

[27] Reliable and up-to-date statistics on current employees are hard to obtain due to rapid fluctuations in the workforce. The estimates for the socialist period are further complicated by the fact that employees in the leather and shoe industry are often included in the count, given that they are traditionally represented by the same trade unions. The most severe job losses took place in Croatia (16,300 workers in textile and 9,600 in the leather and shoe industry, as opposed to 126,000 in late socialism for these sectors combined) and Slovenia (5,000 current employees in textile, as opposed to 37,000 before 1989). The workforce in Croatia and Slovenia, which are now part of the European Union, is better paid, hence less competitive. Textile production is still significant in less wealthy post-Yugoslav states which are not part of the European Union, where the cost of the workforce is more competitive: in Macedonia there are approximately 40,000 employees (from 64,000 in late socialism), while Serbia has around 47,000 workers (from 160,000 in late socialism). Bosnia-Herzegovina lists some 20,000 workers today, a fifth of those employed before the war (100,000).

[28] The Clean Clothes Campaign estimates that employees in the Serbian textile and shoe industries amount to 100,000 when adding up the formal and the informal sector. See Clean Clothes Campaign, *Country Profile Serbia* (2017), available at: https://cleanclothes.org/livingwage/europe/country-profiles/serbia/view (accessed 20 January 2018).

informalization mainly affected female workers, given that they constitute over 80 per cent of the workforce in textile and garment factories.

With the demise of market socialism and the introduction of neoliberal capitalism in the region, the 'working mother' gender contract faded away, even if its memory still persists among former workers. Across Europe, both post-socialist and capitalist gender regimes have started to converge towards a new neoliberal model, in which 'market individualism has attacked the collective assumption of western welfare states and the whole way of life of the planned economies of former communist countries'.[29] The shrinkage in state intervention has brought reduced spending on childcare, education, health, pensions and child benefits.[30] In the field of textile production, which was already heavily feminized during socialist times, market capitalism led to increased gendered segregation, precarity and exploitative labour conditions. Unemployed or precariously employed women dedicate an increased amount of time to make ends meet, and the double burden that was typical of socialist times results in an even heavier burden when wages have to be secured through informal labour and underpaid labour, as in the case of contemporary textile production.[31] In the next sections I will highlight specific cases of workers' experiences of deindustrialization and post-socialist transformation in today's garment and textile factories across the region.

'Before it was different, it was easier': Work across generations

The town of Štip is located in Eastern Macedonia and has a population of around 50,000 inhabitants. The region was known for its production of silk, cloth and laces in the nineteenth and early twentieth century, and Štip became an industrial textile centre during socialist times. What makes the town an interesting case study for a comparison of working conditions before and after privatization is the fact that the now privatized textile production

---

[29] Gillian Pascall and Jane Lewis, 'Emerging gender regimes and policies for gender equality in a wider Europe', *Journal of Social Policy*, 33/3 (2004), pp. 373–94.
[30] Ibid. For the post-Yugoslav context see also Domagoj Mihaljević, 'Tržište rada kao faktor rodne nejednakosti u zemljama bivše Jugoslavije', *Bilten*, 16 December 2015. Avalable at: www.bilten.org/?p=10776 (accessed 20 January 2018).
[31] Bonfiglioli, 'Gendered citizenship in the global European periphery'.

is still the largest industrial sector, with over fifty-eight firms employing approximately 45 per cent of the local active population, according to a 2005 report.[32] Textile workers represent 34 per cent of total employees in the manufacturing sector in Macedonia, with exports being directed mainly to Germany (51 per cent), Greece (19 per cent) but also to Holland, the UK, Italy, the United States, Serbia, Montenegro, Turkey, Croatia and Belgium. A majority of female workers are employed in small *konfekcije*, namely, small private firms performing the finishing phases of outsourced production for Western clients, while men are driving taxis or working in logistics. Present working conditions, however, sharply differ from working conditions in socialist times, whose memory is still vividly present among the town's inhabitants.

Štip's main kombinat – that is, a colossal textile complex combining different production processes for yarn, raw fabrics and finished products – was the Makedonka (Macedonian woman) factory, which employed several thousand workers, predominantly women. Makedonka was created in the early 1950s as a result of the industrialization drive, and their products were mainly sold on the internal market. The number of workers increased from 3,500 in the mid-1960s to more than 6,000 in the late 1980s. A centralized heating system and a railway line were included in the Makedonka complex. Cotton was produced in Macedonia in the early socialist period but in the 1970s and 1980s cotton was mainly imported from countries that were allied with Yugoslavia through the Non-Aligned Movement, such as India and Egypt. Weaving plants and apparel producers linked to the Makedonka complex were gradually built in Štip and the surrounding towns and villages to absorb the great number of unemployed people living in the region. Makedonka included a restaurant for the workers serving one free meal per day, discount stores, childcare facilities, a library and a choir that performed around town. The factory also provided housing for its workers, through a complex of apartment buildings, as well as holiday facilities on the shores of Lake Ohrid, a summer resort on the mountain Plačkovica, and a hotel at Lake Dojran. Workers could also take interest-free credit and advances on their wages for a variety of purposes. The other main factory for the production of ready-made garments, Astibo, was founded in the 1960s, and employed thousands of workers in Štip and the surrounding villages. In the 1970s, Astibo had sixty shops selling casual apparel all over Yugoslavia, and also gained a licence for

---

[32] Center for Research and Policy Making, *The History of the Macedonian Textile Industry with a Focus on Shtip* (Skopje, 2005).

the production of Wrangler jeans.³³ In the early 1980s, Astibo employed 3,700 workers, and the factory included 'a health care institution, a restaurant, and a day care centre for employees' children'. The health care institution also had 'a unit for gynaecological treatment offering, among others, counselling about the usage of contraceptives, a lab, a paediatrician, and a dentist unit'. The company also built houses for its workers across town.³⁴

As mentioned in the previous chapter, the welfare services provided at factories such as Makedonka did not always live up to workers' expectations, particularly when it came to childcare facilities and housing distribution, which were perennial gripes. In comparison to the post-socialist period that followed, however, the golden days of Makedonka and Astibo came to set the standards of desirable working conditions and social security. Makedonka underwent restructuring in the early 1990s, with several waves of layoffs. Privatization started in 1995, and eight different entities were created from the existing subsections of the factory. In 2000 the Macedonian government started a bankruptcy procedure, and attempted to sell the whole complex, but these attempts at privatization failed and the company was put into liquidation and sold piece by piece from 2001. Many costly machines were stolen, or sold as scrap metal. When I visited the complex in 2013, the former kombinat was largely in ruin, with a small warehouse selling the last scrap material from the building, mainly metres of cloth, tools, rubber and bolts. A portrait of Tito still stood in the concierge's cabin, as a reminder of Makedonka's better times (Figure 8). The only renovated area of the Makedonka complex is the former workers' canteen, which has been turned into a private restaurant. The Astibo complex, in contrast to Makedonka, was bought by a consortium of enterprises in 2002, and its main management building is also fully renovated.

Deindustrialization and post-socialist transformations in Štip went hand in hand with an extreme precarization of living and working conditions when it came to textile industry workers employed in newly established private factories. As advertised by the official website *Invest in Macedonia*, besides the proximity to Western Europe, another main competitive advantage of the local garment industry is its 'high flexibility and readiness to adapt to the demands of foreign markers'.³⁵ The working time and wages in the local

---

[33] During late socialism, there was a strong competition in jeans production, as local factories gained the licence for different foreign brands, to be sold on the local market but mostly abroad. Astibo produced Wrangler jeans, while Varteks in Varaždin produced for Levi's and Beko in Belgrade produced for Lee Cooper.
[34] Center for Research and Policy Making, *The History of the Macedonian Textile Industry*.
[35] Official website 'Invest in Macedonia'. Available at: www.investinmacedonia.com (accessed 20 January 2018).

Figure 8 A portrait of Tito in what remains of the Makedonka factory, Štip, 2013. Photo by the author.

textile industry, therefore, are largely dictated by global competition and by the needs of 'just-in-time' fashion that requires very rapid response times. All over the town, one can hear complaints about strenuous working rhythms, constant overtime work and low wages that do not nearly approximate a living wage, namely, a wage that is sufficient to guarantee a proper standard of living in relation to current prices for food and living expenses. This situation is common throughout Macedonia. The newly harmonized minimum wage for the Macedonian textile, clothing and leather sector for 2017 is established at 9,590 denars, the equivalent of 156 euros per month.

The textile sector remains one of the lowest paid, with evident gender discrimination, due to the fact that 85 per cent of its workers are women. The exploitative conditions in the textile industry in Macedonia have been the object of several reports by international organizations such as the Clean Clothes Campaign and the Fair Wear Foundation, which highlighted multiple violations of workers' rights.[36] Poverty wages, forced overtime,

---

[36] See: Clean Clothes Campaign, *Made in Europe: Swiss, Austrian and German Workwear Suppliers Profit from Macedonian Workers' Poverty and Fear* (2012). Available at: http://www.sachsen-kauft-fair.de/wp-content/uploads/2012/08/madeineurope_engl.pdf (accessed 20 January 2018); Fair Wear Foundation, *Macedonia Country Study*, (2010). Available at: https://www.fairwear.org/resource/macedonia-country-study-2010/

precarious contracts, insecure working conditions and lack of trade unions representatives are the main areas of concern. Injuries and deaths from poor working condition and overwork have also been reported. Journalist Natasha Dokovska reported the case of a woman, Marijana Stojčevska, forty years old, who died after thirteen hours of consecutive work at the machine in a Greek-owned factory in Bitola in the summer of 2007. The owner of the factory allegedly prevented a doctor from entering the premises and issuing a death certificate. In another factory in Kočani, six workers were brutally attacked both verbally and physically by the factory owner when they demanded their unpaid wages. They were working over ten hours a day for a daily salary of 4–5 euros, producing garments for Western luxury brands. During his attack, the owner allegedly screamed: *'This is not socialism here!-I'll give you your money, your rights!'* In another case in Prilep, thirty workers were locked inside the workshop to finish an order for export.[37] As a result of the amendments made to the Macedonian labour laws in the 1990s and 2000s to make the country more competitive for foreign investments, workers were deprived of many rights and came to be seen as easily replaceable due to the very high unemployment rate.[38]

Such a situation clearly affects the subjective experiences of textile workers, who express feelings of precarity, social uncertainty and injustice. Among my narrators in Štip, the early post-socialist period is recalled as a traumatic one. Nada, for instance, aged forty at the time of the interview in 2013, is the daughter of two skilled white-collar workers employed in the Makedonka socialist plant. When her parents lost their jobs in the 1990s, she had to abandon her studies of English literature in the capital city of Skopje and started to look for work back in Štip, where she found a job in a private factory, working at the button-hole machine. Thanks to her knowledge of English, she could also work as an intermediary for foreign clients. She could then support her parents for eight months, until they found again work in the private textile sector. Working conditions in the 1990s were particularly exploitative, as new entrepreneurs took advantage of political uncertainty

(accessed 20 January 2018). See also the documentary by Macedonian author Biljana Garvanlieva, titled *The Seamstresses*, short version available at: https://vimeo.com/54517757 (accessed 20 January 2018).

[37] Natasha Dokovska, 'Sweatshops Producing Big Western Brands in Macedonia Continue Unchecked Leaving Twenty Women Dead This Summer'. *The Wip*, 18 August 2007. Available at: http://thewip.net/2007/08/18/sweatshops-producing-big-western-brands-in-macedonia-continue-unchecked-leaving-twenty-women-dead-this-summer/ (accessed 20 January 2018).

[38] Zdravko Saveski, 'The process of the reduction of workers' rights in Macedonia in the period 1993-2003', *South-East Europe Review*, 2 (2005), pp. 95–109.

and poorly defined legal regulations. Many workers were not formally registered and lost several years of social contributions. Nada herself, who had moved to sampling and control jobs, lost four and a half years, which are now missing from her *radni staž*, that is, the years of service necessary to obtain a pension. At the end of the 1990s, Nada recalled being always at work, and so exhausted on a daily basis that she did not realize that she was four months pregnant, until she fainted in the factory:

> When I became pregnant, I didn't realize, because I was working the third shift (night), and then second shift (afternoon), and then first shift (morning), so I thought, since I am not eating regularly, I am not sleeping regularly, the menstrual cycle stopped, like with people in concentration camps (*u logorima*). And then once I fainted at work and went to the doctor. ... I was four months pregnant! And I didn't know. I cried a lot. It was such a rush, we were always at work.[39]

Interestingly, Nada compares her working experience with the experience of concentration camps' inmates in the Second World War through the word *logor* (lager). This reference is not confined to Macedonia but is often used in the post-Yugoslav press when referring to new capitalist factories across the region and to their exploitative working conditions. As Nada testifies, workers in private textile companies often feel at the mercy of their bosses when it comes to working rhythms and targets, and experience a lack of legislative and social protection:

> This is not a career, you cannot call it a career, it is very heavy work. You always work, curb your head and do what they tell you to do. The problem here is that the owners are careless, and they will tell you 'this should be finished', they don't care about sickness and neurological disorders, if the nerves leave you. And on the other hand they will always find some trick to diminish your wage.[40]

Overtime is a common occurrence in Macedonian garment factories, and often the working day is unsustainably long. While interviewing Nada together with her colleague Ana, a quality controller in a private firm in her thirties, Ana recalled that often she had to stay at work from Saturday at 6.00 am until late at night, one time even until Sunday at 4.00 am, since

---

[39] Nada and Ana, Štip, February 2013.
[40] Ibid.

some orders had to be finished and shipped back. Nada then compared the current conditions with the working conditions experienced by her parents at Makedonka. 'Before it was different, it was easier!' she said: her parents had a shorter working week, free weekends, paid overtime work and night work, and a canteen providing free meals. While Nada's parents were white-collar workers, and thus they were not submitted to night shifts, blue-collar workers at Makedonka had to perform night shifts as well as working Saturdays, as in other textile factories, but this mostly happened once a month on rotation and not on a systemic, arbitrary basis.

Another element that is strikingly different, in comparison to socialist times, is the utter disrespect for workers' social rights, such as holidays, maternity leave, sick leave and commuting expenses. Summer holidays on the Adriatic Sea, in particular, are seen as the privilege of older generations, who could stay in subsidized resorts for a symbolic price. For many current workers, holidays on the seaside have become unaffordable, or very difficult to obtain since summer is the peak time for textile production. When Ana wanted to take a holiday with her family in August, for instance, the result was a wage cut of 100 euros. Maternity leaves are also under threat. Workers in Macedonia are formally entitled to nine months of paid maternity leave, extendable to twelve months in case of the birth of more than one child. A new 1998 law amendment, however, authorizes employees to come back to work before the termination of the leave, practically allowing employers to exercise pressure on their workers.[41] In the case of my narrators, Nada could not obtain paid maternity leave after the birth of her second child in the early 2000s, and she was forced to pay for a private crèche when the child was only eight months old. In another factory where she worked, she left in protest after her boss denied her two days of sick leave for a medical examination that had to be carried out in Skopje.

Textile workers also experienced deskilling, namely, a devaluation of existing skills, and a drop in purchasing power in the past thirty years. Nada's mother, Vera, in her mid-sixties, used to be an accountant at Makedonka, but her skills were no longer deemed useful after the closure of the factory. After a few years of unemployment, she found a manual job in a private foreign firm, where she works with a very tiresome press machine. Her living standards, however, are very far from the ones she experienced as a white-collar worker in the past. Vera states that she works 'like a horse', but that she cannot make ends meet, nonetheless. 'I work and I like to work,' she says, 'but this is not important. What's important is that I cannot get to the end of the

[41] Saveski, 'The process of the reduction of workers' rights'.

month with my wage.' Of her 200 euros wage, she spends half on electricity bills. Until 1993, instead, Vera earned 700 Deutsch Marks, the equivalent of 350–400 euros. She could buy an entire kitchen on credit 'without noticing it', she states, while today she cannot buy anything, 'not even a television'. In addition, when working for Makedonka, Vera felt like 'working for something that was *ours*'.[42] Next to material losses, the loss of symbolic recognition and factory loyalty experienced during socialism is something that is painfully felt by the older generation. Former employees of socialist factories do not feel recognized in contemporary private factories where the logic of profit trumps factory loyalties. This is exemplified by the moving account retold by Nada about her mother Vera, which deserves to be quoted in its entirety as it shows the contrast between workers' structure of feeling developed during socialism, and present day post-socialist values:

> Four years ago my grandma – the mum of my dad – could not move from her bed, she was very sick and was about to die. … And my parents agreed that my mum would leave her job and would take care of the old lady. So my mum spoke with the factory owners, who are very happy with her, and told her to take the time she needs and to come back to work afterwards. … My grandma died some six months later, everything was done properly. And then my mum went back to work three days later. My mum is highly respected there, she works a lot, more than me. And she always helps young people to learn and the owner trusts her a lot. And then the owner of the firm gave a prize to workers who are working there for ten years. But my mum did not get it, since she took six months off, unpaid. She was told that she did not have ten years of service, so she could not have the promotion. My mother cried! She said, 'it's not because of those 100 euros! but because I did my best to be a good human being, to let my mother-in-law die as a human being, as she deserves, and I am not deserving anything for that. They just ask me, "where have you been in the last six months"'. And she did not want to quit and to find another job where the quality would be lower. She did not want to revolt. But she cried. And I felt very sorry.[43]

While this anecdote may appear banal or not particularly brutal in comparison to other stories of post-socialist exploitation, it nonetheless highlights the significance of symbolic recognition for workers who were trained in the socialist era. Additionally, this passage highlights women's

---

[42] Vera and Nada, Štip, February 2013.
[43] Nada and Ana, Štip, February 2013.

traditional caretaking roles and intergenerational solidarity, as well as the demise of the previous 'working mother' gender contract, which provided working women with some flexibility when it came to combining productive and reproductive work, and which recognized that family obligations were as important as working requirements. Vera still complied with this moral vision grounded in socialist values, while her employer could not recognize such logic, and thus did not provide the additional symbolic recognition she thought she deserved.

Intergenerational solidarity is still widespread in Štip, where older women help their daughters or younger relatives with childcare, while younger women are generally taking care of the elderly and ill. Nada could count on her mother-in-law for help with childcare, and took care of her before she died. Intergenerational solidarity also works with housing, particularly since the older generation could access social housing through factory work. Nada, for instance, swapped her smaller apartment with her parents' larger one once she had children. Overall, the case of Štip shows that the worsening of labour and welfare conditions in the garment industry leads to widespread feelings of precarity and insecurity among workers of different generations, and to a general view of the socialist past as a desirable model in terms of working and living standards. Female textile workers lost not only living wages and consumer power, but also a wide array of benefits attached to the 'working mother' gender contract typical of socialism, such as paid maternity leaves, subsidized holidays and shorter working weeks. Many of them currently struggle with overtime work, job uncertainty, poverty wages, and with combining such strenuous working conditions with caretaking responsibilities in the private sphere. In the following section, another case of deindustrialization and labour intensification will be addressed, namely, the ones of textile workers in the town of Osijek, Croatia.

'Only duties and no rights': The subcontracting limbo

The town of Osijek is located in Slavonia, close to the Croatian border with Serbia, and has a population of over 108,000 inhabitants. During the Austro-Hungarian times, but also in the interwar period, several textile workshops and small industries were created in Osijek, in addition to other industrial sectors. During socialism, the town was a major agricultural and industrial centre, exporting wood, textile, leather and rubber, footwear, as well as cattle and meat. Chemical and metal industries were also prominent. Close to the Croatian martyr city of Vukovar (besieged and destroyed during the Yugoslav Wars) and home to a sizeable Serbian minority, Osijek also suffered damage during the conflict, and in the 1990s most industrial complexes underwent ruination and bankruptcy. Industrial workers numbered 26,000 in the late 1980s but are now reduced to 4,500.[44] Due to the depressed economic conditions of the area and thanks to Croatia's access to the European Union in 2013, which opened up new possibilities for travel and migration, many young people have been migrating en masse to Ireland in recent years, alongside more traditional destinations such as Austria and Germany. The city centre itself appears largely empty, with many shops closed or for sale. Former textile factories were numerous in town, as the textile industry employed approximately 7,000 workers in Osijek. Today, formerly successful factory such as IMK Slavonija, Mara, Tekos, Svilana and LIO – as well as the important Kožara, the leather factory – are lying in ruin in the outskirts of town. The only remaining textile production is the one catering to the needs of an Italian multinational garment company, which holds a main subcontractor in town, which I will name Vesuvius (the branch used to carry the main multinational name in the near past) as well as several smaller subcontractors in Osijek as well as in surrounding towns in Slavonia.

During my stay in Osijek, I interviewed workers of different generations in two different focus groups. Some older workers experienced working conditions in socialist factories (in this case IMK Slavonija, a typical *konfekcija* or garment factory, and Tekos, a childwear factory), as well as in subcontracting firms in the post-socialist era. Other workers, between thirty and fifty years of age, were mainly employed by Vesuvius or by smaller subcontractors, and thus only experienced textile work in post-socialism, sometimes as a first job but also sometimes as a second career after losing a job in the administrative or trade sector. What is striking about the collected narratives is the widespread feeling of workers' devaluation, and current workers' struggle for daily survival. Poverty wages, precarious working contracts, intensified working times and the disrespect of basic rights such as sick leave, together with episodes of mobbing are commonly mentioned in the stories and weighed against workers' social and labour rights in socialist times.

The welfare protections that went under the 'working mother' gender contract typical of socialism – and the general spirit of socialist times, which my narrators defined as 'humanist', namely, positive in moral and ethical terms – have been completely subsumed by the logic of maximized profit

---

[44] Marija Jakovljević and Luka Matić, 'Osijek i Kruševac: postranzicijsko ogledalo', 23 December 2015. Available at: http://www.osijek031.com/osijek.php?topic_id=60210 (accessed 3 December 2016).

that is typical of neoliberal capitalism. To have an idea of the magnitude of these transformations in societal values, one can consider a passage from a commemorative brochure produced by the local knitwear factory Mara, which employed 664 workers, of which 553 were women, in the mid-1980s. Even if Mara exported up to 91 per cent of its production to foreign countries, and was thus subjected to world market competition, it was acknowledged that female workers were potential working mothers who needed to accommodate family life with work responsibilities. As the brochure mentioned, sick leaves and maternity leaves were numerous at Mara due to its young, female labour force. However, working mothers' social contribution to the reproduction of society was valued alongside women's productivity:

> It is known that our socialist society guarantees a special health protection to pregnant women and mothers, so that a healthy and unhindered development of the child would be assured. Therefore, society as a whole gains from the birth of each new member, and those lost hours due to these justified leaves are not lost in their totality.[45]

As this passage highlights, the 'working mother' gender contract took into account the contradictions between the logic of productivity and the logic of human and social reproduction, even in a factory that mainly produced for export in exchange for hard currency.

In present textile firms in the Osijek region, instead, the logic of productivity and profit is the only one that counts, against workers' structure of feeling, which is deeply rooted in the 'humanist' vision inherited during socialism, which has also been transmitted across generations to younger workers. Both old and young workers see workers' welfare and solidarity as values to be cherished, in contrast to increasing precarious conditions. Since the 1990s, precarity is rife in new private companies that produce textiles in the Osijek area. Vesna, a seamstress in her late 1950s, worked for the Tekos childwear company from 1980 until 1991, when she started working in the private sector. Vesna worked in five private companies since then, including the restructured former socialist factory IMK Slavonija. She describes socialism and the subsequent post-socialist transformation as follows:

> For me it was good. Really, the first job I took at Tekos was ... I was happy to go to work. And I loved the work and it was hard for me when they stopped working. And when I started after that, after the war, from

---

[45] Mara, *Mara, 1909-1984*, commemorative publication (Osijek, 1984), Osijek State Archive library, p. 41.

company to company, that was killing me (*ubitačno*). You go to work with some kind of depression, fear, you don't know what to expect and so on. An enormous difference between then and now. Then workers were respected, and went forward, and were awarded, and they never behaved inhumanly (*neljudski*) towards you, while now there is nothing of that anymore.[46]

Vesna and her colleagues from the older generation listed various material factors that shaped these feelings, notably various instances in which they worked without being paid, both in private firms and in the former socialist IMK Slavonija, which went bankrupt and closed in 2013 despite the fact that the state retained 80 per cent of ownership. In private firms, also, many times the current owner declared bankruptcy and promptly opened a new firm under another name, without paying wages in arrears. But unpaid wages were not the only issue. The lack of symbolic respect as workers, and what Vesna defined as 'inhumane' treatment, also play a big role in workers' feelings in post-socialism. As Vesna reinstated later in the interview: 'Then I was happy to go to work, now I go because I have to. Because I am not a worker now, [allegedly] now I don't know how to work.' Old, experienced workers are often treated as incapable since they are unable to adapt to the new productive rhythms, and mobbing episodes are common. Within the restructured IMK Slavonija, for instance, Slađana, Vesna's colleague, felt mistreated by an Italian female supervisor, and decided to resign because she didn't want to cope with that stress. Other workers were mistreated, and one in particular suffered a nervous breakdown due to the arbitrariness of this supervisor, so much so that the worker's son and husband came to the factory looking 'to beat up' the Italian supervisor.

Another source of contention are the prizes and symbolic awards that were a constant of factory life during socialism, and which are no longer distributed in the same way in post-socialist times, as shown in the case of Vera in the previous section. While in socialist factories workers were used to New Year celebrations with a special children's programme and special rewards, Vesna felt humiliated in a private subcontracting factory when the boss asked her to sign a paper stating that her children received a Christmas' gift of 400 kunas (approximately 55 euros), while in fact they didn't receive anything, and the boss used the bill to cover for some other expenses. 'I signed', she said, 'but I cried so much, it was so hard for me. Isn't it enough what I do for you, do you have to earn money on my children?'[47] Against

---

[46] Vesna and colleagues, Osijek, April 2016. Co-interviewed with Nikolina Hrga.
[47] Ibid.

the post-socialist logic of profit, socialist times are described as a time of good social standards and fair work relations. According to workers from the older generation like Vesna and Slađana, during socialism workers were more productive and even better disposed to work overtime, because they were asked 'in a nice way' and without it being considered an obligation, instead of being constantly forced and humiliated. Besides precarious working conditions, former workers also experience devaluation in the form of lack of purchasing power and very low retirement wages. Such is the case of Walter, a retired male worker who became shop-floor supervisor at Tekos during socialism, and who gets a monthly retirement pension of 2,100 kuna (300 euros). After complaining about his low pension and about the ways in which it was calculated, which do not reflect his earnings during the socialist era, Walter says that he 'cannot comprehend' how workers during socialism managed to earn good wages and even have savings, while today people work to survive and cannot put any savings aside.

Younger workers are also experiencing stress and devaluation, both as a result of material working conditions and of sketchy social rights in private subcontracting firms. In this sense, it is interesting to compare working conditions in the main subsidiary branch of the Italian multinational giant producing in Osijek, and in the wide array of subcontractors that are also producing for the multinational company. Subcontracting is a phenomenon that is typical of the global garment industry, which had extensive repercussions for garment workers all over the world, particularly in Asia where sweatshops have been growing exponentially since the early 2000s. As noted by Hale and Willis:

> through the management of complex supply chains, leading corporations are able to use geographical differentiation in production costs, legal regulations, trade quotas and labour supply to maximum effect, sourcing their products at the requisite quality and the cheapest price from the most suitable suppliers.[48]

Subcontracting allows multinational brands to reduce production and labour costs, and to eschew responsibility for human rights violations, as in the case of the Rana Plaza building collapse which occurred in Bangladesh in 2013, killing 1,129 workers and injuring over 2,500.[49]

---

[48] See Angela Hale and Jane Wills (eds), *Threads of Labour: Garment Industry Supply Chains from the Workers' Perspective* (Hoboken, NJ, 2005).
[49] Siegle and Burke, *We Are What We Wear*.

In Osijek, workers are aware of the fact that working conditions are better at Vesuvius, the main subcontractor of the Italian multinational company, rather than in smaller subcontracting firms. The employees' working day is clearly defined and their wages are regular. Also, at Vesuvius there is a collective bargaining agreement so that workers are more protected from the supervisors' arbitrariness. Nonetheless, even in the main subsidiary working conditions are far from ideal, according to workers' testimonies. In particular, workers have difficulty taking breaks, as the new automatized knitwear production performed in the factory proceeds at lightning speed, and each worker is in charge of sixteen machines that need to be constantly monitored, by changing thread, collecting items, controlling the quality, etc. If a worker takes a short break to go to the toilet, there might be mistakes in the final products. Since Croatian labour law (2014, art. 73) establishes that for every six hours of work there should be a thirty-minute break, without timing specification, Vesuvius workers' paid break usually takes place at the end of the six-hour shifts, when they are ready to go home, so that production has the least possible interruptions during the shift.

Current labour intensity has also changed following the renovation of textile machines. Previous machines, made especially for the company, were mainly operated by a male workforce, since they required some heavy lifting. Those machines, however, were also semi-automated, so that workers could switch them off or regulate the speed of operations, which is no longer the case today. Besides the speed of working rhythms, wages are always minimal, with little incentives for workers with a long service. Working contracts are often precarious (one month, three months, six months), and stable contracts are hard to obtain, and, as a narrator told, they amount to a 'lottery'. Working conditions in the factory, moreover, are hard to bear, especially due to poor lightening during the night shift. Leave days are very difficult to obtain and must be demanded in written form seven days in advance. Often, the only way to have a day of leave is to ask the doctor to write a medical certificate. According to my narrators, doctors generally retain a 'humanist' attitude, as opposed to factory managers.

Such working and welfare conditions, inevitably, have an impact on personal life. Many younger workers live with their parents, because they are not able to support themselves with their wages. Textile workers are definitely better off if they can count on the salary of a spouse in a more secure sector, such as public administration. If they are the ones who provide for their family with minimal wage, however, their position is very difficult. A number of blue-collar male workers at Vesuvius, for instance, have another job in the informal sector, and come to the night shift after having worked all day. Women are also particularly exposed to this situation, which marks a clear demise of the 'working mother' gender contract typical of socialism and which makes it difficult to combine work and family obligations. As Lana, a female worker at Vesuvius in her forties, stated:

> We all have children, a family, duties, not to mention a possible loss in the family. [The bosses keep saying:] 'That is not possible, that's not possible'. I don't know, people know that you live with a spouse, with parents, with someone. If someone in the house dies, it is your duty to bury that person. But no, it's not your duty, it's not your problem. That day you must be at work. What option do you have? Go to the doctor and plea for a sick leave. Explain what is the situation and nothing else. Another thing. I have now a permanent contract, but many young women … a colleague who worked for three years, they sent her then to the unemployment bureau for three months, then they called her back and gave her a contract for two months. If she would by chance become pregnant, surely they wouldn't renew her contract. She did a lot for the firm in three years, and is doing a lot now, but still they wouldn't give her a permanent contract.[50]

The logic of neoliberal productivity doesn't take into account social reproduction and its costs in terms of time and labour, so that workers' private obligations become an additional source of pressure due to their lack of leave days and job security. 'We only know our duties and not our rights,' summarized Lana, who related that she had to sign a paper in which she agreed to night work in order to keep her job, even if her child was still under three years of age and thus she was not supposed to take up night work yet. In fact, Croatian law does not forbid night work for women with small children, but states that special categories of workers (pregnant women, parents with children under three years and single parents of children under six years) may only work overtime or with an uneven distribution of working hours after giving written consent. Lana's memory of night work prohibition is thus probably connected to late socialist time regulations, during which women with children up to three years were entitled to part-time work. This provision is now only limited to parents who have children with special care needs. Also, while Croatia has a relatively generous maternity leave provision in comparison to other Western European countries, the established fully paid leave from twenty-eight days before childbirth up to child's first six months, based on 100 per cent of average earnings, is only allowed for workers who

---

[50] Lana, Tanja and colleagues, Osijek, April 2016. Co-interviewed with Nikolina Hrga.

have been in regular employment for twelve months, otherwise the basic allowance drops to approximately 200 euros.

Despite their precarity, workers at Vesuvius are seen as privileged in comparison to other textile workers who are working for private subcontractors engaged by the Italian multinational brand present in Osijek, as well as by other famous multinational brands, such as Moncler and Missoni. Working conditions in subcontracting firms are characterized by extreme arbitrariness and uncertainty, and by irregular wages. Many owners easily close and reopen firms without paying their debts, including arrear wages, or displace production to cheaper settings, notably to Serbia, Romania and other neighbouring countries with a cheaper labour force (the Italian multinational companies that own Vesuvius closed its plant in Labin, Istria, and opened new ones in Osijek and in Niš, in the South of Serbia). While the workers I talked to often successfully took runaway owners to court, they were still not fully compensated for their losses. Also, in subcontracting firms overtime on Saturdays and Sundays is common, and daily overtime hours are often unpaid under the pretext that workers did not reach their piece-rate daily norm and thus have to 'catch up'. Workers' strict control and monitoring doesn't allow for any break or distraction during the shift. As Tanja, a worker for an Italian subcontractor, testified: 'At our place we work eight hours, non-stop. There are sixteen cameras connected to the laptop. The boss sits in front on the laptop and zooms in and out, zooms in and out and controls you (*zumira i normira te*).'[51] The intensity of piece-rate work is so strenuous that Tanja has to produce one collar per minute on average, but she always keeps two or three aside to be able to rush to the toilet. Even after a major operation, after which she received a 70 per cent invalidity certificate, her boss contested the fact that she would take a few minutes to go to the bathroom. She replied that he should be ashamed, and he told her: 'I will only be satisfied with you when your hands are as fast as your tongue.' Western entrepreneurs in the region often treat local workers with contempt. As a male young worker at Vesuvius stated, 'In their view we should be happy that we are working.' When workers complained about minimal wages, Vesuvius' female director replied that they could not raise wages, and suggested workers to find an extra job, on the side, or 'to go to Ireland and earn money there', as many are actually doing already.[52] Many workers are afraid of speaking out about working conditions in the company for fear of reprisals.

---

[51] Lana, Tanja and colleagues, Osijek, April 2016. Co-interviewed with Nikolina Hrga.
[52] Ibid.

Such precarious and exploitative working conditions are common not only in Croatia, but across the post-Yugoslav region, as shown by the Macedonian case analysed in the previous section, and as highlighted by the recent press coverage of workers' exploitation within foreign companies in Serbia, which benefit not only from low wages and a liberal labour law, but also from state subsidies for each new work position. Recently, the Italian GEOX shoe factory in Vranje was denounced in the local press for a wide array of alleged labour and human rights violations, which led several workers to look for psychological treatment on the grounds of mobbing.[53] The South-Korean Yura cable factory in Leskovac, on the other hand, was recently exposed by the press for firing a single mother who was undertaking medical treatment for cancer (the woman was subsequently re-employed after widespread public outcry).[54]

In Leskovac, a former industrial centre in the South of Serbia which is by now almost completely deindustrialized, the remaining 870 workers of the Leteks textile factory worked without receiving any pay for two years between 2001 and 2003, when the plant still belonged to the Serbian state (Leteks employed up to 3,000 workers during socialism). An entrepreneur of Serbian origin residing in Australia bought the factory in 2006, but instead of reinstating production, sold the machinery as scrap. The contract of sale was then annulled since the buyer had failed to fulfil contractual obligations and the factory once again became state property in 2008. The Municipal Court in Leskovac then declared that the Serbian state was once again responsible for paying salary arrears. Since the state did not pay, 167 former Leteks workers filed a lawsuit at the European Court of Human Rights (ECHR) in Strasbourg (Case of *Anđelić and others v. Serbia*, applications nos. 57611/10 and 166 other applications). Five years after the initial lawsuit, on 28 May 2013, the ECHR ordered the Serbian state to pay salary arrears plus 3,100 euros of compensation for each worker, a total sum of 540,000 euros.[55]

---

[53] Mašina, 'What is the real price of Geox shoes?', 16 March 2017. Available at: http://www.masina.rs/eng/real-price-geox-shoes/ (accessed 20 January 2018); Mašina, 'Working for GEOX in the 21° century – The case of Serbia'. 12 April 2017. Available at: http://www.masina.rs/eng/working-geox-21-century-case-serbia/ (accessed 20 January 2018)

[54] Daliborka Alijodžić, 'Dobila Otkaz Telefonom: U "Juri" otpustili samohranu majku, koja se na bolovanju leči od raka!', 1 December 2016. Available at: http://www.novosti.rs/vesti/naslovna/reportaze/aktuelno.293.html:637692-DOBILA-OTKAZ-TELEFONOM-U-Juri-otpustili-samohranu-majku-koja-se-na-bolovanju-leci-od-raka (accessed 20 January 2018).

[55] Vesna Rakić-Vodinelić, Saša Gajin and Mario Reljanović (eds), *Europa ne stanuje u Babušnici. Građani protiv Srbije pred Sudom u Strazburu* (Belgrade 2013).

Nowadays, apart from some small factories, the only notable textile factory in Leskovac is the German firm Falke, producing high-quality socks, which opened in early 2012. The firm obtained 2.4 million euros from the Serbian government, as part of Serbia's incentives to FDI. Falke has been built on the premises of the former socialist factory named Inkol. Falke bought Inkol for 33.7 million dinars, but the majority of Inkol's 500 former workers are still due forty months of wages. At the end of the 1990s, the local government promised textile workers that they would receive unpaid wages once Inkol, then bankrupt, was sold, but this never happened. Inkol workers have been fighting for compensation ever since.[56] These are just a few examples that highlight industrial workers' disempowerment and dispossession during the processes of post-socialist transformation. In the following section I will address another case study, that of the industrial region of Varaždin, and examine this case through the perceptions and narratives of local trade unionists, who share workers' structure of feeling, and often use the socialist experience as a benchmark for what constitutes decent work.

Trade unions in post-Yugoslav states

Scholars of labour and post-socialism have been discussing the role of trade unions in relation to the contemporary weakness and disempowerment of workers. In the volume *Workers after Workers' States*, published in 2001, Ost and Crowley claim that 'labour weakness' is a legacy of socialism, as trade unions throughout Eastern Europe were 'on the same side of the management' during socialist times: 'their chief role was in performing social functions, particularly distributing benefits such as social security payments, sick pay, vouchers for factory vacation centres or summer camps for children, and consumer goods through the workplace.'[57] The weakness of unions during socialism, therefore, was further enhanced after post-socialist changes, when unions could not reorient themselves to defend the interest of their members in the new capitalist setting. In the same volume, Arandarenko discusses the Serbian case, and similarly argues that the legacy of the Yugoslav system of self-management disempowered workers, since workers had no real decision-making powers in workers' councils, and unions were basically part

---

[56] Danilo Kocić, 'Protest radnika konfekcije "Inkol"', 9 January 2012. Available at: https://www.juznevesti.com/Drushtvo/Protest-radnika-konfekcije-Inkol.sr.html (accessed 20 January 2018).
[57] Crowley and Ost (eds) *Workers After Workers' States*.

of the state apparatus. In investigating the economic collapse that affected post-socialist Serbia in the 1990s, Arandarenko mentions the importance of the informal economy, which functions as a social buffer, 'employing wide masses of unemployed and even the working poor'. In his view, this process further reinforces 'labour quiescence' among the population, also due to the co-optation of the former socialist trade unions by the Milošević regime.[58]

This earlier interpretation of the self-management legacy in the current post-socialist context deserves to be juxtaposed to other points of views that allow for a wider array of complexity, and for a deeper understanding of workers' structure of feeling in relation to trade unions and the self-management legacy. Other scholars dealing with the post-Yugoslav region attributed labour weakness not only to the legacy of state socialism, but also to the current neoliberal context. Writing on the Croatian case, Kokanović suggested that the legacy of socialism represented a disadvantage in current times, as workers lacked the experience of fighting for their interests due to the paternalism of the socialist state and trade unions, a point which also clearly emerges in my interviews. At the same time, as Kokanović argued, workers' disempowerment was very much the product of current circumstances of economic collapse, factory closures and war, rather than the legacy of socialist times:

> The Croatian worker has lost the factory she worked in, her workplace, the possibility to ensure a decent life for herself and a future for her children. Workers are also bereft of the possibility to influence their own lives, sentenced to struggle for survival from one day to another.[59]

Kokanović, moreover, emphasized the delegitimation of trade unions in a context of war and nationalist propaganda, an issue that definitely received less attention from scholars. The impact of what is commonly defined as 'criminal privatization', which happened with the complicity of local state elites in the 1990s, is something that workers and existing trade unions were ill-prepared to fight, especially at a time of authoritarianism and nationalist revival, which went in parallel with hopes of economic improvement and growth through the liberalization of the economy. Trade unions leaders and members were divided over how to deal with ongoing privatization processes, particularly privatizations through shareholder quotas, which were often

---

[58] Mihail Arandarenko, 'Waiting for the workers: Explaining labor quiescence in Serbia', in Crowley and Ost (eds), *Workers After Workers' States*, p. 169.

[59] Marina Kokanović, 'The cost of nationalism: Croatian labour, 1990-1999', in Crowley and Ost (eds), *Workers After Workers' States*, p. 142.

opaque and difficult to understand. Also, power hierarchies were largely tilted on the side of new capitalist and state elites in the 1990s, and trade unionists risked their lives if they took oppositional stances. On this point it is worth mentioning the case of Milan Krivokuća, a social-democratic trade unionist of Serbian ethnicity, president of the first independent trade union in the railway sector, who was killed in his home in Velika Gorica in 1992 Croatia, and whose murder circumstances were never fully clarified. During wartime, similarly, several trade unionists in Croatia were threatened and attacked as potential traitors of the state and as opponents to the newly established government led by the Croatian Democratic Party (HDZ). As stated by the then president of the Union of Independent Trade Unions of Croatia (*Savez Samostalnih Sindikata Hrvatske*):

> Every trade union action was met with the roughest, organized and orchestrated attack, especially through the media. Unionists who led these campaigns were labeled as national traitors, traitors to the homeland, foreign mercenaries, Yugonostalgics, Chetniks. Dealing with trade union work and representing the interests of workers was not only difficult, but also extremely risky. Intelligence services were particularly active and created strife within the movement. There was provocation, destruction and the spread of misinformation.[60]

Still, this did not stop a wide array of strikes against the privatization measures to take place throughout the 1990s across all working sectors in Croatia.[61] Similarly, in Serbia, as Tibor T. Meszmann notes, trade unionists were caught between the government co-optation of the former socialist trade union and repressive forms of demobilization for those who did not comply, with vocal union activists being defined as 'troublemakers representing foreign interests'. Opposition intellectuals, furthermore, portrayed 'workers en bloc as gullible Serb nationalists'.[62] Striking miners organized in new independent trade unions, however, had a crucial role in the fall of the Milošević government in 2000. Workers also opposed the neoliberal reforms introduced in the post-Milošević era, which affected most of the industry, and several local strikes were organized in different industrial sectors throughout the last two

---

[60] Ladislav Tomčić, 'Zašto su Raznici Zgaženi 90-IH: "Tada su sindikalci bili izdajnici domovine, strani plaćenici, jugonostalgičari, četnici"', 21 May 2014., Available at: http://www.lupiga.com/vijesti/zasto-su-radnici-izgubili-borbu-sa-najezdom-skakakavaca-koji-su-opustosili-hrvatsko-gospodarstvo (accessed 20 January 2018).
[61] Ibid.
[62] Meszmann, 'The lingering constituency', p. 675.

decades.⁶³ While some strikes were successful, many others were so-called 'strikes of despair' enacted by workers who were about to lose their jobs. Workers underwent hunger strikes, chained themselves to factory buildings, and even resorted to extreme gestures such as the one carried out by Zoran Bulatović, a worker and trade unionist in the Raška textile factory in Novi Pazar, who cut off his finger in 2009.⁶⁴ Bulatović and his colleagues were on a hunger strike to demand the payment of up to twenty-six months of wages in arrears. Bankrupted in 2013, the Raška kombinat employed up to 4,000 workers in its heyday.

These latter type of protests reflect the weakening of trade union membership and of workers' organizing that has been typical across post-Yugoslav states since the 1990s, with the partial exception of Slovenia, where a gradualist corporatist system of negotiation between employers and trade unions was introduced in the early 1990s and remained in place until the early 2000s. Overall, across the post-Yugoslav space, union membership affiliates around a third of the workforce, and mainly covers workers in the public sector, particularly workers of older generations, while younger workers and workers in private firms are more exposed to precarious contracts and weak unionization.⁶⁵ This is mostly the case with textile firms and with new private companies, which often oppose trade union presence and membership of their employees (trade union membership in the textile sector in Macedonia, for instance, is no more than 9 per cent).⁶⁶

On the one hand, in this new context of weakness, atomization and fragmentation, the paternalism of the self-management system is certainly not equipping workers with activist experience or skills that could be mobilized. On the other hand, workers' socialist structure of feeling, which is still lingering and widely present and which incorporate paternalist elements, is often evoked as a cultural and political repertoire to demand social justice and social rights in the present context. As Grdešić argues, blue-collar

---

⁶³ Darko Marinković, 'Strike at Kolubara – A Case Study', *South-East Europe Review for Labour and Social Affairs*, 6 (2003), pp. 41–72; Musić, *Serbia's Working Class in Transition*.

⁶⁴ Upchurch and Marinković, 'Serbia from the October 2000 revolution to the crash', p. 245; Musić, *Serbia's Working Class in Transition*; Crowley and Ost (eds), *Workers After Workers' States*. The town of Novi Pazar witnessed a booming of informal, private textile companies in the 1990s, which mainly produced counterfeited goods, especially jeans. See Aida A. Hozić, 'The Balkan merchants: Changing borders and informal transnationalization', *Ethnopolitics*, 5/3 (2006), pp. 243–56.

⁶⁵ Marko Grdešić, 'Workers and unions after Yugoslavia', in Horvat and Štiks (eds), *Welcome to the Desert of Post-Socialism*.

⁶⁶ Milka Kazandziska, Marija Risteska and Verena Schmidt, 'The gender pay gap in the former Yugoslav republic of Macedonia' (Skopje, 2012).

workers were celebrated in the socialist system and self-management gave workers a 'real sense of empowerment, entitlement and, when reality did not correspond to their expectations, a powerful sense of frustration'.[67]

In another earlier contribution, Grdešić argues that in Yugoslavia, thanks to self-management, 'labour was empowered in its dealings with the political elite in a way that did not occur elsewhere in Eastern Europe'. The Yugoslav system of social ownership, notably, 'produced a feeling of closer attachment and identification of workers with their companies'.[68] The concepts of 'labour weakness' or 'labour strength', therefore, as aptly pointed out by Grdešić, appear to be oversimplified, since they do not account for workers' agency, and neither do they encompass the variety of workers' experiences of post-socialism in different post-Yugoslav states. Workers' overall disempowerment in the post-socialist context coexist with major and minor instances of resistance and resilience in which the legacy of socialist self-management and workers' rights is mobilized as a benchmark for workers' demands of fair labour conditions and basic dignity.[69]

An example in point is a collective conversation I had with five union representatives, three men and two women affiliated to different unions, in the industrial cities of Varaždin and Čakovec. Three of them were employed as blue-collar workers in textile earlier in their careers. Both Varaždin and Čakovec, located in the North-West of Croatia at the border with Slovenia, are known for their important textile industry, first of all for the Varteks plant, but also for VIS (Varaždinska Industrija Svila), as well as Čateks and MTČ (Međimurska trikotaža Čakovec). The Varaždinska and Međimurska counties are the most prosperous in Croatia, and 75 per cent of the Croatian clothing and shoe industry is still concentrated in the area. Even though some restructured former socialist factories are still in production and new private factories have appeared, deindustrialization and crony privatization practices have also affected this part of Croatia.

In Čakovec, for instance, the MTČ factory employed up to 4,200 workers during socialism, while now only a couple of small firms with a few hundred workers retain the brand. MTČ was divided into nine shareholders' companies in the 1990s, and a big factor in its demise was the so-called 'coupon privatization' (*kuponska privatizacija*) put in place by the HDZ government, when free shares of state companies were distributed to war veterans, refugees and to various other sectors of the Croatian population

---

[67] Grdešić, 'Workers and unions after Yugoslavia'.
[68] Marko Grdešić, 'Mapping the paths of the Yugoslav model: Labour strength and weakness in Slovenia, Croatia and Serbia', *European Journal of Industrial Relations*, 14/2 (2008), p. 138.
[69] Ibid.

for electoral purposes. In fact, this process favoured extreme speculation from a restricted capitalist class who could buy the majority of quotas on the market and healthy assets while debts remained unpaid and many factories ended up bankrupt. The loss of the Yugoslav and Soviet markets and the entry of cheaper Asian products after 2005 further penalized the existing local industry. Čateks, also in Čakovec, which employed 1,200 workers before the end of Yugoslavia, is also surviving in a reduced capacity of 330 employees, thanks to the fact that workers still own 50 per cent of factory shares. In Varaždin, former socialist factories are also barely surviving after restructuring. At Varteks, one of Croatia's oldest firms, which used to employ up to 10,000 workers, 1,300 workers remain. There are now thirty Varteks shops across Croatia, while eighty existed before the war all over Yugoslavia. After the 2012 closing of the Tivar section, which was the last weaving mill in Croatia, the Varteks company, which traditionally specialized in male and female suits of high standard, is surviving not only through its own *pret-à-porter* collection but also through outsourced production for foreign brands such as Hugo Boss, which are sewn by workers paid the minimum wage of around 2,500 kunas per month. The last strike, to obtain wages in arrears, happened in July 2016. VIS, which was also a gigantic complex during socialism and which employed 4,700 workers, is now reduced to a workshop of 320 workers who perform outsourced work for foreign clients such as La Perla, Hugo Boss, Wolford and others.

In this context, the new sectorial trade union, the Independent Trade Union of Workers in the Textile, Clothing, Leather and Rubber Industry (*Samostalni sindikat tekstila, obuće, kože, gume Hrvatske*), as it is called, has little over 5,000 members, while its corresponding socialist trade union had 112,000. Faced with such a drop in membership, the trade unionists I met described how they are attempting to defend workers' position in restructured, formerly socially owned factories. Factories as Varteks and Čateks, despite their problems, are portrayed by trade union representatives as still relatively respectful of workers' rights, especially in comparison to multinational companies who invested in the region and who attempt to bring workers' earnings and welfare rights to the legal minimum allowed by law. The Italian stocking brand Calzedonia, the British HX shoe company, the Austrian shoe company Paul Green and the Austrian Boxmark leather company all have opened greenfield plants in the area, with significant tax break advantages in comparison to pre-existing local firms and with enormous profits.[70]

---

[70] Nada Landeka, 'Nenad Leček; Uvoz i loša politika uništili su domaće tekstilce', 9 May 2014. Available at: http://www.hazud.hr/nenad-lecek-uvoz-i-losa-politika-unistili-su-domace-tekstilce/ (accessed 20 January 2018).

According to local trade unionists, new foreign firms are often 'stealing' workers from existing local firms, such as the Meiso and Ivančica shoe factories, by promising higher wages and by later changing contract agreements, or by hiring workers from local firms on the verge of bankruptcy. Due to the presence of foreign companies, moreover, it is becoming accepted that every Saturday is a working day, whereas in existing local firms such as Varteks the working week is 40 hours. Trade union organizing is also close to impossible in foreign firms, and workers are afraid to meet with trade union representatives for fear of losing their jobs. Some local factories, also, have extremely low working standards, especially when performing outsourced jobs for these same multinational companies. In the words of my narrators, some local firms also have become 'working camps' (*radni logori*). The shoe industry is particularly heavy and labour intensive and many workers have permanent health problems and end up with invalidity pensions. Due to the fact that state regulations are not sufficiently strict when it comes to financial and industrial crimes, small local entrepreneurs have ample margins of manoeuvre and profit, and trade unionists are ill-equipped to relieve workers from extreme exploitation. The following case, reported by one of my male narrators, is illustrative of the overall situation in the area:

> This is a concrete example in …, of a privately-owned knitwear factory, three companies are registered at the same address. … They largely work for the Italian market, from Benetton, to Max Mara and others. They have their own website and their list of customers is huge. We founded a union there because of the catastrophic working conditions. And when we made some formal demands and they could no longer manage with us in the way that we were too big a threat, then they set up a new company. And then they offered new contracts to all workers, mainly female workers, under condition that they renounced all their rights held under the previous company and that they would not be members of the trade union. And our union representatives did not get a new contract. And then, after a year and a half, when they got into debt with the company, then they set up another company and all at the same address, with the same machines. … Every year and a half, every two years a firm is closed, and a new firm is set up.[71]

As my narrators retold, after the periodical closing of the firm, once again 'problematic' workers were dismissed, while others had to give up all their

---

[71] Trade unionists, Varaždin, February 2016.

rights, including trade union organizing, to continue working. In another firm, a worker who became union representative was intimidated through severe mobbing practices, so much so that she had to undergo psychological treatment. Additionally, she was fired, and she received compensation only after she sued the company for discriminatory treatment. After mentioning such examples, local trade unionists were keen to stress that they are not against foreign investments per se, but are against exploitation and mistreatments. They are also opposing the unfair privileging of so-called *green field* companies at the expenses of local companies where workers still retain some rights, and which function as a social buffer for middle-aged, low-skilled workers who could not be employed anywhere else. As another male representative stated:

> What we are asking from the state is to think about that, that these people have to work somewhere, not everyone can be director, IT worker or nurse ... also during former Yugoslavia all those textile firms were not always profitable, but they had a socially useful role.[72]

Besides textile factories' social role, my narrators recalled the symbolical recognition enjoyed by garment workers during socialism, as well as the material advantages brought by being employed in textile. In contrast to today, wages were secure and always paid on time, and even if the textile sector was considered as a low-paid one, wages usually reached the republican or federal average. As one female trade unionist stressed, if someone would buy a *fićek* (a FIAT 500), a popular model of car at the time, people would be sure that it was a Varteks worker with a good wage. Another female trade unionist recalled that as a regular worker in production in 1986, with a single wage she once bought a solid fuel cooker, four winter tyres, a bicycle, paid all bills and lived normally for the rest of the month with two children. While this sketch might be an idealized portrait of life in socialism filtered through contemporary memories and experiences, trade unionists were keen to stress how purchasing power dropped and social inequalities raised in the post-socialist era, especially when it came to the distribution of profits inside the workplace. Their observations about low wage differentials between factory directors and regular workers in the socialist era, as opposed to current high wage differentials, are backed by existing studies.[73] Also, the symbolical

---

[72] Ibid.
[73] According to Wachtel, 'By 1967, the highest paid skill group (white-collar workers with high school education and above) was earning only 2.5 times the lowest paid group (unskilled blue-collar workers)'. Howard M. Wachtel, *Workers' Management and*

devaluation of manual workers became rife in the 1990s as a result of widespread unemployment: it was common to hear catchphrases like 'every granny knows how to sew', or, in the case of a new director which arrived in the early post-socialist era in one of the abovementioned factories, 'You kick the bush and five seamstresses come out', to indicate the abundance of undervalued and easily replaceable textile workers.

Workers' devaluation also happened through the demise of traditional celebrations like Women's Day (celebrated on March 8), when members of management would distribute flowers to female workers and women would have a small celebration in the factory. After the end of socialism, such celebrations gradually disappeared and even started to be stigmatized. As a male trade unionist recalled:

> When after a couple of years I bought flowers for all female union members, there were laughs among the management, and from our local simple people. [They would ask:] 'What stupidity are you doing?' They all forget that their pay comes from the work of those women. And even today there are smiles sometimes. I cannot name one company where the director would come and wish the people a happy 8th of March.[74]

The idea that industrial work was ultimately the only productive work, which funded the 'superstructure' of administrative staff and directors, was a constant element of socialist discourse and a popular argument advanced by blue-collar workers against managers and white-collar staff. As this passage makes clear, trade unionists, who are also former industrial workers, share the same structure of feeling of the workers they represent, and use working practices in the self-management era as a repertoire of 'best practices'. Notably, trade unionists regret that some of the welfare and labour rights practised in the socialist era have now been dismissed, while they are still customary in Germany and in other places. Welfare services of a certain standards, in fact, came to be seen as an unwanted socialist heritage, as summarized by one of my male narrators:

> Unfortunately, under the guise of capitalism, we have destroyed everything that was good and what was in the favour of the workers,

---

Workers' Wages in Yugoslavia: The Theory and Practice of Participatory Socialism (Ithaca, 1973), p. 146. Another case study of a textile factory in Slovenia found that 'the general manager's income is 4.3 times higher than that of the janitor'. Ukandi G. Damachi, Hans D. Seibel and Jeroen Scheerder, *Self-Management in Yugoslavia and the Developing World* (London, 1982), p. 150.

[74] Trade unionists, Varaždin, February 2016.

and automatically to the benefit of society. Because the directors thought they would be exposed to the pillar of shame if they would keep some sort of 'socialist heritage', such as holiday resorts, canteens, clinics, general practitioners, gynaecological and dental services, and so on and so on. So they quickly liquidated such services, even if all this still exists in Europe.[75]

While the opposition between the 'wild capitalism' of the Balkans and the 'good capitalism' of Western Europe is in itself a simplification (one only has to consider the working conditions in places like the Amazon depots in Germany), and while middle-age trade unionists seem to refer to a 'golden age' of Fordism that has passed in Western Europe as well, it is certain that the peripheral position of industrial workers in the Balkans and the stigmatization of anything that belonged to the past period made post-socialist transformations more sudden and more traumatic for many, as Kideckel also argued for the Romanian case.[76] Symbolic stigmatization added to this feeling of sudden devaluation. As a male trade unionist noted:

> I am not, how to say, Yugonostalgic, or socialist or anything else, but at that time you were happy to go to work. Because at that time you really could count on one hand the times when a supervisor, boss, director, technical director would call you 'cow', 'goat', and I am not mentioning the other insults.[77]

Currently, instead, management's insults towards female workers are an everyday occurrence, despite the fact that these are 'valuable workers and good mothers and wives'. The words of the male trade unionist are permeated once again with the socialist structure of feeling, and with its gendered aspects, indicating female workers' deservingness in the public and private sphere.

Besides workers' devaluation, trade unionists feel that the negative media image propagated about unionism doesn't help to establish trust among workers, as media frequently portray trade unions as useless and their leaders as moneymakers with a negligible interest in workers' lives. Solidarity between workers of different factories is difficult to establish as a result of the socialist structure of feeling that encouraged workers' extreme loyalty to their

---

[75] Ibid.
[76] Kideckel, 'The unmaking'.
[77] Trade unionists, Varaždin, February 2016.

own firm only. Solidarity within the same firm itself is also hard to reach, as a result of the current climate of fear for one's job and owners' intimidation. According to my narrators, moreover, workers are often reluctant to pay membership fees (amounting to 1 per cent of their gross income) or to organize, but are quick to expect the trade union to do something for them, or quick to accuse trade unionists of not protecting them enough, even when they never subscribed for membership. Collective agreements reached by trade unions, however, apply to all workers, even to those who never joined the union. Trade unionists, therefore, also feel devalued, both by workers and by the general public.

In my other interviews with blue-collar workers across the post-Yugoslav space, socialist trade unions' paternalism is positively remembered in relation to specific welfare services (i.e. food distribution, free schoolbooks, excursions) but post-socialist trade unions are almost inevitably denounced for not being able to support workers and for being complicit with factory management in critical moments of bankruptcy and privatization – something that trade unionists were also mostly unable to prevent.[78] Very rarely workers see unions as something they could be part of, or be responsible for, while they expect unions to take care of them, as it happened during socialism. While assessing concrete interactions between workers and trade unionists during specific labour conflicts is beyond the scope of this book, with this last section I wished to highlight that despite the current social and political rift between workers and trade unions, the middle-aged trade unionists I spoke with also share the structure of feeling typical of socialist factories, as well as a 'humanist' vision of workers' social citizenship. Trade unionists, therefore, often use the socialist period as a benchmark for proper, normal 'social standards', against the current practices of exploitation and precarious labour that are typical of local private and multinational companies. In the following chapter I will continue my exploration of workers' structure of feeling after deindustrialization, focusing on former workers' narratives of deindustrialization after factory closures.

---

[78] See for instance recent reports denouncing trade union officials' uncooperative attitudes with workers and complicity with management in the cases of the Kamensko, INKOP and Orljava factories in Croatia published by the webportal www.radnicki.org, and particularly Dimitrije Birač, 'TOKG iznevjerio radnike', 15 September 2016, Available at: https://www.radnicki.org/tokg-iznevjerio-radnike/ (accessed 20 January 2018).

4

Workers' structure of feeling after deindustrialization: Loss, nostalgia and belonging

I close the door, I close my eyes and with a strong desire I relive the memory of full offices and corridors, the murmur of clerks bustling around, wonderful. When I open my eyes and see the desolation, tears often start flowing, but they quickly pass. That is why my friends often call me the princess in the bewitched castle – smiles the woman who works without having to, and who does it without receiving a wage.
 'The woman who married her firm', 4 May 2013.

In May 2013, a local online news portal in Southern Serbia showcased a singular story. The piece was titled *Žena koja se udala za svoje preduzeće* (The woman who married her firm), and retold the daily life of Mirijana M., a bookish-looking, smiling fifty-seven years old who was once the accountant of the Graditelj building complex in Leskovac, which used to employ 1,700 workers.[1] Despite the fact that the factory had been bankrupt for years, and in a state of complete abandonment, Mirijana went to work every day without being paid, sitting from 9.00 am to 2.00 pm in the management building of the enterprise, among mice, dust and cockroaches and mainly taking care of papers that could attest to the years of service of former employees, to obtain pension rights despite the bankruptcy. According to the news portal, the accountant, who never married and had no children, felt that her place was at Graditelj, where cases with papers and bills had become 'her children'. Computers had been stolen from the factory and Mirijana did everything by hand. Still, she felt that it was her duty to help former employees, whose gratitude compensated her for the unpaid work.

---

[1] Jugmedia, 'Žena koja se udala za svoje preduzeće', 4 May 2013, Available at: http://jugmedia.rs/zena-koja-se-udala-za-svoje-preduzece/ (accessed 20 January 2018).

A 'princess in a bewitched castle', as her female friends mockingly described her, Mirijana fought the existing desolation by dreaming of the firm's better times, and by clinging to the familiarity of her daily work, still useful for many. This account is illustrative of the strong degree of loyalty and belonging developed among the employees of former socialist firms, for whom the factory often had become a second home and a fundamental source of identity and self-realization. It is also a testimony to the importance of community networks and intergenerational solidarity in post-Yugoslav states. Such accounts are not atypical: I was retold a similar story about a former accountant who saved some of the employment books of the Sana textile factory in Bosanski Novi/Novi Grad from destruction during the Bosnian war, and who kept helping former employees to track back their years of service on a voluntary basis.

This chapter highlights the ways in which the industrial structure of feeling proper of socialism persists among workers of the older generations across the post-Yugoslav space. In dialogue with recent scholarly work on the subject, I discuss textile workers' articulations of post-socialist nostalgia, which expresses itself in different forms. On the basis of case studies of Pula, Sinj (Croatia) and Bosanski Novi/Novi Grad (Bosnia-Herzegovina), I analyse workers' nostalgic attachments not only to welfare and labour entitlements, but also to the sociability created within textile factories; workers' loss of existential security and predictability is also prominent, and so is the regret for the lost multi-ethnic coexistence and solidarity that was in place before the Yugoslav Wars. Workers' nostalgia for certain aspects of socialism, however, coexists with ambivalent and critical narratives about other less positive features of the past regime, namely, its reproduction of social and gender inequalities, which are still part of working-class citizens' memories. New dominant ethno-nationalist narratives, moreover, are also coexisting in unpredictable and contradictory ways with the structure of feeling inherited from socialist times.

Deindustrialized landscapes across the post-Yugoslav space

Scholars have extensively studied the effects of deindustrialization on cityscapes, between ruination, gentrification, 'ruin porn' and 'smokestack nostalgia'.[2] They have also investigated the relation between deindustrialized

---

[2] High, 'Beyond aesthetics'.

landscapes and their inhabitants, including former industrial workers. As Alice Mah has argued in her study of industrial ruination as a lived process in North America, the North of England and post-Soviet Russia, 'abandoned industrial sites remain connected with the urban fabric that surrounds them: with communities; with collective memory; and with people's health, livelihoods, and stories'.[3] In this section I will provide an overview of the relation between deindustrialized landscapes and social memory – particularly former workers' memory – across the post-Yugoslav space, with a focus on the town of Pula and on other examples from the region, and with the help of some photographs collected within deindustrialized places on-site. This change in industrial landscapes – which brought to an increasing marginalization of workers' memories – has happened alongside wider process of reconfiguration of the local public space as a result of post-socialist and post-conflict transformations.

The most apparent and mundane transformation in post-Yugoslav states has been the widespread renaming of streets according to new historical revisionist narratives and new hegemonic national narratives.[4] The reconfiguration of public space has been even more prominent in the case of the monuments from the socialist era that commemorated antifascist resistance during the Second World War, which were often destroyed, vandalized or abandoned to ruin.[5] While scholars have dealt extensively with such reconfiguration of public memory in a nationalist sense, urban reconfigurations which entailed the local industrial heritage have been researched to a lesser extent, specifically in relation to local inhabitants' lived experience of deindustrialization. Such reconfigurations of local industrial landscapes, in most cases, happened as a result of the devastating processes of criminal privatization described in the previous chapter, during which managers, corporations and local political elites had the upper hands, while workers faced dispossession and disempowerment. A case in point is the one of Pančevo, an industrial town with a specific Austro-Hungarian heritage located some 14 kilometres from Serbia's capital, Belgrade, which used to host the oldest brewery in the Balkans. As anthropologist Ildiko Erdei shows, the brewery was first bought by the Turkish Efes brand in 2003 and then by

---

[3] Mah, *Industrial Ruination, Community, and Place*, p. 3.
[4] Srđan Radović, 'Politike simbola na gradskim ulicama: obrasci preimenovanja javnih prostora u postjugoslovenskim zemljama', *Narodna Umjetnost*, 51/2 (2014), pp. 117–32.
[5] Sandina Begić and Boriša Mraović, 'Forsaken monuments and social change: The function of socialist monuments in the post-Yugoslav space', in S. L. Moeschberger and R. A. Phillips De Zalia (eds), *Symbols that Bind, Symbols that Divide: The Semiotics of Peace and Conflict* (Switzerland, 2014).

the Heineken multinational company in 2008, which promptly shut it down despite its significance for the urban and cultural heritage of the industrial town. Over 100 workers were fired in the process. Yet the event met with an astounding public silence and with 'social oblivion' in an already largely deindustrialized and individualized setting.[6]

Industrial ruination has been affecting all industrial sectors across the post-Yugoslav space, and industrial heritage has been often associated with an undesirable socialist past. This happens even in towns and regions that are perceived as progressive, like the town of Pula, located in the border region of Istria. Since the 1990s Istria has been governed by the local regionalist Istrian Democratic Party (IDS), which has been opposing hard-line Croatian nationalism on the basis of a local regional and multi-ethnic identity (and, critics argue, locally embedded clientelistic practices). Unlike in other parts of the country, the local partisan monuments from the socialist era are very well preserved, with local political and cultural authorities frequently commemorating the legacy of antifascist resistance. At the same time, as elsewhere across the region, Pula's authorities are underplaying the town's industrial heritage, especially for purposes of tourist rebranding. The town has been recasting itself as a tourist hub and as a popular seaside destination, with local and national investors planning to build a new luxury marina and tourist resort in the abandoned premises of the former Yugoslav naval base. The Uljanik shipyard, founded when Pula was part of Austria-Hungary and turned into a symbol of socialist industrialization, is undergoing a profound crisis despite several attempts at restructuring. The shipyard risks closure due to liquidity problems (and, many argue, deliberate plans to get rid of the industrial giant in order to further expand the town's tourist capacity). After going on strike to reclaim unpaid wages, Uljanik's workers are now facing an uncertain future.[7]

The obliteration of the local industrial heritage becomes particularly evident in the case of the Arena knitwear factory. As already mentioned in Chapter 1, the factory started its production under the name of the local partisan heroine Olga Ban in the late 1940s. Renamed as Arena in the 1960s, it employed over 1,000 workers in the early 1960s, and around 700 on average in the 1970s and 1980s. The innovative designs of Arena fashion creator

---

[6] Ildiko Erdei, 'Stepeni tuge: ekonomska devastacija i društveni zaborav', *Issues in Ethnology Anthropology*, 9/2 (2014), pp. 351–69.

[7] Andrew Hodges, 'Worker narratives of blame and responsibility during the 2018 crisis: The case of the Uljanik Shipyard, Croatia', *IOS Working Paper*, November 2018. Available at: https://www.dokumente.ios-regensburg.de/publikationen/mitteilungen/mitt_67.pdf (accessed 20 January 2018).

Marija Vareško led to several prizes being awarded to Arena at different fashion fairs. Arena successfully exported high-quality knitwear to the West, the Eastern bloc, and Non-Aligned countries allied to Yugoslavia, such as Libya, Iran and Iraq (Figure 9). The growing value of the factory's export – and the forward-looking imaginary of that time – is well exemplified by the English text printed on a multilingual brochure of the factory in 1983:

> Pula ... is a modern town with all the characteristics of a Mediterranean region – intensive colours, temperamental people, a port with hundreds of anchored ships, yachts sailing under a variety of flags and a great shipbuilding yard. Three thousand years of history have been built into the town of Pula, including a great Roman amphitheater, Arena, after which our factory was named. ... What is being presented here is only a fraction of what we produce, as our products are made and worn in

Figure 9 Arena collections, design by Marija Vareško. Reproduced with permission from the Arena factory archive in 2015.

countless fashionable shades over the whole of Yugoslavia, and with regard to our significant exports, we can say over the whole of the world.[8]

Such cosmopolitan imaginary of modernization, which integrated industrial production into the local cultural and historical heritage, has been gradually fading away after the end of Yugoslavia. When I arrived in Pula at the end of November 2014, the factory had been declared bankrupt just a few months earlier, and its imposing three-storey building facing Pula's historical harbour in the city centre was in the process of being sold floor by floor. During the process of cleanup in view of the sale procedure, the factory was still open for potential investors and buyers. Two remaining workers were supervising the cleaning up of the premises, and I was able to tour the abandoned factory, where all the machines and furniture were still in place and for sale. In one corner stood an abandoned small statue of the Golden Deer (*Zlatna Košuta*), a once prestigious prize that was assigned at Belgrade fashion fairs, won by Arena creator Marija Vareško. The abandoned statue symbolized the dissolution of the factory, of its production and of its material and symbolic value (Figure 10). Remaining clerical staff kindly allowed me to browse through the remnants of the factory archive, specifically through old photographs and catalogues (much had already been thrown out by the time I arrived, except papers necessary for bookkeeping and pension claims). The

Figure 10 The abandoned Golden Deer, Arena factory, 2015. Photo by the author.

---

[8] Photograph in possession of the author, private collection of Marija Vareško.

last stocks of clothing were also available for sale, so I bought a few garment items as a memory of the local disappearing knitwear production, whose quality was praised by women of all generations across town. By the end of 2015, the factory had been largely emptied of its machinery, and only a few items of furniture were sold in a warehouse for symbolic prices. As a sentimental token, but also for practical purposes, I bought an old standard office desk, used by white-collar workers, for 70 kunas, or 10 euros.

During my last stay in Pula in summer 2017, the different levels of the factory had been sold to various investors. On the ground floor, notably, where another small garment factory and an antique shop were hosted earlier, an English pub named Shipyard had been opened. The new shiny pub sports a stylish post-industrial décor, and various old photographs of the local Uljanik shipyard on its wall. The pub has a hip, spacious vibe that attracts local middle-class professionals. At the same time, its classic pub features are heavily standardized, so that international visitors during the tourist season can come in and feel as if they would be visiting any other English pub in Western Europe. While images of the local shipyard – without its workers – can fit the hip profile of the seaside pub, the memory of women's textile work is completely obliterated from the space, except for the small plaque from socialist times that survives on the corner of the building. Lately, a bank was opened in the lower part of the building facing the waterfront, and a privately funded 'House of Olive Oil' was inaugurated in another part of the building. The new facility showcases the history of local olive oil production from the Roman times to the present and provides tourists with a traditional gastronomic experience. This last attraction appeals to the pre-industrial, agricultural character of Istria, like the infamous Croatian tourist advertisement that used to promote the country internationally with the slogan 'The Mediterranean as it once was'.[9]

The example of Pula is illustrative of the processes of gentrification and rebranding driven by the local tourist industry. Another comparable case, which I will discuss in the next chapter, is the one of the Kamensko garment factory in Zagreb. Due to the location of Kamensko's main building – close to the city centre – the firm was privatized through shady agreements in view of real estate speculation and profitable reconversion for residential purposes. Most deindustrialized textile landscapes in the Balkans, however, are in a permanent state of ruination and have not been reconverted. This is the case of the textile industrial district in Leskovac, in the South of Serbia, which is completely in ruin, except for the German factory Falke and for another small Turkish jeans producer. Similarly abandoned were, at the date of my

---

[9] I have to thank here Igor Duda for highlighting this parallel and for sharing his critical insights on the obliteration of Pula's industrial heritage.

visit, the Dalmatinka spinning mill in Sinj, Croatia, and the IMK Slavonija factory in Osijek, also in Croatia. At Dalmatinka, a workers' canteen which had been modernized during socialist times still appeared in perfect shape in comparison to the general abandonment of the building. Within IMK Slavonija, a relatively new bowling room reminded visitors like me of workers' heydays of labour and leisure.

In other instances across the post-Yugoslav space, part of those textile plants had been privatized – usually the canteen – and turned into small businesses, to the dismay of local workers who had contributed to their construction with their wages and got nothing in return. This is the case for the workers' canteen in the Makedonka factory in Štip, Macedonia, and in the Sana factory in Novi, RS, which has been turned into a private bingo-tombola place where I was not allowed to enter to take photographs, since it was 'clients-only'. Parts of Sana had been rented out to a small textile workshop, while a new Konzum supermarket also occupied part of the premises. I encountered a similar situation in Murska Sobota, Slovenia, in the premises of the recently bankrupted Mura textile factory, also occupied by small subsidiary companies and warehouses. Likewise, the Klupko textile factory in Pančevo has now been replaced by the Israeli retail mall Aviv. Such processes are part of the general reconfiguration of post-industrial urban spaces, which are now oriented towards individualized consumption rather than towards collective production.

Workers' loss of centrality within the urban landscape was almost always indicated by my narrators through a reference to the 'emptiness' of industrial and urban landscapes in the present days, in comparison to the crowds of workers that inhabited urban space during socialism. Jasminka, for instance, a blue-collar worker who lost her job in 2014 with the bankruptcy, recalled what happened at 3.00 pm every day, when Arena female workers would come out of their afternoon shift, together with male workers of the Uljanik shipyard:

> When Uljanik [workers] got out, and Arena [workers], you know how many women … there were such columns of people. And now when we go there, two women are left. Or when I am going home passing Uljanik, there is no one on the harbour. Once at 3.00 pm there was a crowd, now there is no crowd. There is nobody, everything is sad.[10]

The memory of crowds of workers inhabiting the city and the comparison with the current emptying out of public space as a result of deindustrialization are

---

[10] Jasminka and Alida, Pula, May 2015.

constant motives of workers' oral history narratives across the post-Yugoslav space. Former Dalmatinka workers in Sinj compared the crowds coming out of the factory to the crowds who use to visit the Catholic pilgrimage site of Međugorje in Bosnia-Herzegovina, to give me an idea of the amount of people that used to leave the factory after each shift. In the Slovenian town of Murska Sobota, similarly, after the closure of the Mura factory that used to employ over 6,000 workers, public space appears largely deserted. In front of the former Mura premises, one can get an idea of the past crowds of workers that used to come out of the factory from the current empty parking lot where factory buses used to be, which is as big as Murska Sobota's main bus station. In Štip, where the Makedonka factory is now abandoned and in ruin, former white-collar worker Vera, whose life story I discussed in the previous chapter, recalled:

> Makedonka had 6,400 workers, meaning 9 buses, 6 times per day, going to Makedonka. Three times bringing the workers there, three times bringing them back. In the afternoon, three times bringing them, three times back. In the evening, again, three going in, three out. Nine buses. Today there is not even one bus.[11]

Besides their lost centrality to the surrounding urban space, workers also miss the space of the factory itself, its modern canteens, bathrooms and showers, but also its well-kept gardens and courtyards with statues, sports fields and flowers. These spatial arrangements symbolized the overall societal respect for labour and for workers' time of leisure next to the time of production. During our interview, Vera recalled the beauty of the Makedonka factory garden before deindustrialization. In her narrative, the orderly kept garden of the socialist factory, with different kinds of birds, became a metaphor for the proper moral order or society, in comparison to the ruthlessness of post-socialist times:

> Do you know how was that park? Let me tell you. There were swans, ducks, green grass, bushes and birds, so many birds in that park, peacocks, I cannot describe it. ... At that time, people had *esnaf*, that is to say, respect, at home and outside the home. So that when someone would see you, they would see a human being. Now you don't see a human being, you see a wolf.[12]

---

[11] Vera and Nada, Štip, February 2013.
[12] Ibid.

This poignant metaphor of a society in which humans have become wolves towards each other, a modern version of the Latin *homo homini lupus*, echoes other workers' narratives about the end of solidarity and of socialization in post-socialist times. As noted by Ivana Spasić, the Yugoslav model functions in ordinary citizens' memories not only as a model of normal life in a material sense, but also as an ethical form of life.[13] In the following section I discuss workers' narratives of loss after deindustrialization and factory closures and the ways in which white-collar and blue-collar identities permeate current memories, alongside the industrial structure of feeling acquired during socialist times.

Threads of belonging:
Remembering the factory as a second home

Textile workers in socialist factories developed a specific industrial structure of feeling, which was declined along the social axes of class, gender and generation and which was characterized by particular attachments to the welfare entitlements and to the 'working mother' gender contract typical of socialism, as I have shown in previous chapters. Despite their relatively low wages, work-intensive tasks and double burden of productive and reproductive labour, the former workers I interviewed across the post-Yugoslav space overwhelmingly expressed a strong sense of attachment and belonging to their factory, which they associated with terms such as 'home' and 'family' to indicate the strong place occupied by the firm in the creation of their daily routines and in the construction of their identities. During socialism, moreover, employees relished the idea of their factories' success on the Yugoslav and international market. Such pervasive sense of pride is a feeling I encountered among male and female workers across the post-Yugoslav space when describing the past success of their firms. Textile towns such as Maribor and Leskovac, and many others, were frequently described as local 'Manchesters', and countless textile workers assured me that their factory produced the items with the highest quality that could be found. One former male worker from Leteks, Leskovac, recalled that a yellow high-quality cloth was named after the wife of the US president at the time and was thus called *Gospođa Carter* (Mrs Carter). Alongside past pride, however, workers felt a strong sense of loss for the end of factories that

---

[13] Spasić, 'Jugoslavija kao mesto normalnog života'.

were built thanks to the sacrifice of several generations of workers, who had taken part in the progress narrative of the Yugoslav regime. As I will show throughout this chapter, the socialist discourse of intergenerational solidarity and sacrifice for the future promoted by workplace newspapers remains a strong interiorized value for former workers.

In the Istrian town of Pula, the local Arena knitwear factory had closed in spring 2014 after bankruptcy, and former workers' feelings of sadness and bitterness were still very fresh across the city when I arrived, particularly among workers who had lost their jobs. Older workers who had retired before bankruptcy were also very saddened by the end of the firm in which they grew up and in which they had invested the best part of their lives – some younger and older workers declined to take part in interviews due to overwhelming feelings of loss. Those who agreed to be interviewed were very keen to stress the significance of the factory and its success, also as a way to underline the magnitude of its loss. As Arena's former manager, Pavlica, a strong-willed middle-class woman in her eighties, retold with visible pride:

> I believe that no one else in Yugoslavia had what we had. Our factory … we had everything, from the doctor who was there all day, to the nurse, to specialists who came once a week, so that women would not lose much time to see a specialist. We had the dentist, the orthopaedist, everything. We had everything.[14]

The feeling of 'having everything', meaning all necessary welfare services inside the factory, reinforced this sense of community. The belief that no one had such standards in Yugoslavia points at the fragmentation of workers' loyalty, and at the attachment to their own local factory, rather than to a Yugoslav idea of the working class as such. Social mobility, together with the Fordist ideal of a 'job for life', was an important factor that strengthened these loyalties, especially for the old generation. Most women started working in the factory during their training in technical school, or immediately after finishing school, at sixteen or seventeen, and spent all their lives within the factory until retirement.

Pavlica, born in a poor family, the last of nine children, started to work in the mid-1950s. Thanks to a stipend received by the factory, she gradually advanced on the social scale and later became a qualified manager in charge of all the foreign exports of the factory. For her, 'the factory was home. There you grew up, became a woman and a mother, and all that.' Once again, her

---

[14] Pavlica, Pula, May 2015.

narrative strongly emphasizes the interrelation between the public and the private sphere. After childbirth, Pavlica refused to stop working, despite her husband's requests. The factory 'was all for her', also due to their high responsibility. When she went into retirement, she cried, 'as if you were leaving your home', and fell into a period of depression. She recalled with amusement that the psychologist had proposed that she undergo ten sessions of therapy at 250 kunas each to cure her depression, but this made her conclude that she could better get well on her own. Deeply attached to the factory, Pavlica still kept at home the heavy golden ring that she received for her first twenty-five years of service, which represents a seamstress encircled by the local Roman amphitheatre.

White-collar workers as Pavlica tend to have a more idealized picture of working and welfare conditions inside Arena, and to emphasize the factory's paternalism towards its employees, as opposed to blue-collar workers, who appear more critical of gendered and class inequalities in the socialist era. Dissimilar to the managers' narratives, blue-collar narratives frequently point at work alienation, fatigue and personal sacrifice. As they recalled, the *norma* (timed, piece-rate production) was always hard, either during socialism or capitalism, especially when coupled with night shifts, which were common at Arena. In a way, workers' narratives indicate the chief mechanism of value production which was behind successful branding and exports: female workers' intensive, exhausting and often even disabling piece-rate work at the machine. Welfare provisions, therefore, are seen as a rightful compensation for such hard work. Ines, a seamstress who started working in 1977, summarized the situation at Arena as follows:

> We had a real restaurant, the cooking was good. We had a clinic. The worker was taken care for, and the work had to be done (*Brinulo se o radniku, a raditi se moralo*). All according to the [piece-rate] norm, from handmade to all other phases, everyone had to work to get something. Because we know that textile work has always been poorly paid, then and now. We did not know better, and you've got to do what you've got to do.[15]

The idea that seamstresses 'did not know better' and easily complied with hard work frequently comes up in the narratives. During our collective conversation, a colleague of Ines, Romana, stated jokingly that blue-collar workers were 'dobro zdresirane', meaning well trained to follow orders

---

[15] Ines and colleagues, Pula, January 2016.

during socialist times: 'We knew nothing else. So we accepted and worked. The worker was always at the bottom (*Radnik bio je brižan vajk*, in Istrian dialect).'[16]

Challenging the official socialist discourse on workers' rights, Ines recalled that she would avoid taking sick leave in order not to lose the production prize, which represented a substantial addition to the basic salary. Three times, she told me, she took a box of antibiotics when sick to get on with work: 'You cannot go on sick leave, you take five, six pills and get going, you would not think of going home or taking sick leave.'[17] Ines also paid a local woman to take care of her children during shifts. As mentioned in Chapter 2, for blue-collar workers it was often a problem to combine productive and reproductive labour, especially when living outside town, as Ines did. In Pula workers generally used municipal crèches and kindergartens, as Arena had no childcare facilities. Village women most often left children with female relatives, usually a grandmother.

Despite the fact that blue-collar workers provide a critique of gender and class inequalities that persisted during socialism, their narratives nonetheless describe the factory as a space of socialization, solidarity and personal fulfilment. Ines, for instance, was once talking to a relative and former colleague, and admitted that she missed the factory after retirement. Her relative asked her: 'Are you crazy, don't you like to stay at home?' to which she replied:

> It's nice at home, but it was nicer when I would get ready in the morning, take the bus or get a lift from my husband and go to work. It was how it was, but we worked, we were young, we sang, we had fun, and so on. There was a party once in a while, we would bring something, treat ourselves, and so on. During the night shift, for the whole night shift you work, and work, but you also sing, not because you are happy, dear God, but like that, together with others [*u društvu*], you were also somehow happy, weren't you.[18]

Similar to the Moulynex workers studied by Clarke, and to the Polish seamstresses interviewed by Pine,[19] Arena workers describe the factory floor as a space that allowed class and gendered sociability and solidarity. Most interviews evoke the good working atmosphere that reigned in the factory

---

[16] Ines and colleagues, Pula, January 2016.
[17] Ines, Pula, October 2015.
[18] Ibid.
[19] Clarke, 'Closing Time'; Pine, 'Retreat to the household? Gendered domains in postsocialist Poland'.

and the sense of conviviality that was felt as members of the community. Words like family and home are frequently used to convey this sense of community. Alida, another worker, stated: 'In fact we were like one family, if something bad happened to someone, God forbid, everyone would collect money'. She then recounted a solidarity initiative taken by all the workers to help a woman who had a baby out of wedlock:

> There was a woman who got pregnant and the baby had no father. She surprised us with her pregnancy, she carried it for nine months, she worked with us until the end, and we did not know that she was pregnant. She worked at the ironing machine until the last days before childbirth. At the end we took our van, someone gave a small bed, someone a pram, someone clothes, everyone collected something, we filled the van and brought it to the village where she lived. She later told us that her parents and everyone else cried when they saw the van. They were stunned. This is to say that we were like one family, there were tears and laughs, but it was also beautiful.[20]

Other shop-floor stories of women's solidarity and sociability at Arena include the pans of food brought into the factory during the night shifts, or the time when Arena workers dressed up with the shirts that had to be packed and shipped for Germany the next morning. Women also warmly remember the frequent celebrations organized by the Arena management, when all the women would congregate in the House of the Army (now Veterans' house). Such celebrations were organized for New Year, or for Women's Day. All female workers would then dress like 'Jovanke', namely, like copies of Jovanka Broz, the wife of Yugoslav president Josip Broz Tito, known for her glamorous style. Former blue-collar workers Tanja and Božica, who started working in the Arena workshop located in Pazin and later moved to Pula, recall that they were feeling like 'real ladies' on Women's Day (8 March) celebrations, with new dresses and new shoes. Tanja still has the dress at home as a souvenir. Božica emphatically stated that everyone was equal then, and that 'you could not distinguish the director from the worker'. Of course, this display of equal recognition was only limited to special occasions, while social hierarchies were firmly in place on the shop floor, as the last section of this chapter will make clear.

Besides annual commemorative events, Arena workers were also often called to greet and celebrate Tito and Jovanka when international guests were received in the harbour adjacent to the factory, on their way to the

---

[20] Jasminka and Alida, Pula, May 2015.

presidential residence on the Brijuni islands facing Pula. Dorina remembers well when Arena workers were called to honour Ethiopian emperor Haile Selassie. Workers had to keep the place assigned to them in the parade, but it was 'phenomenal', as Tito could be seen at close distance. Politicians' visits to textile factories were relatively common, as shown by a video of Tito visiting Makedonka, and by pictures depicting an official visit to Arena by first female Yugoslav prime minister Milka Planinc. Such visits stand in opposition to present times, when local politicians generally neglect to visit textile workers. In the case of the state-owned Orljava textile factory in Požega, workers were recently prevented from meeting the Croatian president Kolinda Grabar-Kitarović for fear that they might complain of poor working conditions.[21]

In their narratives, blue-collar workers remember socialism as a time in which interpersonal relations and work relations were more 'humane' and based on mutual understanding. Moreover, the socialist era is seen as a time during which people were more easily willing to help each other, and more keen on conviviality and socializing (*druženje*). Class is a central element in such articulations of memories. In a recent article, Dražen Cepić has analysed the 'crisis of sociability' among working-class Croatians employed in different industrial sectors in post-socialist times.[22] This crisis, he argues, can be attributed to the waning of trade unions' initiatives within the factory (excursions, sport, summer holidays), as well as to rising inequalities and to a shortage of leisure time due to the worsening of labour and welfare conditions. Alison Stenning made similar observations in her accounts of Polish workers in Nowa Huta after the end of socialism, noting that the current lack of time and money and job insecurity have a great role in restricting leisure and sociability.[23]

Even in a restructured former socialist factory like Varteks, which survives against all odds, the general precariousness of contemporary Croatian workers affects the ways in which sociability and leisure are enjoyed and experienced. Leda, a white-collar trade unionist in Varteks, summarized the changes that occurred as follows:

> You know what is, in my view, one of the biggest problems, the difference between then and now? Once people had very good relations, we really were like one big family. Now interpersonal relations have greatly

---

[21] Dimitrije Birač, 'Ponižavanje radnica Orljave', 6 February 2017. Available at: https://www.radnicki.org/ponizavanje-radnica-orljave/ (accessed 20 January 2018).
[22] Dražen Cepić, 'The crisis of working class sociability in Croatia: Challenges of de-unionization', *Ethnologia Balkanica*, 18 (2015), pp. 337–53.
[23] Stenning, 'Where is the post-socialist working class?'.

deteriorated. There is no trust anymore. Not just in the trade union, but generally, no one trusts each other. ... The worker doesn't trust the worker, nor the boss, nor the boss trusts the worker and then some kind of animosity ensues. There is no social life (*nema druženja*), there is not enough money for sociability. Once we had our own holiday resort, we went to the seaside, to excursions, we had sport meetings. Today there is nothing of that as trade unions have not enough financial means, wages are low, people have their worries, they are indebted, they worry how they will pay, their wages are not regularly paid, hundreds of worries. This is a big problem that puts distance between each worker.[24]

For female workers in the textile sector, whose spaces of sociability and leisure were already restricted during socialism due to familial obligations, post-socialist transformations and deindustrialization signified a further limitation of spaces of leisure and collective sociability. The end of union-based sociability is deeply felt by workers across the post-Yugoslav space. Despite such wide-ranging social and cultural changes, workers strive to keep in touch with their colleagues and to maintain informal networks even after retirement or the closure of the factory, as in the case of my narrators in Pula or Varaždin. At times, they even manage to self-organize, as in the case of the recreational centre founded in a village near Čakovec by a textile worker, and modelled after earlier factory initiatives.[25] After the analysis of workers' attachment to the sociability provided by factory life, in the following section I get back to another theme that is deeply characteristic of workers' industrial structure of feeling, namely, their attachment to the job security and predictability provided by the socialist factory, and their difficulty in coping with job losses and precarity after deindustrialization.

Missing the future: The end of intergenerational solidarity

The current post-industrial landscape, devoid of factories and of working-class presence, contrast with textile workers' structure of feeling, rooted in the times of Fordism and industrialization. Citizens in Yugoslavia were largely part of global Fordist imaginaries which generated wide-ranging attachments across the world, and particularly 'commonly held

---

[24] Leda and blue-collar workers, Varaždin, May 2016. Interview conducted by the author and Nikolina Hrga.
[25] This case is described in Cepić, 'The crisis of working class sociability', p. 348.

attachments vis-à-vis the future – a future marked by a predictable, measured incrementalism mediated by the state'.[26] Similar to the Yugoslav state, textile factories were conceived as permanent entities, which structured the life and time of their workers as well as the life of entire communities. Entire families worked in the same factory and parents expected their children to witness a continuous improvement of their life conditions thanks to their wages and savings. Deindustrialization, however, brought increasing precarity and insecurity for working-class citizens and their families. Worries about the future of their children and grandchildren, often educated but without a job, are constant in textile workers' narratives. Textile workers often compare their experience of finding a job immediately after vocational school, with the plight of unemployed young people today, and have trouble to explain how this can be possible or accepted on a wide scale. Some former workers even told me that they wished that young people could experience the same carefree stability they were able to enjoy in their own youth. The difficulty in coping with the consequences of deindustrialization is apparent in the dialogue between Alida and Jasminka, two Arena workers who live near each other in a working-class neighbourhood of Pula. As I mentioned earlier, Jasminka lost her blue-collar job in 2014, while her neighbour Alida, also a blue-collar worker and a concierge in later years, retired shortly before the collapse of her factory. The two neighbours' narratives make clear the shock and loss of meaning that was felt with the end of Arena, and compare the factory's closure to the break-up of Yugoslavia. The dialogue goes as follows:

Jasminka:	It's like the break-up of Yugoslavia! The same! We fell from the clouds. Will Yugoslavia break apart? Of course not, there is no chance it would happen … no chance. And then it happened. The same goes with the factory. You simply cannot grasp it is all gone … that's it, you cannot …
Alida:	Such an important firm, I will never forget, when I was working at the door, there came all the pensioners. … They were the ones who put the factory on its feet, who took money out of their wages so that things could be good for us afterwards. They had no toilet or canteen or health clinic or anything, the workers made all that. Someone led those workers, well done to Škrinjarić [former factory director],

---

[26] Andrea Muehlebach and Nitzan Shoshan, 'Introduction, special collection on post-Fordist affect', *Anthropological Quarterly*, 85/2 (2012), p. 333.

>   I am not saying it wasn't good for him, but it was good for us as well. As when Tito was there, everyone says he was a dictator, this and that, but it was good for us while he ruled, we did not miss anything, we got flats, we had workers' self-management. Someone directed it, but you felt like you were worth something, differently than now. And now there is democracy ...
>
> Jasminka: And there is more fear than before. Young people are afraid about work, of where they will be when everything closes, and of how they would manage to create a family. There is no security, no job, no flat, nothing. There is no security.[27]

Similar to the end of Yugoslavia, the closure of Arena could not be foreseen. Even if welfare services such as the canteen and the health clinic had gradually been dismantled in the 1990s, and even if the working atmosphere worsened to a certain extent – a sign of this was the closure of the main factory gate during each shift[28] – Arena nonetheless managed to withstand global competition and to survive through outsourced orders for major brands such as Stefanel and Benetton. Until its last days, and until the closure of its two main shops in the historical centre, Arena's reputation stayed strong in the minds of Pula's citizens, particularly among its clientele of local middle-class women. Alida, who worked as concierge, could witness the popularity of Arena knitwear across town thanks to all the messages of praise she received. Frequently meeting the older pensioners, she also witnessed the ways in which the factory had become successful, thanks to the daily sacrifice of several generations of women. Arena's enduring prestige made workers proud and partially compensated the fatigue of everyday work, as Alida made clear when she stated: 'when you are working you can't stand the shirts anymore, you hate them, out of tiredness, but when you hear all those compliments, you feel proud, and you are happy to have been part of the firm.'

Workers' pride in relation to the success of the firm coexisted with workers' respect for the former director, who was likened to a local Tito, for directing the firm while taking care of its workers. Social security featured among the valuable elements of working for a socialist factory, and another recurring theme of workers' narratives was the phrase: 'wages were low, but

---

[27] Jasminka and Alida, Pula, May 2015.
[28] The closure of the main factory gate during shifts was lived by workers as an arbitrary imposition. Often workers had to wait 1 or 2 hours for the concierge to open the gate, especially after overtime work. See Maksić, *Trikotaža Arena Pula*, p. 13.

they were regular," in comparison to the frequent occurrence of unpaid wages in contemporary Croatia. Jasminka, who regretted the present insecurity, had lost not only her job but also her savings due to the criminal disappearance of funds deposited in the internal bank. She revealed how she felt compelled to keep her savings there rather than in a regular bank, as like many others, this way she felt she would contribute to keeping the factory going, while receiving a slightly higher interest rate. Again, this was both a matter of economic interest and of loyalty to one's firm.

Feelings of insecurity and devaluation were particularly strong among those sixty-two workers who had lost their jobs in 2014, mostly women in their mid- or late fifties who needed a few more years to achieve retirement age and who felt that their loyalty had been misplaced. Suzana, for instance, was one of the last to leave the factory, assisting sale proceedings in the winter of 2014. I interviewed her in the bankrupted factory, when potential buyers could come and look at the industrial equipment and factory furniture for sale. The structure of feeling and the work ethic shaped by socialist factories clearly appeared in Suzana's narrative:

> When you think how much of your life has been spent here, and all of a sudden ... we never went to the unemployment bureau, only when we got employed. And now we have to go to the unemployment bureau. It is so unusual for me, to go there. After all these years. I feel like ... how shall I say ... as if we had no value here. As if we gave nothing to the company. But we gave our maximum. Not just us, also the women who came before, we continued their work. That's why, when I look at the machines and at what's on sale ... so little money is being asked for it, and we, how shall I put it, earned it with our blood, for the factory to get to this point.[29]

Similar to Alida's account in the earlier passage, Suzana's narrative also recalls the sacrifice of the previous generations of women, who accepted difficult working conditions and sacrifice in order to achieve collective progress and well-being. As mentioned earlier, this discourse of sacrifice was very much part of the structure of feeling created by self-managed socialism in Yugoslavia, and its legacy can still be perceived among workers, who frequently recall the difficult post-war beginnings of the factory. The closure of Arena, however, disrupted this linear vision of time. Workers had difficulties in coping with the idea that their hard work had no meaning, or

---

[29] Suzana and Milka, Pula, January 2015.

value, since during socialist times their contribution had been valorized both symbolically and materially. Arena workers who lost their jobs had to go to the unemployment bureau for the first time after decades.

Similar feelings of loss, devaluation and sacrifice related to the expectation of a promising and stable future were also expressed by former workers of the bankrupted Dalmatinka spinning mill in the town of Sinj, in the Dalmatian region of Croatia, whose early socialist history I described in Chapter 1. After its expansion in the 1970s and 1980s, the factory employed over 2,000 workers and supplied 60 per cent of the Yugoslav market, exporting worldwide. It was renovated completely in the mid-1980s. In 1991, the existing management was removed for political reasons, and new staff loyal to the Croatian Democratic Party (HDZ) was appointed. During the war, due to the closeness of Sinj to the front, the factory temporarily served as a refuge for the local hospital, including the maternity ward, so that one former worker we met during our visit revealed that she had given birth within the factory itself in wartime. After the war, the Dalmatinka spinning mill gradually accumulated debts and finally went bankrupt in 2001. In 2004, two Italian entrepreneurs and brothers bought the privatized premises. They were supposed to relaunch production, but instead speculated on the company's remaining stocks and assets and avoided paying workers for months, until bankruptcy was declared again in 2008. Most workers lost their job before retirement age and were left fighting for survival. In 2009, a group of former workers laid flowers on the grave of Vice Buljan, the communist politician who had been decisive to the establishment of the factory in the early 1950s. The local newspaper *Slobodna Dalmacija* reported the event with the headline: 'You died, the factory died, and we do not feel so good either.'[30]

When I visited Sinj in spring 2016, the spinning mill was abandoned and in disrepair (in late summer 2018, the factory was eventually demolished, to build a wedding hall in its place) (Figure 11). During the collective interview session with former workers that I conducted with the help of local activists in charge of the Dalmatinka heritage project, the anger, bitterness and sense of injustice caused by deindustrialization and criminal privatization practices were still very palpable, particularly among workers who lost their job before retirement age. For textile workers in Sinj, Dalmatinka embodied the possibility of normal life and of a normal future. As mentioned emphatically by Nataša, a former accountant and trade unionist: 'We are the generation

---

[30] Vito Perić, 'Umrlo si ti, umrla je tvornica, a ni mi nismo baš najbolje', *Slobodna Dalmacija*, 23 March 2009. Available at: http://www.slobodnadalmacija.hr/dalmacija/split-zupanija/clanak/id/45434/umro-si-ti-umrla-je-tvornica-a-ni-mi-nismo-bas-najbolje (accessed 20 January 2018).

Figure 11 The Dalmatinka factory in 2016, before its demolition in 2018. Photo by the author.

whose grandmothers provided for our future through the factory. And we thought we would be able to build an even better future for our children and grandchildren.' This hope, however, did not materialize. Dalmatinka, the 'mother' of the local community, was lost with factory closure, as highlighted by Nataša in another poignant statement:

> Dalmatinka was the mother of all the inhabitants of the city of Sinj and of its surroundings. She fed us, our children, our grandchildren, and we had a future. However the war came and things did not stay like that. While we worked, there was welfare for all, possibilities, good wages, houses were built and the future of our children was built. ... Now the factory is so abandoned, so pillaged, so destroyed, that it is terrible and ugly to tell our children and grandchildren that we once worked there.[31]

It is interesting to note the usage of such a maternalist discourse to describe the factory, also bearing in mind that it even served as a maternity ward during wartime. The fact that Nataša mentioned children and grandchildren

---

[31] Nataša and colleagues, Sinj, April 2016. Co-interviewed with Dalmatinka Sinj project team (Nikola Krizanac, Silvia Milić, Jelena Pavlinušić).

indicates how the factory was experienced as a provider for the entire community and for working women's families. Yet the end of Dalmatinka as a community provider, coupled with women's devaluation as workers, became a source of shame – former workers feel ashamed to indicate that their beloved factory has turned into a wasteland. Work and family life were intimately interrelated in Sinj. Nataša's colleague, Petra, said that it was great to work for Dalmatinka during socialism, and immediately added that she had three children for whom she could buy whatever was needed. Another worker, Jadranka, mentioned free schoolbooks for children, Women's Day celebrations and the voluntary blood donors' association as the highlights of her factory experience. Bathrooms with proper showers and running water were also a distinctive feature of the factory, at a time in which many women did not have a proper bathroom at home, particularly in the villages surrounding Sinj (one of the activists who co-conducted the interview, for instance, recalled that her grandfather was the first in the village to have a bathroom built in his home in 1973, thanks to his savings as a *gastarbeiter* in Germany). Besides its avant-garde facilities, Dalmatinka also sponsored the construction of housing for workers and of various sport facilities, such as an Olympic swimming pool that is seen as the pride of local inhabitants to these days.

The outstanding contribution of the Dalmatinka plant to the local industrial, economic and social development was recognized even by former workers with no sympathy whatsoever for socialism as a political regime. Together with the local activists of the Dalmatinka project, I interviewed Marija in her house located in one of the surrounding villages of Sinj. Born in a poor family of ten children, Marija started working at Dalmatinka in the early 1970s after finishing a vocational school, and she worked until 1999. Raised in a village that was considered to have sided with the Ustasha during the Second World War, and of Catholic faith, Marija did not feel politically aligned to communist rule during her time in the factory. She recalled how she was scolded by the management for invoking the name of Jesus once, and how women who came from so-called 'partisan villages' could at times obtain easier jobs and better privileges in contrast to those from the 'Ustasha villages' as herself. Also, she experienced the factory's work discipline and piece-rate *norma* as extremely hard, especially in the beginning in the learning phase. During the interview she compared work discipline at Dalmatinka to 'Auschwitz', 'a prison' and to 'collective torture'.

At the same time, Marija also felt that during socialism workers had many more social entitlements and protection than today. She mentioned the canteen with its warm meals, the sanitary facilities for women, the twenty-four-hours doctor and nurse service, maternity leave, the subsidized holiday facility on the coast near Split, the frequently organized excursions she attended visiting many places across Yugoslavia, and credits for house building at 2 per cent interest which she took together with her husband. She also recalled a time in which she cut a finger at the machine, and was afraid to let her supervisors know, but was instead sent home on sick leave without any problem. Partially attempting to reconcile her political feelings with her positive narratives of social welfare during socialism, Marija stated: 'We had all privileges then, more than in this system. I am glad about the new system. Croatia is my Croatia. But it was beautiful.'[32]

Besides welfare entitlements, Marija recalled the socializing routines that she shared with other girls from her village, who finished the same textile school, as well as the sense of independence that she gained thanks to her wage and thanks to the fact that she left the village to move to Sinj in a rented room. Working outside the home meant that she was able to buy what she liked, to meet new people, to access some culture: 'What would I have if I would stay in the village? Nothing. In this way I became my own master since I was eighteen years old. You could do whatever you liked.' One of the former workers who lost her job with the bankruptcy, Milica, voiced a similar feeling about Dalmatinka's wages and women's autonomy. In her words, a secure wage meant a secure life, a future. 'When you have means in your pocket, you have means in life,' she stated. The empowering character of factory work outside the home for women of rural and working-class background in socialist Yugoslavia has been often downplayed in the existing scholarly literature, especially due to widespread patriarchal domination in the private sphere and due to women's persistent double burden throughout the socialist era. As I have shown in Chapter 2, however, while socialist authorities tended to naturalize women's double burden, there were also plenty of discussions on women's positions as workers and mothers, which enhanced women's awareness of the value of their work and of their welfare entitlements. Working-class women who lost their jobs with deindustrialization remember their factory as a source of empowerment, job security and sociability. Workers' structure of feeling is specifically gendered, as a result of the socialist legacy of the 'working mother' gender contract. In the following section I will analyse another source of post-socialist nostalgia, namely, the longing for pre-war, peaceful times, with a special attention towards the post-conflict setting of Novi in Republika Srpska, one of the two entities of Bosnia-Herzegovina.

---

[32] Marija, Sinj, April 2016. Co-interviewed with Dalmatinka Sinj project team (Nikola Krizanac, Silvia Milić, Jelena Pavlinušić).

Feeling Yugoslav: Nostalgia for brotherhood and unity

While nostalgia for socialist welfare is pervasive in my narrators' narratives, this sentiment is often interrelated with another type of nostalgia, which is voiced often implicitly and less emphatically, as it contrasts with the new nationalist discourses that have been dominating public space in post-Yugoslav states in the course of the last three decades. This other type of nostalgia can be defined as nostalgia for pre-war times and for the daily practice of peaceful multi-ethnic coexistence that became common in many urban settings during socialist Yugoslavia, and which led to numerous mixed marriages among citizens of different religious faiths or ethnicities.[33] As mentioned in the introduction to the book, the break-up of Yugoslavia and the Yugoslav Wars of the 1990s represented a tragic process of disruption and discontinuity for ordinary citizens, alongside privatization, deindustrialization and widespread job losses.[34] During the Bosnian War, in particular, which made over 100,000 victims and many more internally displaced, ethnic cleansing and war rapes were widely used in mixed territories to create homogeneous ethnic constituencies. In the city of Bosanski Novi, renamed Novi Grad by Serb authorities to eliminate the linguistic marker of its 'Bosnian' identity, local Muslim citizens were expelled as early as July 1992, when Bosnian-Serb forces 'blackmailed' UN officials to remove all 8,000 Muslims from Novi through humanitarian convoys. Refugees were made to sign a paper with which they renounced all their property.[35] In 1995, during a Croatian-led operation across the border with Republika Srpska that made military victims on both sides, fifty-four Serb civilians were also killed in Novi and in the surrounding villages.[36] The Sana factory was also partially damaged in 1995, after a period of wartime production, during which employees were summoned to work as a contribution to the war effort, despite the risk of concrete attacks

---

[33] Monika Palmberger, 'Nostalgia matters: Nostalgia for Yugoslavia as a potential vision for a better future', *Sociologija*, L/4 (2008), pp. 355–70.
[34] See Catherine Baker, *The Yugoslav Wars of the 1990s* (London, 2015).
[35] Charles T. Powers, 'Serbs accused of "blackmail" on refugees', *Los Angeles Times*, 29 July 1992. Available at: http://articles.latimes.com/1992-07-29/news/mn-4653_1_refugee-problem (accessed 20 January 2018); Peter Maas, 'Muslims forced to leave Bosnia', *Washington Post*, 25 July 1992. Available at: https://www.washingtonpost.com/archive/politics/1992/07/25/muslims-forced-to-leave-bosnia/f81d0b25-4e0c-4bb2-80f5-bc6d09715c56/?utm_term=.4ea44972254b (accessed 20 January 2018).
[36] Paulina Arbutina, 'Unska slagalica strave', *Novosti*, 29 October 2010. Available at: http://arhiva.portalnovosti.com/2010/10/unska-slagalica-strave/ (accessed 20 January 2018).

(the so-called *radne obaveze*).³⁷ During and after the war, many *Novljani* of different ethnicities left the town, looking for better life opportunities in Western Europe, North America and Australia. The town is now largely emptied out of a pre-war population of 41,665 inhabitants, and in the municipality some 27,115 remain. Novi is also deindustrialized – most factories have closed, including the local wood and metal factories.

In December 2013 I visited Novi with a local friend who now lives outside Bosnia, but whose parents still live in town. I wanted to interview women who had worked in the Sana textile factory, which employed 3,000 women in its heydays (including workshops in surrounding villages) and which had been chosen as the setting of the 1985 television series *Priče iz Fabrike*, discussed in Chapter 2. In a few days I met six former workers among my friend's neighbours and acquaintances. These workers were all of Serbian descent. My friend tried to contact, via a Muslim friend, a woman of Muslim descent, Meriba, who also worked at Sana in the past. Unlike Serbian women, Meriba was very wary of a formal interview, and only allowed us to have a quick chat outside her home, in the freezing December weather, while her dog barked the entire time. She briefly recalled the happy time in the factory, the singing and the Women's Day celebrations, and how it all ended with the Bosnian war – meaning not just factory life, but also peaceful coexistence between workers of different ethnicities.

Serbian women, with whom I could have in-depth interviews, shared similar feelings. The war clearly defined the moment of disruption in the narratives, separating the *before* and *after*, also since the Sana factory only worked in a limited capacity after 1995, up until 2002. My first interview was with Danijela, a former seamstress who worked at Sana from 1972 to 1992. But the dialogue also involved her husband, Miro, as well Ljilja, the mother of my friend, a former waiter turned shopkeeper who is generally more critical of socialism than former blue-collar workers. In my presence, the past period was summarized as follows in a polyphonic and somehow chaotic dialogue, intended to explain local historical transformations to an outsider like me:

Danijela: It was good until we worked, we all worked.
Ljilja: And no one hated each other then.
Danijela: No, we were singing when going to work. ...
Miro: There was no nationalism. Muslims, Serbs, Croats ... everybody ... we did not know [who was who].

---

³⁷ I heard similar reports about work during wartime for the Dalmatinka factory in Sinj, Croatia and the Leteks factory in Leskovac, Serbia. I was unable to trace the amplitude of this phenomenon and more precise data on it.

Danijela:	They asked me once what I was [in ethnic terms] when seeing my ID and I did not know.
Ljilja:	I knew.
Danijela:	I only knew that I was Yugoslav. I said 'Yugoslav'. That stayed in my memory. We did not know.
Miro:	And then war came, and people were supposed to hate each other. ...
Danijela:	It was better then, whatever others might say.[38]

Since both Danijela and her husband remained without jobs after the war and were still waiting for retirement age, the previous time was positively associated with regular wages, prosperity and sociability, next to multi-ethnic coexistence and Yugoslav belonging across ethnic background. Positive memories of pre-war times and of brotherhood and unity were presented alongside wartime stories related to the Croatian military operation and bombing of 1995, which my narrators experienced personally in their neighbourhood. Miro, especially, who saw me as 'neutral', was keen to denounce the killings of local civilians by Croatian forces, and to stress instead the hospitable manners and good nature of the local Serbian population. He was particularly keen to counter the stereotypical negative images of Serbs that he saw as widespread in 'the West' and Western media.[39] Overall, my narrators in Novi adopted similar narratives on war times, and never mentioned the ethnic cleansing of local Muslim inhabitants by Serbian forces.

In my narrators' narratives, working-class nostalgia for the socialist past could coexist with specific ethno-nationalist narratives constructed during war times, precisely because of the strong temporal disruption between *before* and *after* caused by the war, to which these respective narratives belong, and because of the strong un-mixing of population that followed the socialist era. At the same time, interethnic solidarity was maintained as a moral value, while the socialist period continued to be singled out as a benchmark of normality, decency and prosperity. Dragana, who worked at Sana for thirty-two years from the mid-1960s to the early 1990s, said that she still felt 'Yugoslav', and that Yugoslavia could have been 'stronger than America' if the war had not happened. She recalled the heyday of the factory when she started as a fourteen-year-old trainee in 1966, and when everything was available for

---

[38] Danijela, Miro and Ljilja, Novi, December 2014.
[39] See Zala Volčič, 'The notion of "the West" in the Serbian national imaginary', *European Journal of Cultural Studies*, 8/2 (2005), pp. 155–75.

workers, from warm meals in the canteen to the kindergarten, from regular wages to subsidized holidays. Then the war came, she said, perhaps because of the history of hatred that is present in the region. In relation to this she referred to a traditional theme of local ethno-nationalist discourse, namely, the massacre of Serbian inhabitants by Ustasha forces during the Second World War, in which the entire family of her husband got killed. Hatred came back, she seemed to suggest, despite coexistence: 'We grew up together, Muslims, Croats, Serbs, we went to the same schools and to the same parties, but this started to unravel little by little.'[40] While stressing the humanity of the local Serbian population and her own concrete gestures of solidarity towards Muslim neighbours and colleagues, Dragana also denounced the Croatian shelling of the town and the killing of local Serbian civilians.

In Dragana's narrative, essentialist narratives of recurring violence in the Balkans ('In Bosnia there is no family where a house can be transmitted for three generations, things get destroyed and reconstructed') coexisted with a strong nostalgia for socialist times: 'Everyone screams at socialism, but no one was hungry back then. Eight hours work, eight hours leisure ... you work the regular working day, having a proper weekend.' The structure of feeling interiorized during socialism became particularly evident when discussing the construction of the factory and its ending during wartimes, which countered the predictability and the promise of future prosperity on which daily sacrifice was based:

> That factory, we built it for fifty years. I had a neighbour, an elderly woman, she brought the wood to heat the factory in 1948, people slowly built the factory on Saturdays and Sundays. When we were not at work we had voluntary actions (*radne akcije*). We supported each other, we worked hard. You work, and work, and you think that you have something, but you have nothing.[41]

Interestingly, Dragana's narrative of *radne akcije* on Saturdays and Sundays contradicts her previous story about free weekends during socialist times – still, voluntary actions for collective good are remembered positively, in contrast to contemporary neo-capitalist labour exploitation, as shown in Chapter 3. Besides the social damages created by wartime divisions, former Sana workers, like other textile workers across the region, are suffering the consequences of deindustrialization and privatization, which manifest themselves in extremely low early pensions before reaching retirement age,

---

[40] Dragana and colleagues, Novi, December 2014.
[41] Ibid.

Figure 12 The Konzum supermarket in the former Sana factory, Novi Grad, 2014. Photo by the author.

and in very precarious working conditions in the few private workshops that produce outsourced garments in town and in the surrounding villages. The struggle for survival results in an increase of informal work, for instance in Dragana's informal textile workshop, where she offers repairs services with some of her colleagues. As Dragana and as another former worker in Novi similarly stated during two separate interviews, 'before we worked eight hours, now we work twelve', even if they are formally unemployed. Parts of the Sana factory, as mentioned earlier, have been partially reconverted into a Konzum supermarket, into a textile workshop and into a bingo-tombola facility, while the rest of the factory lies abandoned in the centre of town. Another landmark of the city, the modernist Hotel Una, which figured prominently in the series *Priče iz Fabrike*, is now abandoned on the bank of the river, after serving as a detention centre during the war, and after being damaged in the fight between Croatian and Serbian forces. The televised series from 1985, which former workers recall as a truthful representation of factory life, is a stunning representation of past industrial modernity when compared to the current urban landscape in Novi (Figure 12).

While Novi combines the features of post-conflict and post-socialist transformations, textile workers' nostalgia for multi-ethnic coexistence and solidarity in pre-war times is not to be found only in contexts directly affected by war such as Bosnia-Herzegovina. In the city of Pula, as well, home to a sizeable Italian minority and to many citizens from all former Yugoslav republics since the Second World War, nationalist tensions were experienced by some of my narrators. Alida, for instance, whose father was a Serbian officer in the local navy base, told me how he was deprived of his pension when the war started, and had to go to Italy to work as a gardener, together with his wife, who took up work in elderly care as many other women in Pula. It was a difficult period, she stated. Alida herself was asked to show proof of her citizenship during the war due to her father being Serbian, while her colleague Jasminka was questioned by authorities about her neighbours, if they were taking drugs or talking ill of the government, due to the fact that they were of Serbian ethnicity. Other narrators in Pula related similar episodes, when they had to resist new dominant ethno-nationalist categorization because of their minority status, or because of regime change. Romana, for instance, born in 1948 in an Italian speaking village, was forced to attend Croatian school without knowing Croatian when the local Italian schools were closed in the 1950s. After the war in the 1990s, she said that she felt discriminated again because of the nationalist atmosphere in town. Her elderly mother, notably, the native of a local village who only spoke Italian, was mistreated by a Croatian doctor who came from outside Istria, who asked why she had not left for Italy after the Second World War.

Stories related to nationalist pressure were retold as well by Ines, who is perhaps more sensitive to this issue due to the fact that her mother is one of the few survivors of the fascist massacre that occurred in the village of Bokordići near Svetvincenat, where the entire local male population was killed in 1944. Ines told me that all female workers at Arena were the same, even if some from the surrounding town of Vodnjan/Dignano only spoke Italian, and even if some came from the rest of Yugoslavia together with their husbands who were in the Yugoslav army. During socialism, she stated: 'We were all the same, no one asked where you are from and what you are, we were all the same.' During the war, however, someone started saying that her neighbour and colleague of her husband, from Bosnia, was a Serb: 'But what Serb, he has never seen Serbia, like me. I said, the best person in the world … It is not important, it is just a person, who cares who he is, what he is, where he is from.' The same went for some other neighbours of Roma origin, with whom she is in very good terms: 'We are all human beings. I say, for everyone there is a mother who suffered when giving birth, isn't it?'[42] Echoing

---

[42] Ines, Pula, October 2015.

the maternalist discourse characteristic of the socialist era, Ines coined her own values of 'motherhood and unity', based on women's common suffering during childbirth.

The concept of past 'brotherhood and unity' among different people was also related by Ines to concrete examples of daily solidarity and sociability, as when all neighbours and acquaintances helped to build her local village house with their manpower:

> Once it was like 'brotherhood and unity', now it is funny to say, but people helped each other with everything. We built the house without paying one kuna. I cooked lunches and dinners, and there was always more men than needed at the machines and at work. In the same way, my husband helped all his friends and brother and everyone else. People were more connected than today.[43]

As this passage shows, 'brotherhood and unity' could be read and appropriated not just as an ideological statement related to multi-ethnic coexistence, but also as a more general ethical stance of mutual aid, solidarity and conviviality – even if the formula, as Ines said, sounds 'funny' in today's dominant discourse. Collective solidarity was supposed to sustain workers' sacrifice for the factory and for the country's future, but was also a concrete mean of support in daily life, as in the case of self-made housing. As mentioned in the second section of this chapter, however, workers' social networks very much declined with the weakening of trade unions and the closure of factories, which represented major sites of sociability and of interethnic mixing.[44] New nationalist narratives also privileged ethnic categorization and homogeneity over humanist, universal values – although as discussed in this chapter this phenomenon is often resisted or at least selectively accepted by ordinary citizens due to previous experiences of multi-ethnic coexistence, even in settings like Republika Srpska where public discourse is heavily dominated by ethno-nationalist narratives. In the following section, I will address how, despite their attachments to socialist welfare and labour rights, textile workers do express class-based critiques of power inequalities experienced during the socialist era.

---

[43] Ibid.
[44] Cepić, 'The crisis of working class sociability'.

Matters of gender and class: Critical Yugo-nostalgia

Scholars of post-socialist nostalgia in the post-Yugoslav space have underlined the gap between new official public discourses and the generally positive memories of socialism brought forward by ordinary citizens, which often represent a form of counter-discourse to present injustices and a way to articulate utopian feelings of resistance and hope.[45] The theme of 'Yugo-nostalgia', initially considered in its cultural and consumerist implications, has been analysed recently in relation to wider social and economic transformations and from the point of view of different categories of industrial workers affected by post-socialist transformations.[46] The study of nostalgia in relation to specific class positioning, however, has been theorized to a lesser extent, particularly when it comes to the material roots of post-socialist nostalgia.[47] The continuities between class formation and class positioning in the socialist and post-socialist era also deserve further comparative attention across post-Yugoslav states. When it comes to textile workers' structure of feeling as expressed through oral narratives, for instance, it is important to note that the widespread post-socialist nostalgic longing for the socialist welfare state coexist with a number of critical remarks about the reproduction of power inequalities in the socialist era – particularly class-based and politically-based inequalities.[48] Oral history interviews, therefore, should not be treated simply as inevitably 'nostalgic' and thus 'unreliable' in relation to the past. Rather, in combination with archival sources from the socialist era, post-socialist oral narratives can enable us to trace how structural inequalities characterized the socialist era, and how these inequalities were reshaped after the end of socialism.

Present inequalities and injustices, certainly, are the ones that matter most to former industrial workers, but this doesn't make them unable to reflect upon a number of problems and limits that characterized socialism itself.

---

[45] Velikonja, 'Lost in transition', p. 14.; Palmberger, 'Nostalgia matters'.
[46] Spasić, 'Jugoslavija kao mesto normalnog života'; Petrović, '"When we were Europe"'; Vodopivec, 'Past for the present'; Stef Jansen, *Yearnings in the Meantime: 'Normal Lives' and the State in a Sarajevo Apartment Complex* (Oxford and New York, 2014); Sanja Potkonjak and Tea Škokić, '"In the world of iron and steel": On the ethnography of work, unemployment and hope', *Narodna umjetnost*, 50/1 (2013), pp. 74–95.
[47] For a recent case study of nostalgia and class in Serbia, see Ognjen Kojanić, 'Nostalgia as a practice of the self in post-socialist Serbia', *Canadian Slavonic Papers*, 57/3-4 (2015), pp. 195–212.
[48] On social inequalities during socialism, see Archer, Duda and Stubbs (eds), *Social Inequalities*.

Nostalgic attachments, therefore, appear to be *reflective*, or *interpretative*, and permeated with awareness of the limits of both the socialist and post-socialist era in a number of cases.[49] Ambivalences and contradictions in the narratives are of course always present, but they can often be explained through a genealogical exercise based on a historical contextualization that takes into account workers' industrial structure of feeling, and particularly the gap between the interiorized values, discourses and norms proper of socialist factories and the speaker's embodied experiences of socialism and post-socialism, which often contradicted these same values and discourses. I will consider two specific examples here: workers' memory of self-management, trade unions and factory politics more generally, and workers' memory of welfare resources that were unevenly distributed during socialism.

When it comes to issues of self-management and factory politics, textile workers' narratives are not at all uncritical and nostalgic. As I mentioned earlier in the chapter, blue-collar workers tend to be very critical of the strict labour discipline enforced through piece-rate production. A similar critical stance is evident when it comes to the theme of factory politics. Narrators seem to confirm the findings of social historians about self-management – ordinary blue-collar workers, especially women, hardly felt motivated to take part in politics, and they did not want to lose precious time in bureaucratic meetings which were seen as largely formal and predetermined in advance.[50] Workers' councils, in which some of my narrators took part as delegates, are remembered in a similar way by blue-collar workers, as made clear by these quotes taken from separate interviews conducted in Pula:

> Milka: Workers' councils were there, but you know how it was, you sat and raised your hand (*laughs*). There wasn't much debate, it was quite formal. ... There was a vote, who got more votes was elected ... the last world was always theirs. We talked more of technical issues.[51]
>
> Dorina: Listen, we just had to be present more than anything else, few people always decided. That's how it was. Politics.[52]

---

[49] On reflective and interpretative nostalgia, see Tim Strangleman, 'The nostalgia for permanence at work? The end of work and its commentators', *The Sociological Review*, 55/1 (2007), pp. 81–103. See also Boym, *The Future of Nostalgia*.
[50] See earlier discussions of the self-management system in chapter one.
[51] Suzana and Milka, Pula, January 2015.
[52] Božica and Dorina, Pula, March 2016.

Romana: When you had to vote for something, they called you, they told you in advance for whom to vote.[53]

The distance between blue-collar workers and management was undoubtedly significant, as the 'us' and 'them' distinction shows. Most female textile workers did what they could to stay out of 'politics', as discussed in Chapter 2. On the other hand, as I already mentioned, socialist discourse emphasized workers' rights and entitlements in the self-management system, including women's specific social rights. Female workers interiorized such entitlements, which they recall in positive terms, in contrast with the present situation characterized by workers' symbolic and material devaluation. During the dialogue between Jasminka and Alida, workers' councils were remembered as formal and dominated by the management, but nonetheless it was recalled that workers felt freer to express their criticism to their supervisors and bosses:

Jasminka: [During meetings] it was always like they decided, but still ...
Alida: But still they would listen to you. You could speak out and you would not be reprimanded for it. That's how society was taught then *(Nekad se to tako naučilo društvo)*. And after [socialism], you did not dare to say anything, not to the boss nor to anybody.[54]

Power hierarchies, in the eyes of my narrators, were legitimated then by true meritocracy and skills, and by the fact that managers were taking care of the common good, rather than of their own interest. According to Zorica, a middle-range supervisor at the Arena knitwear factory in Pula, some white-collar employees were only interested in career advancement, while others displayed a more humanist (or paternalist) attitude:

I remember a technical director who told me when he retired: 'those who are smart, they have to take care of those who are not so smart, they are the one who can enable others to be in a good position.' And afterwards capitalism came, and it did not look like that, you only have to run for profit.[55]

---

[53] Ines and colleagues, Pula, January 2016.
[54] Jasminka and Alida, Pula, May 2015.
[55] Zorica, Pula, June 2015.

As discussed earlier, and especially in Chapter 1, paternalism did not seem a problem to most workers, since it was an integral part of the industrial structure of feeling acquired in socialist factories and a characteristic of the Fordist mode of production. The strong authority of politicians and experts was generally respected, since it did not translate into great wage differentials and was compensated with regular wages and additional welfare benefits for blue-collar workers.[56] Trade unions are also positively remembered for their paternalist assistance, and for 'really caring' about workers back then, through the redistribution of various social benefits, as opposed to post-socialist trade unions who have been generally equated with the despised realm of 'politika' in the eyes of blue-collar workers (see Chapter 3).

While socialist welfare is positively remembered in contrast to the present precarious setting, however, workers' memories of making use of actual welfare resources, such as holiday resorts, or housing, is not devoid of contradictions. Blue-collar workers, for instance, often recalled that white-collar workers had privileged access to holiday facilities and subsidized excursions.[57] The class-based character of social memory was made particularly evident during an exchange occurred in the course of a collective interview in the Varteks factory in Varaždin, where I met with a number of blue-collar workers together with the local trade union delegate who is part of the management staff. The trade unionist, Leda, was telling me about two different holiday resorts, one near Varaždin on a lakeside, in Trakošćan, and the other on the coast near Zadar, Turanj. She explained how each worker could sign up for such resorts and pay symbolic sums, which they would pay back in instalments from their wage. While Leda was painting an idealized picture of such services and of workers' holidays, however, blue-collar workers interrupted her and started a collective debate on who really managed to access such facilities:

- The ordinary worker did not go there, only *those* (*oni*) went ... (*General laughs*)
- Nobody, Leda, not to the lake, nor to the sea, nowhere.
- Some went, but not us from the sewing department (*konfekcija*).
- Old women also told me that they never went to the seaside.

---

[56] Bob Deacon summarized the welfare state contract of socialist regimes as 'provision of highly subsidized prices on food, housing, transport and basic necessities, guaranteed employment, adequate health and education provision and small differentials between the wages of workers, professionals and managers, in return for the political quietude of the population.' Bob Deacon, 'Eastern European welfare states: The impact of the politics of globalization', *Journal of European Social Policy*, 10/2 (2000), pp. 146-61, p. 147.
[57] On socialist tourism and class differences, see Duda, 'Adriatic for all'.

- Well, I am old and I never went!
- Bosses and some others in that category, but workers never ... .[58]

Overall, ordinary workers questioned the idea that each worker had the same access to holiday facilities, especially low-skilled women employed in the sewing department, which was always more labour intensive and less valued than the more men-dominated spinning mill, named Tivar, which was closed in 2012. Welfare redistribution within the factory was supposed to follow universalist criterias, but in fact the social difference between white and blue collar, as well as within party members and non-members, influenced distribution as well as subjective feelings of entitlement. Alida and Jasminka, former blue-collar workers at the Arena knitwear factory in Pula, recalled, for instance, that they felt less entitled to welfare services than their supervisor, Zorica, who was aware of all available social benefits and felt entitled to claim them due to the fact that her parents were also white-collar workers at Arena. She was thus perceived as closer to circles of power within the factory. When it came to housing, Alida managed to obtain one of the last social flats in 1986 through the Uljanik shipyard where her husband worked, while Jasminka was unable to do so, presumably because she had no children and thus was lower on the list. She mentioned the case of a colleague with the same career credentials, who obtained housing thanks to her larger family. In the case of blue-collar workers at Arena, class belonging has a clear role in shaping memories of socialism, even when such memories are generally positive when contrasted with perceptions about the post-socialist era.

The importance of class positioning in shaping memories of socialism becomes even more evident when contrasting blue-collar and white-collar narratives of past and present. Generally, the former designers, technical directors and commercial directors I interviewed had more cultural and political resources to adapt to the mutated post-socialist context, and were able to translate the skills learned during market socialism into valuable skills for market capitalism, especially in the 1990s when new outsourced garment production required transferrable professional training and high flexibility. White-collar workers' narratives, therefore, are more likely to express middle-class values of individual success and entrepreneurship, which were already highly praised during self-management, and to stress the successes of each factory in the international and Yugoslav market

---

[58] Leda and blue-collar workers, Varaždin, May 2016. Interview conducted by the author and by Nikolina Hrga.

during socialist times, which translated into frequent experiences of international travels.[59]

Older managers, especially former directors and secretaries, display the kind of socialist paternalism I already discussed, and often highlight what they did to help ordinary workers and their families. An exemplary story, for instance, is the one of Jože, a former Slovenian factory director in his eighties, who, to my surprise, contacted me online through a social network after reading about my research in a Croatian newspaper. The son of a poor seamstress who fed the family with her sewing machine and with smuggling trips to Italy, he became a textile engineer in the 1960s, and later an important entrepreneur specialized in the production of jeans and sports clothes. In his account, he told me how he 'saved' one factory in crisis after another, challenging the communist party with his entrepreneurial skills and the high wages accorded to his workers. Jože managed to get by as a consultant in the 1990s, and still spends his summers in a holiday house on the Dalmatian coast, where he directed a subsidiary branch of the main Slovenian factory, and where all former workers, he says, know him and respect him. Such paternalism was less prominent among commercial directors and former designers, who did not seem attached to the collective space of the factory or to its welfare services, but rather insisted on their individual experiences of cosmopolitanism through work and trade. Female designers, in particular, portrayed themselves as uniquely creative subjects, misunderstood by socialist bureaucrats, forced by them to comply with the rigid working schedule of the factory, even if the process of artistic creation happened mostly outside factory walls. Work during socialism was mainly associated with travels abroad and awards received at fashion fairs for some specific collections.

The managing staff, already embedded in middle-class values and equipped with cultural capital, could benefit from a general re-evaluation of bourgeois qualities in post-socialism, and at times 'helped' working-class subjects to acquire bourgeois values to survive in the new context. Such is the case of Alan, who started working as commercial director in the early 1990s in one of the Croatian factories I studied, and who found himself busy with the renovation of the one of the firm's shop in the city of Zagreb. The shopkeeper was a Bosnian woman of Croatian ethnicity, Kata, who had left Bosnia and had replaced the previous Croatian seller of Serbian ethnicity, who had left for Serbia during the war. Alan said he was very disappointed

---

[59] About the predominance of middle-class values during socialism and after post-socialist transition, see Škokić and Potkonjak, 'Working class gone to heaven'.

with the appearance of Kata, and during coffee she gave her some advice for a better adaptation into the new post-socialist world of trade:

> I told her that I wanted her to get to the point where she was going to speak *kajkavski* [Zagreb dialect], meaning that she should not speak Bosnian but *kajkavski*, that she should get regular hairdos and manicures, and that she should become a *Zagrebačka dama* [Zagreb lady], because she has to sell to Zagreb ladies. How can you sell to Zagreb ladies with a Bosnian accent? Years later … I went to Zagreb and we went for coffee. And she told me honestly that at that moment when I told her those things she wanted to kill me, that she hated me from the depths of her soul. But today, she told me, she is grateful that I pushed her in that direction, it completely changed her life. She also became a Zagreb lady. She has her own shop now, she sells clothes and is a real lady.[60]

Alan's anecdote is illustrative of long-standing urban-rural divides, which flourished during socialism,[61] but also of the reaffirmation of bourgeois values in the new post-socialist context, and of ordinary workers' need to adapt to the mutated circumstances in order to 'make it'. Gendered, ethnic and class hierarchies were reinforced in the course of such transformations, and one way out was to transform the visible markers that would sustain such hierarchies. A shopkeeper like Kata, however, was better placed than ordinary seamstresses in such process of transformation. Blue-collar workers had very few possibilities to become 'Zagreb ladies', even if, as I will show in the next chapter, some former workers have been constantly taking care of their external appearance as a way to stress their ongoing dignity in difficult economic circumstances.

Besides class positioning, gender also has a fundamental role in shaping memories of work during socialism. In the case of male respondents, who are generally also former directors, supervisors or technicians, workplace stories take centre stage in their structure of feeling, while issues of private life and family are casted in the background. Men are also less keen to retell their personal hardships related to processes of post-socialist transformation, while women have no difficulty to admit them. Generally, however, class belonging seemed to be a much more significant factor of differentiation than gender in the narratives. Women generally spoke of gendered themes

---

[60] Alan, Pula, March 2016.
[61] About gendered discourses of urban and rural belonging, see Ana Hofman and Polona Sitar, '"Buy me a silk skirt, Mile!" Celebrity culture, gender and social positioning in socialist Yugoslavia', in Archer, Duda and Stubbs (eds), *Social Inequalities*.

such as maternity leaves and childcare facilities only when prompted to do so by my questions. As I showed in Chapter 3, at times they underlined their difficulties in combining productive and reproductive work in post-socialist times, particularly in relation to excessively exploitative working days and inability to take time off the firm. Such narratives, however, would only be related to episodes of extreme or untenable conditions in present times, while the 'working mother' gender contract of socialism (or rather its late socialist variety, with longer maternity leaves and added welfare services) would be remembered as a 'normal' arrangement which allowed to combine work outside the home with caring responsibilities at home.

Women's double burden during socialist times, especially women's difficulty to sleep after the night shift or to deal with childcare, was acknowledged matter-of-factly by the narrators, and described as an inevitable and common occurrence of women's everyday life. As I discussed in Chapter 2, the double burden was valorized, but also naturalized, during socialism. Women mostly had to rely on private solutions to cope with family obligations in each given context, and therefore workers' memories of combining productive and reproductive work are fragmented and individualized, as opposed to memories of collective welfare structures within the factory. Moreover, as during socialism, working-class women generally accept both productive and reproductive duties as a fundamental part of their female identity. While patriarchal norms remain a constant element of women's lives in the region, most socialist factories are no longer there to provide working-class women with economic independence, job security, sociability and welfare services that could partially ease their dependency from private family networks. In parallel to nationalist, re-traditionalizing discourses that symbolically represented women as 'mothers of the nation', working-class women have been pushed further back into the private sphere and into informal labour by material processes of privatization and deindustrialization.

5

Beyond nostalgia: Workers' struggles for social justice and everyday resilience

> *When we were sewing in three shifts for the army during the Homeland War, then we were a European fashion house. When we were sewing tailored suits for the first Croatian president, we were also a European fashion house, but now when we ask for unpaid wages we are only the house of European shame.*
> Declaration by a Kamensko worker, September 2010.[1]

In September 2010, a group of twenty Kamensko workers decided to go on a hunger strike, working during the day and then spending the night in the park across the factory. The wages of the 426 employees of the Kamensko garment factory had not been paid for seven months, and workers engaged in a desperate protest to gain visibility and to reclaim their wage arrears. The Kamensko struggle gained particular prominence in the Croatian media, especially due to the fact that student groups and civil society organizations supported female workers in their mobilization.[2] Alongside the Kamensko workers' struggle, many other strikes and hunger strikes were documented in the textile sector across the post-Yugoslav space in recent years.[3] This

---

[1] 'Kada smo u Domovinskom ratu šile u tri smjene za našu vojsku, onda smo bile kuća evropske mode, kada smo šile odjela po mjeri za prvog hrvatskog predsjednika bile smo kuća evropske mode, a sada kada tražimo plate samo smo kuća evropske sramote', 'Nakon poslova štrajkuju gladu', 25 September 2010. Available at: http://www.capital.ba/nakon-posla-strajkuju-gladu/ (accessed 20 January 2018).

[2] Andrea Milat, 'Pobuna radnica Kamenskog i kako se oduprijeti kapitalizmu (I.)', *Slobodni Filosofski*, 20 September 2012. Available at: http://slobodnifilozofski.com/2012/09/andrea-milat-pobuna-radnica-kamenskog-i.html (accessed 20 January 2018).

[3] In recent years, the press reported strikes at the Javor factory in Ivanjica, Serbia (2014), at the KTK factory in Visoko, Federation of Bosnia-Herzegovina (2016) and at the state-owned Nikola Tesla factory in Bileća, Republika Srpska (2015). In Croatia, workers from the DTR factory in Zagreb have regularly been striking and protesting in the centre of the town. In 2016, textile workers from the Estare Culto factory in Veliko Trgovišče, Croatia, blocked the main local road to reclaim their unpaid wages.

last chapter addresses the return of industrial workers' mobilizations, particularly textile workers', in the post-Yugoslav space, considering not only how workers' mobilization came into being, but also the ways in which new forms of solidarity with industrial workers were created among civil society organizations, left-wing groups and activists in the arts, heritage and cultural sectors.

New mobilizations across generations and classes have been enhanced by recent political movements for social justice that have emerged across the post-Yugoslav space in the past years, from the Zagreb students' protests of 2009 and the Maribor uprisings of 2012, to the Bosnian Spring of 2014, the 2015 anti-government protests in Macedonia and the 2017 'Right to the City' demonstrations in Serbia.[4] New forms of alliances and solidarity with workers were established by student organizations and local NGOs, while the proud, dignified image of male and female workers typical of socialism was reactivated within the imaginary of a still politically marginal, but increasingly visible, new left. A notable, earlier example of this collaboration is the case of the Jugoremedija pharmaceutical factory located in Zrenjanin, Serbia, which was self-managed by workers between 2007 and 2013, and whose workers waged a long battle against criminal privatization together with the independent activist organization named Freedom Fight Movement (*Pokret za Slobodu*).[5] A more recent example of workers' prominence within wider social mobilizations is the movement of the so-called Bosnian Spring of 2014, sparked by workers from deindustrialized factories in Tuzla, in alliance with new social movements. This resulted in a new form of workers' management of the DITA detergent factory.[6] In Croatia, the struggles of Kutina Petrokemija workers against privatization and the worker-owned metal factory named ITAS in Ivanec, supported by local activists groups, are also important examples of resistance against the neoliberal status quo, and

---

[4] For a comparative analysis of these mobilizations, see Štiks, '"New left"'. See also Goran Musić, 'Between Facebook and the picket line: Street protests, labour strikes and the New Left in the Balkans', *Debatte*, 21/2–3 (2013), pp. 321–35. See also the recent special issue of *Europe-Asia Studies* 69/9 (2017) on 'Activist Citizenship in Southeast Europe'.
[5] See notably the following publications: Pokret za slobodu, *Deindustrijalizacija i Radnički Otpor. Borbe i Inicijative za Očuvanje Radnih Mesta u Periodu Tranzicije* (Belgrade, 2011); Pokret za slobodu, *Borba za Budućnost. Ka Balkanskom Pokretu Otpora. Otpor Deindustrijalizaciji i Dtimanju Zemlje* (Belgrade, 2013).
[6] Anđela Pepić, 'Reclaiming the factory: A story from Bosnia', *Open Democracy*, 15 June 2015. Available at: http://www.opendemocracy.net/can-europe-make-it/andjel a-pepic/reclaiming-factory-story-from-bosnia (accessed 20 January 2018). Elvira M. Jukic, 'Workers' takeover saves iconic Bosnian firm', *Balkan Insight*, 1 July 2015. Available at: http://www.balkaninsight.com/en/article/workers-takeover-saves-tuzla-s-iconic-detergent-company (accessed 20 January 2018).

point at the potential of new political alliances around workers' struggles.⁷ In Slovenia, the strength of trade unions and the new activist mobilizations of 2012 led to the creation of the United Left political party, which gained 6 per cent of votes in the 2014 elections. This party gathered members of previously existing NGOs and civil society initiatives, such as the 'Workers and Punks University'.⁸

Together with workers' forms of collective resistance and instances of civil society solidarity with workers' movements, the chapter will also deal with individual workers' everyday stories of resistance, resilience and agency during post-socialist transformations, and especially with biographical accounts detailing women's ways of coping with precarious and exploitative labour, unpaid wages, factory closures and job losses. Workers faced these challenges by making use of gendered tools that have been common to other post-socialist societies, such as informal work, work migration, subsistence agriculture and extended family networks. At the same time, forms of individual resistance include everyday skills such as *snalaženje* (getting by), irony, cultivating one's feminine appearance despite deprivation and lack of resources, reactivating one's sewing and knitting skills, and intergenerational transmission. In my narrators' narratives, their industrial structure of feeling – and particularly the memory of dignified work during socialism – is mobilized as a way to counter processes of dispossession and devaluation of women's labour. Also, new activities outside the realm of industrial production are used to find a renewed meaning for one's life after deindustrialization, as well as new forms of sociability after the disappearance of factory life and of its social networks.

Industrial workers' struggles in the cultural, artistic and academic realm

In recent years, workers' struggles and grievances have made an unexpected return in the field of post-Yugoslav popular culture. In 2015, the popular

---

7   On the Petrokemija case, see Ivandić and Livada, *Lines of (Dis)Continuity*; on the ITAS case, see, Ognjen Kojanić, 'Countering Dispossession with Worker-Ownership. The case of ITAS in neoliberal Croatia', unpublished conference paper, EASA 2016.
8   On the Slovenian context see Musić, 'Between facebook and the picket line'; Alen Toplišek and Lasse Thomassen, 'From protest to party: Horizontality and verticality on the Slovenian left', *Europe-Asia Studies*, 69/9 (2017), pp. 1383–400. See also Gal Kirn, 'Slovenia's social uprising in the European crisis: Maribor as periphery from 1988 to 2012', *Stasis*, 24 January 2014. Available at: http://www.stasisjournal.net/all-issues/24-1-2014-revolutions-and-protest-movements/60-slovenia-s-social-uprising-in-the-european-crisis-maribor-as-periphery-from-1988-to-2012 (accessed 20 January 2018).

Croatian rock band *Hladno Pivo* (Cold beer) released a new single titled *Firma* (Company), which portrayed the plight of workers from deindustrialized factories. In the text of the song, a male worker walks towards his abandoned factory, remembering the days in which black limousines stopped in front of it, inaugurating the beginning of privatization. The refrain of the song captures the economic and social changes of the last thirty years: 'God, Homeland, Nation/All Freeze!/This is privatisation!/ Free up space/for "200 families"'. As noted by Igor Štiks, the song points at the conservative ideology that became dominant, and at the demobilization of workers in the process of privatization, for the benefit of 200 families who were supposed to be in charge of the Croatian economy according to its nationalist president Franjo Tuđman.[9] The infamous '200 families' promise resounded with the words of Ines, a retired seamstress from Pula. She stated: 'Yes, there were good things then, there are good ones now, there were bad ones then and now. ... When the new Croatia came, as they said, only 200 families had to be rich, no one else. And so all had to be destroyed. And that wasn't right. That's why we are all like beggars. ... Destroy everything, close everything, *as if nothing from before had value*.'[10] The song's text, similarly, points at workers' powerlessness over this social and political backlash. Another verse of the song recalls how firms 'collapsed without firing a bullet', namely, without any workers' resistance.

The video accompanying the song, however, adds a combative tone to the piece, and relies on the aesthetics of workers' collective heroism, combativeness and dignity. It also combines male and female workers' perspectives on deindustrialization. The band sings in blue-collar factory outfits in a deindustrialized factory hall, while female and male workers from dismantled factories appear as subjects of the video, in a dignified pose, walking and singing, alone and in groups, standing near the factory gates, drawing the silhouette of their work machines on the walls of the abandoned firms and reciting their own spoken narratives in between the song. The video is opened by a Kamensko female worker, who states: 'We were good when we were enlarging the suits of politicians, even better when we sew a new one for them, as they could not fit the old ones. And where are we now?' This passage comes from a real and very metaphorical story, of a finance minister who kept bringing his suit to Kamensko textile workers for them to fix it, because he was growing larger, while 'workers in the meantime were growing thinner and thinner' due to unpaid wages, as it was retold by one of

---

[9] Štiks, "'New left'".
[10] Ines, Pula, October 2015.

my narrators. Male workers from the Dioki petrolchemical factory and from the Gredelj metal factory, both bankrupt, also appear in the video. The worker from Dioki says: 'With regret I have to note that I cannot enter the firm to raise the trade union flag that stayed in my wardrobe, because the factory went bankrupt,' while the Gredelj worker concludes the video with the words: 'The famous slogan "Factories to workers" has no value today – there are no factories and there are no workers.' The ambivalence of industrial workers' presence and absence in post-Yugoslav states is well illustrated by this last statement, which points at the gradual dismantlement of the industrial structure of feeling built during socialism, and at the lingering presence of men and women whose work identity is no longer valued.

The haunting presence of former workers from dismantled industries is being increasingly tackled in popular culture, as in the case of the *Hladno pivo* song, but also in realm of art and culture, notably theatre. The Kamensko workers' struggle against criminal privatization, for instance, inspired at least three theatre dramas. The first, titled *Neraskidive niti* (Unbreakable Threads), was staged by director Lenka Udovički in 2011 and involved Kamensko workers as actresses in the play. Another later play, titled *Projekt višegodišnjeg nasada jabuka* (Project of a multiannual apple plantation),[11] was written by Nina Gojić and Bojan Mucko. Cultural workers wrote the piece in collaboration with Kamensko workers, particularly in order to understand the complicated, shady financial operations that led to the dismantlement of the factory in view of appropriating its building for real estate speculation. A third theatre piece written on the Kamensko case was *Radnice u gladovanju* (Starving female workers) by Goran Ferčeg, a Brechtian-style piece which dramatized workers' hunger strike.[12] Besides Croatia, workers' struggles were dramatized in other post-Yugoslav states, for instance in Bosnia-Herzegovina, where Selvedin Avdić's biographical essay *Moja fabrika* (My factory) on the industrial city of Zenica and of its metal plant, was turned into a theatre play.[13] In Serbia the issue of work in post-socialism has also been addressed in the play written by Olga Dimitrijević, titled *Radnici umiraju pevajući* (Workers Die Singing), and in the play by Igor Štiks titled *Zrenjanin*, the name of a Serbian post-industrial town.

---

[11] A trailer from the performance *Projekt višegodišnjeg nasada jabuka* is available at: https://vimeo.com/169520373 (accessed 20 January 2018).
[12] The full text of the drama *Radnice u gladovanju* is available at: http://drame.hr/drame/358-radnice-u-gladovanju (accessed 20 January 2018).
[13] Selvedin Avdić, *Moja fabrika* (Zenica, 2013).

Such representations of social struggles in popular culture go hand in hand with young generations' renewed interest in workers' lives in the socialist and post-socialist era; these representations are also as a result of young people's daily experiences of unemployment and precarious labour in contemporary post-Yugoslav states. The exploration of workers' existences in capitalist times is part of a wider philosophical and cultural interrogation on the meaning of life and labour in the post-industrial and post-Fordist era.[14] In the cultural field, workers' struggles during socialism and particularly during the post-socialist era have been the object of numerous exhibitions, installations and cultural heritage initiatives in recent years. Most of these initiatives, led by a young generation of activists who came of age after socialism, have been aimed at uncovering the lost archives of deindustrialized factories, and the lost memories of former workers hit by privatization, often the mothers, fathers and relatives of the young activists in question. The younger generations are clearly interested in learning more about the social welfare and job security enjoyed by the older generations, which became almost unimaginable and difficult to articulate in contemporary post-Yugoslav societies. Kinga Pozniak has observed similar forms of intergenerational transmission in her ethnography of the post-industrial town of Nowa Huta, Poland, where young people revive the legacies of work and community ties in order to cope with increasing precariousness and unemployment.[15]

When I started researching the history of the garment industry, I could count on a number of research projects that were already in place, most notably the project related to the Dalmatinka textile factory in Sinj, Croatia, led by cultural activists Nikola Križanac, Dragana Modrić, Jelena Pavlinušić and Silvia Milić. Besides collecting archive material, personal photographs and oral history interviews, this group also produced a short documentary with former Dalmatinka workers, and a successful exhibition on the history of the factory.[16] Countering societal amnesia about the socialist period, the project addressed issues of housing, working conditions, community building, solidarity and women's position in society: 'workers' memories

---

[14] See for instance the interview with Goran Ferčeg, and his comments on the connections between Kamensko workers' and cultural workers' precarious lives. Bojan Munjin, 'Goran Ferčeg, Kapitalizam je ucjenjivački mehanizam', *Novosti*, 28 June 2017. Available at: http://www.portalnovosti.com/goran-fercec-kapitalizam-je-ucjenjivacki-mehanizam (accessed 20 January 2018).

[15] Pozniak, *Nowa Huta*, p. 190.

[16] *Dalmatinka Sinj* (Dragana Modrić, Jelena Pavlinušić, Nikola Križanac, 2014). Available at: https://vimeo.com/104534639 (accessed 20 January 2018). The exhibition 'Što je nama naša Dalmatinka dala?' (What did our Dalmatinka gave us?) was held in Sinj in autumn 2017.

provide us valuable information for the young generation, and models that can offer an alternative, the organizers argued.[17] Another important exhibition and activist research project that focuses on similar issues in Croatia is the one addressing the Borovo industrial complex, located in the multiethnic city of Vukovar, which produced shoes, rubber and car tyres. Borovo employed up to 24,000 workers once, in comparison to its current 750 employees engaged in shoe production. The project covered notably the early times of post-socialist transformations, from the late 1980s until the early 1990s, looking at the gradual erosion of workers' power and rights in the final years of socialism.[18] In Ljubljana, Slovenia, the City Museum organized in 2014 an interactive exhibition titled *Adijo Tovarna. Spomini pozabljenih delavcev* (So long, factory. Memories of forgotten workers), which detailed the experience of workers of ten different deindustrialized factories in the city. Workers' memories were published in the major Slovenian newspaper, *Delo*.[19] In Belgrade, Serbia, a recent exhibition by the Museum for Yugoslav History dealt with another important theme related to labour history, namely, the phenomenon of *gastarbeiters*, economic migrant workers who left from socialist Yugoslavia to Germany, Austria and other Western European countries.[20]

Next to artistic and cultural projects with a research focus, a veritable resurgence of interest in labour history can also be witnessed in the academic field, and especially in the amount of recent doctoral dissertations dealing with workers' position in different settings of socialist Yugoslavia and post-Yugoslav states through archival research and ethnography.[21] Collaborative efforts have also been established between academic researchers and workers themselves as a result of activist encounters during recent social mobilizations. In early February 2014, the protests waged by the workers

---

[17] Saša Šimpraga, 'Dalmatinka, Sinj', H-Alter, 10 September 2014. Available at: http://www.h-alter.org/vijesti/dalmatinka-sinj (accessed 20 January 2018).
[18] Centar za mirovne studije/Baza za radničku inicijativu i demokratizaciju, 'Kome treba poduzeće? Borovo 1988. – 1991'. Available at: http://borovo1988.radnickaprava.org/ (accessed 20 January 2018)
[19] Delo, 'Adijo Tovarna'. Available at: http://www.delo.si/adijo-tovarna (accessed 20 January 2018).
[20] Muzej Jugoslavije, 'Jugo moja Jugo'. Available at: http://www.mij.rs/izlozbe/442/jugo-moja-jugo-.html (accessed 20 January 2018).
[21] See for instance: Sara Bernard, *The Return of the Gastarbeiter in Socialist Yugoslavia, 1965–1991*. PhD dissertation (Regensburg University, 2016); Goran Musić, *The Self-Managing Factory after Tito: the Crisis of Yugoslav Socialism on the Shop Floor*. PhD dissertation (EUI, 2016); Ivan Rajković, *Struggles for Moral Ground: Problems with Work and Legitimacy in a Serbian Industrial Town*, PhD dissertation (Manchester University, 2015); Ulrike Schult, *Zwischen Stechuhr und Selbstverwaltung: Eine Mikrogeschichte sozialer Konflikte in der jugoslawischen Fahrzeugindustrie 1965–1985* (Vienna, 2017).

of five deindustrialized factories (Dita, Poliolchem, Polihem, Guming and Konjuh) were joined by civil society activists in the former industrial town of Tuzla, sparking the radical anti-government mobilizations that later came to be known as the Bosnian Spring, and which soon extended to other cities in the country, including Sarajevo.[22] Workers, students and activists were later organized in spontaneous assemblies named 'plenums', which also led to the creation of a new trade union named Solidarity and a new political party, Civic Strength. In the recent volume *Unbribable Bosnia Herzegovina: The Fight for the Commons*, which presents voices and analyses about the Bosnian Spring, two workers' testimonies open the book. For the first time, workers' voices are presented in the book on an equal footing with other academic and activists contributions. Workers are visible here not only as objects of research, but as subjects of social struggles, able to express agency, resistance and resilience. The meaning of resilience is perhaps best expressed by DITA chemical worker and shopfloor supervisor Emina Busuladžić, now retired. A veritable *pasionaria*, Emina fought for a decade against the sell-out and dismantlement of her enterprise, until workers were joined by a wider solidarity movement and managed to revive production through a workers' cooperative. As Emina summarize in her contribution:

> The more you beat me, the more you punch me, the more you spit on me, blackmail me and belittle me, I grow stronger, more audacious and more persistent. I often told my children that they will face many obstacles, pitfalls and problems in life, but that these obstacles are not there to halt them, but theirs to overcome and conquer, because they will make them stronger. We have to be persistent, brave, honest and enduring, because that is the only way we can hope to succeed in life.[23]

The figure of Emina – who successfully pushed her children to complete their higher education despite countless deprivations and who managed to save her factory together with her colleagues against all bureaucratic odds – subverts the trope of the victimized Balkan woman typical of Orientalizing discourses on the region, and shows instead the persistence of female industrial workers' agency and attachment to their workplace, which lies at the root of their industrial structure of feeling. In a more recent testimony, Emina Busuladžić

---

[22] Chiara Milan, 'Reshaping citizenship through collective action: Performative and prefigurative practices in the 2013–2014 cycle of contention in Bosnia & Hercegovina', *Europe-Asia Studies*, 69/9 (2017), pp. 1346–61.

[23] Damir Arsenijević (ed.), *Unbribable Bosnia Herzegovina: The Fight for the Commons* (Baden-Baden, 2014), p. 21.

referred to the period of socialist welfare as a benchmark of security and normality. The recent period, instead, left workers in a totally precarious position due to processes of criminal privatization and dispossession. According to Emina, 'workers in Bosnia are in the worst situation ever.' Her message to other workers is again one of resilience and agency: 'Fight for your rights. No one will do it for you. Get back your dignity, because you are the ones who create the profits for the factory owner.'[24] A similar resilience can be found among Kamensko workers in their struggle against the criminal privatization led by local Zagreb tycoons, or among Arena workers fighting for unpaid wages, as shown in the next section.

Heads up: Textile workers' strikes and collective organizing

When it comes to recent textile workers' mobilization in the post-Yugoslav region, the strike of Kamensko workers in Zagreb is certainly the one that got the most significant media coverage. The Kamensko factory was founded in 1943 in the village of Lika with the same name, as a partisan workshop charged with the supply of clothes and shoes to the National Liberation Front.[25] After the war, the factory was re-established in a former army building in Zagreb, and continued to be a supplier of military clothes, with 432 employees. In 1952, most of the work machines were transferred to Karlovac and Travnik for strategic purposes as a result of the crisis following the Soviet–Yugoslav split. In 1953, for the remaining 450 workers in Zagreb, production was reoriented towards internal consumption for underwear products, while garment production was immediately targeting the international market, namely, Western Europe, Eastern Europe and the Middle East.[26] Employees grew to almost 1,000 and new plants were built in underdeveloped villages in the regions of Lika (Gračac), Gorski Kotar (Grižana) and in other locations. In the early 1960s, the factory was equipped with a holiday resort on the Adriatic coast (lost in 1982 after a conflict with the Crikvenica municipality), as well as with a canteen and the provision of social housing for workers. During late socialism, Kamensko employed 2,600 workers in the Zagreb plant, exporting

---

[24] Maja Isović Dobrijević, 'Emina Busuladžić o 40 godina rada u "Diti": Radnik u BiH nikad nije bio u goroj situaciji', *Buka*, 6 February 2017. Available at: http://www.6yka.com/novost/120369/emina-busuladzic-o-40-godina-rada-u-diti-radnik-u-bih-nikad-nije-bio-u-goroj-situaciji (accessed 20 January 2018).
[25] Kamensko workplace periodical, 1 (1978); 4 (1978)..
[26] Kamensko workplace periodical, 1 (1978).

mainly to Western Europe. The Kamensko newspapers mentioned various problems, such as the high amount of sick leave, especially among working single mothers who did not know where to leave their children, particularly on Saturdays when schools were closed. Workers' activism in the firefighter association was also prominent.[27]

In 1993, the factory was privatized through the shareholders' system, and continued to produce outsourced garments for Western Europe with updated technology and growing profits, up to 2006. Working hours, however, increased during this period, while social rights deteriorated, with overtime work and night work ceasing to be properly compensated.[28] After 2005, when the sale of factory shares to outsiders was permitted, one of the directors started to sell his shares on the market. Construction companies bought most of the shares, since the Kamensko factory building, located in a relatively central area of the Croatian capital, was coveted by the local oligarchy for estate investments. Between 2006 and 2010, the factory started to accumulate losses, particularly as a result of intricated financial speculations that found their roots in the local administration and which involved the usage of fictive creditors' firms that belonged, among others, to the infamous tycoon named Miroslav Kutle. A Bosnian–Croat businessman, Kutle was a major supporter of the Croatian Democratic Party (HZD) in the 1990s, and the owner of a commercial empire that included the Diona retail shops and the Tisak newsagent chain, whose assets were gradually stripped until bankruptcy. Condemned to jail by Croatian courts for embezzlement, war profiteering and industrial crime, he is currently on the run in neighbouring Bosnia-Herzegovina.[29]

In 2009, as a result of such privatization processes, wages payment were delayed for the remaining 426 Kamensko workers; yet, occasional payments would be made to keep workers from going on strike. Despite such delays, workers held on hoping that the factory will be saved, as management kept promising that payments would be made retrospectively. In September 2010,

---

[27] Kamensko workplace periodical, 4 (1978).
[28] Milat, 'Pobuna radnica Kamenskog'.
[29] During the process of asset stripping that affected Kamensko, the obscure mechanisms of criminal privatization were uncovered by civil society activists belonging to organizations such as Pravo na Grad (Right to the City), Zelena Akcija (Green Action) and Centar za Mirovne Studije (Center for Peace Studies). The dynamics of criminal privatization and speculation surrounding Kamensko are explained in detail in the Cenzura tv programmes. Cenzura, 11 March 2011, part one. Available at: https://www.youtube.com/watch?v=4R-WXPMdAWU; Cenzura, 11 March 2011, part two. Available at: https://www.youtube.com/watch?v=fjx9HsDT0RA (both accessed 20 January 2018). See also Pulska Grupa, 'We were destroyed by capitalism! Interview with worker from Kamensko who wishes to stay anonimous and student Jelena Miloš', 15 August 2012. Available at: http://praksa.hr/kamensko/ (accessed 20 January 2018).

Figure 13 Kamensko workers' protest, Zagreb, 2010. Courtesy of Tomislav Medak.

after seven months since the last wage was paid, a group of twenty Kamensko workers decided to go on a hunger strike in the park located in front of the factory, sleeping in the park at night and going to work during the day. Workers organized the strike against the advice of the main union for textile workers (see Chapter 3), which also warned them that a regular interruption of production would put workers at risk of lay-offs. Workers then decided to keep working and to maintain the hunger strike outside of their working time, and managed to hold on for ten days. Despite the lack of union support, workers received support from civil society activists and students, and significant media coverage (Figure 13). Kamensko workers' opposition to real estate speculation was intersecting with wider Right to the City mobilizations against urban redevelopment and the privatization of public space in the city.[30]

Despite such solidarity, however, workers felt isolated and at a loss during the hunger strike. Their narratives relate the existential watershed represented by the closure of the factory in which they had spent most of their adult

---

[30] See Danijela Dolenec, Karin Doolan and Tomislav Tomašević, 'Contesting neoliberal urbanism on the European semi-periphery: The right to the city movement in Croatia', *Europe Asia-Studies*, 69/9 (2017), pp. 1401–29.

lives. Among those who joined the hunger strike there was Dunja, an upbeat and witty woman in her fifties, married with two children, who later found precarious but better paid work in the public sector after losing her position as a blue-collar worker at Kamensko (currently, she is once again unemployed). Dunja started working in the factory in 1981, when she was eighteen years old. She recalled that her first pay was 400 dinars, of which 100 she gave to her mum, 100 she deposited in the bank, 100 she used for shopping and another 100 she kept for coffee and daily expenses. Work during socialism was strictly regulated, and overtime was often required to carry out outsourced orders for Western Europe. Still, work was compensated fairly according to Dunja, with production prizes, a thirteenth wage and an allowance (*regres*) for summer holidays. With her poignant irony, Dunja states:

> At that time, which they tell us was Tito's 'dark time', and so on, you had more rights than today. Young workers could not work at night, or for too many hours, and they had more holidays, there were more and better rights than nowadays. Today they pay 8 hours and you work 10 hours. Before overtime got paid, now you can work from morning until the next day and you won't get paid. This is democracy, while before it was terrorism (*she laughs*).[31]

As a positive element of socialism, Dunja also remembered the rich social life of the factory, such as the parties that were organized for those who retired, and the catwalks where new collections would be presented. The nearby soldiers stationed at the Črnomerec barracks would also join and music would be played – Dunja liked it even if it departed from her usual music choice: 'I was a hippie, I listened to Janis Joplin, Led Zeppelin and Deep Purple, and there they were playing traditional songs, *narodnjaci*, after a while they would get into your ear.'

In the 1990s, Dunja bought shares of the factory worth up to 4,000 euros, in order for the factory not to fall into outsiders' hands. She recalled that people stipulated mortgages and made big sacrifices to buy factory shares, which now have lost all value. In summer 2009 wages started to get paid with delays and in 2010 they were stopped completely. Due to the fact that trade unions advised against a production strike, workers decided to engage in a symbolic hunger strike in front of the factory in September 2010. 'It was great' – recalls Dunja with her usual irony, laughing – 'I lost three kilos. It was the only great thing.'[32] Eventually, the hunger strike was followed

---

[31] Dunja, Zagreb, February 2016.
[32] Ibid.

by a production strike in which all workers were involved. The process of bankruptcy started in October 2010, and workers' pleas for a reorganization of the factory fell on deaf ears, even if there were still Italian clients who were ready to pay for new outsourced orders in cash. The factory was closed at the end of November 2010, and despite court appeals deposited by workers with the help of local NGOs, which led to the indictment of several managers for speculation and fraud, workers have not yet been fully compensated.[33] The building of Kamensko has been sold for a fraction of its real market value, while workers are still waiting for four unpaid wages and for half of their redundancy payment.

In the interview, Dunja recalled the trauma and difficulties of the last months, in which many workers were struggling to survive without a wage, especially those who were single mothers and had to pay a rent. At a certain point, after seeing her colleagues in such a critical situation, she had a nervous breakdown, and a psychologist received her immediately when she heard that she was working at Kamensko. She was prescribed three days of holidays, as well as antidepressants and sleeping pills. Eventually, however, she decided to do without them ('I didn't do drugs when I was young, I won't start now'), and asked her children for positive books to read, in order to put her mind elsewhere. Even if her husband had a job that provided for the family and ensured the mortgage would be paid, Dunja felt very bad about working and leaving her children alone at home without bringing any wage home. She told me that she felt most hurt when one of the kids asked her why she wouldn't buy them chocolate, while the other said 'shut up, you see that she is not getting paid, wait for dad to arrive'. Despite these difficult memories, Dunja kept taking part in all activist initiatives concerning Kamensko, including theatre shows and documentaries, with her usual irony and sarcastic demeanour.

Another proud and resilient figure of the Kamensko struggle is Rada, the president of the new Kamensko cooperative founded by former workers after the bankruptcy of the factory. A widow and mother of two, Rada managed to find another job in the public sector after the bankruptcy until she could obtain an early retirement. After retirement, she founded the cooperative, in which she serves as a president on a voluntary basis. The sewing cooperative employs six women in a workshop in the popular neighbourhood of Trešnjevka. It not only offers small repair services to the local community, but also accepts

---

[33] For an in-depth analysis of the Kamensko workers' struggle, see Sonja Dragović, 'Tailors turned activists: Surviving the demise of the Croatian textile industry', *Intersections*, 2/1 (2016), pp. 32–53.

orders from other clients in towns – for instance, sewing conference bags or other items for specific purposes. Periodical sewing classes and educational activities with several volunteers and trainees are also organized in the same space. Rada deals with funding issues and local bureaucratic hassles. She also liaises with the local and national media and with other civil society groups. As her narrative testifies, she does her work with a heightened sense of responsibility and solidarity towards other women, with whom she shared the difficult moments of the hunger strike and the bankruptcy. She tells me that for a long time she dreamt of a former colleague, who was alone and hungry during the final stages of the bankruptcy and who got a stroke and 'died of all that', without anyone being held accountable for the stress and misery caused by criminal privatization.

Rada sees the cooperative as a way to help people in need, and particularly as a safety net for middle-aged colleagues who lost their jobs at Kamensko and who need a few more years of employment to obtain pension benefits. As well as former workers, she also stresses her desire to help unemployed young trainees as well as workers from other deindustrialized factories who are looking for advice with court cases. Words like 'pride' and 'dignity' are recurrent in Rada's story. Even during the worst times of the strike, when workers were deprived of everything, she says, their personal pride could not be taken away from them. Thanks to the cooperative, she adds, two women could retire 'keeping their heads up' (*dignute glave*), meaning they could have a dignified job until the end of their career. Rada herself, who always wears make up and has a blond, fashionable hairdo, never gave up on her feminine appearance even during the worst time of the strike, and even when by-standers and colleagues commented upon her outlook, which appeared way too 'lady-like' for a garment worker on the brink of poverty. Rada told me that she resisted those who wanted to put her down, more so when it came to appearance:

> I always had my head up, always with make up and always proud. Every woman has some make up on a side that can last. ... I also told it to my kids who do not like make up, everyone has something in life, I have that. I like when a woman takes care of herself, and even in the hardest of moments, no one has to notice, you are the only one to know (*Meni je lijepo kad žena drži do sebe i kad god joj je teško to nitko ne treba primjetiti, to znaš ti sama*). ... It really fascinated some people, that we are proud and that we are not allowing others to make us curb our head.[34]

[34] Rada, Zagreb, February 2016.

Looking like a 'real woman' and maintaining a representative image undoubtedly helped Rada to express her individual agency in times of crisis[35] and to maintain good public relations and networks, in a society in which middle-aged working-class women are more and more discriminated on the basis of their appearance (see the episode about the Bosnian seller having to turn into a 'Zagreb lady' at the end of the previous chapter). Rada herself recalls how she recommended a former unemployed colleague for a job in a chemical cleaning company, and how the colleague came back to her in tears, saying that the owner sent her away because she looked like a 'baba' and was not deemed fit to deal with clients due to her looks. Rada then decided to employ her until retirement, to save her from a desperate situation. She also went on to scold the owner for his ageist behaviour, asking him if he would be happy that someone would do the same to his mother or sister. She reminded him that working skills go beyond external appearance, and that 'women's worth has no expiration date'. Overall, while Dunja's resilience greatly rested on her ironic attitude, Rada built her resilience strategy around her personal idea of working-class pride. Rada described how Kamensko workers refused to submit to trade unions' improper advice, to the blackmail of the former director who came to offer them sausages while they were on a hunger strike, or to the hypocrisy of local politicians. This was due to their dignified stance and due to their consciousness of the value of manual work, which was supposed to command respect on a societal level, like during socialist times. Despite their experiences of victimization, Dunja, Rada and the other Kamensko workers refused to be cast as victims, and took matters into their hands, turning the case of Kamensko into an example of political resistance across Croatia. The fact that their struggle happened in the capital city of Zagreb, where solidarity networks could be more easily fostered and where media attention was easier to gather, in comparison to more peripheral parts of the country like Sinj, certainly helped workers to feel legitimated and supported in their demands for social justice.

A less known, but significant mobilization happened in the Istrian town of Pula among the workers the Arena knitwear factory, founded in 1947, whose history I retraced in previous chapters. As recalled earlier, Arena was declared bankrupt in May 2014, after several years of mismanagement and indebtedness on behalf of main shareholders in connection with the factory management, and in view of real estate speculation connected with the

---

[35] On the ways in which feminine appearance can be used as a tool of agency in times of economic crisis, see Rozita Dimova, 'Between borderlines, betwixt citizenship: Gender, agency and the crisis in the Macedonia/Greece border region', *Women's Studies International Forum*, 49 (2015), pp. 66–72.

rebranding and gentrification of the city as a tourist hub. Even bankruptcy, however, was not easy to obtain for Arena workers. The remaining sixty-two employees had to carry out a three-month strike in spring 2014, from February until May, to receive the official declaration of bankruptcy and to be able to receive social assistance as unemployed. Like Kamensko workers, Arena workers started striking out of desperation, after seamstresses' very low wages of 2,500 kunas (337 euro) were not paid for eight months, from June 2013 onwards. Arena workers also continued to work in the hope that the factory would recover and that wages would be paid at some point in time. They simply could not believe that such an important firm, producing such quality products, could be allowed to go bankrupt by municipal and state institutions.

Besides the workers who lost their jobs, the bankruptcy also hit hard the pensioners of Arena, who had placed their savings in the internal bank of the factory (see Chapter 1) and who now were left without anything, as both the money of the internal bank and of the fund for mutual aid from the factory disappeared during the bankruptcy procedures, creating a veritable process of economic and social dispossession for former workers. As recalled in the earlier chapters, workers contributed for decades to the success of the factory, not just through their work but also through the liquidity provided by their savings, and they were left with neither work nor savings. In front of the factory, during the February strike, a former worker in tears testified that she had been saving for twenty-five years for her old days, and that her 40,000 kunas (around 5,300 euros) disappeared without a trace.[36] The value of the savings contained in the internal bank was estimated at around 6 million kunas (above 800,000 euros), while important amounts gathered from the sale of Arena shops, which were located in prestigious sites in many Croatian towns, were also missing.

Even if the Arena strike was less visible in national media than the Kamensko strike, Arena workers gathered a considerable amount of local solidarity and media attention, particularly on the 8 March 2014 demonstration, during which striking workers, activists and citizens gathered in front of the factory, denouncing the criminal privatization practices that brought Arena to bankruptcy, as well as the indifference or complicity of local politicians, as documented in two local radio programmes dedicated to the case of Arena. Workers also denounced Istrian and Croatian politicians' support for the tourist sector, which only provided work during the summer season; this support was contrasted with the lack of support for the industrial

[36] Ibid.

Figure 14 'Catwalk on strike' in support of Arena workers, Pula, 2014. Courtesy of Dejan Štifanić.

sector, which had suffered a drastic decline across Croatia.[37] In a symbolic demonstration of attachment to the factory, the participants to the protest also wore Arena garments and engaged in one last 'catwalk on strike' (*modna revija u štrajku*), showcasing the quality of locally produced garments.[38] (Figure 14).

During the catwalk, Pula photographer, activist and singer Edna Jurcan sang the traditional Italian folk song, *La Lega*, a song of struggle used among the female rice-growers of the Po Valley and showcased in Bertolucci's famous movie *Novecento*, whose refrain states: 'Although we are women/we are not afraid/ for the love of our children/we join the union.' After this event, and also as a result of other mobilizations against the privatization of public space, Pula saw the creation of Zbor Praksa, an activist choir that performs around Croatia in support of various protests and alternative events.[39]

---

[37] Recordings of the radio emission 'Spolitika', Radio Maestral, 26 February 2014 and 30 April 2014 in possession of the author, courtesy of Ana Orsag.

[38] Pulska Grupa, 'Revija u štrajku – Arena trikotaža – Pula, 8 March 2014'. Available at: https://www.youtube.com/watch?v=dKkYDd6YWNM&t=1s (accessed 20 January 2018)

[39] Antifascist, feminist and LGBTQ choirs have become a prominent phenomenon in post-Yugoslav states in recent years, and their repertoire includes many songs that belong to the internationalist workers' movement tradition, from *The Internationale* to *Bella Ciao*. For a recent history of these choirs, see Ana Hofman, *Novi život partizanskih pesama* (Belgrade, 2016).

Another initiative that occurred in February 2014 was a so-called 'strike of solidarity' of two hours organized by Croatian trade unions in support of Arena workers and unpaid workers of other firms, and against new changes to the Croatian Labour Law, which introduced the possibility for longer working hours, easier lay-offs and flexible working contracts. Arena workers also took part in 1st of May demonstrations in Zagreb, connecting with other workers of deindustrialized factories, and also presented their grievances at the European Parliament with a trip to Brussels.

In the months that preceded the bankruptcy, surviving without a wage was especially difficult for those who were single and paying a rent, as well as for couples that were both employed in the same factory. Suzana, a blue-collar worker whose testimony I already quoted in Chapter 4, and who was living on her own in a rented apartment, testified to the local media:

> I have nothing. I am begging around for each and every kuna, so that I can survive. I am not homeless but I feel homeless, I live in a place where I can be sent away anytime, because I cannot pay.[40]

Workers had to ask for the help of their children, relatives and friends, since their employment was still officially ongoing and thus they had no right to ask for full social assistance. They only received around 1,000 kunas every three months while still employed. Suzana, who was divorced, got some help from her son, while Milka, who was widowed, could count on her mother's pension. Similarly to Kamensko workers, Arena workers experienced the strike as a dramatic moment. Suzana, for instance, described the strike in terms of 'shame', since she had to 'beg' for a wage, something she had honestly earned. She felt 'uneasy' to get out in the street, she said. Her colleague Milka added she wasn't ashamed, as unpaid wages are now the reality in Croatia. In their public statements to Radio Maestral, Arena workers denounced not just the bankruptcy of Arena, but the ways in which society was turning into a post-industrial direction, devaluating former industrial workers who were still able to work and had no place to turn to. Like DITA and Kamensko workers, they also invited other workers to organize collectively as soon as their wage wasn't paid, without hoping in the goodwill of the owners.[41] In the next section, I will continue the discussion of textile workers' multiple strategies of resilience and survival during post-socialist deindustrialization.

---

[40] 'Spolitika'.
[41] Ibid.

Do it yourself: Everyday survival strategies

Alongside collective mobilizations, former workers of deindustrialized textile factories across the post-Yugoslav space have been engaging in a variety of everyday strategies of survival and resilience. Scholars of post-socialism have underlined how processes of post-socialist transformation and marketization led to a reconfiguration of gender and class relations and of the boundaries between public and private. The emergence of the working poor in post-socialist contexts has been analysed, for instance in the Polish and Slovak cases.[42] When it comes to textile workers, several studies have demonstrated that most textile workers in Central, Eastern and South-Eastern Europe are receiving poverty wages, in contrast to a living wage which would allow workers to provide for themselves and their family without battling for survival. Subsistence agriculture, alongside poverty wages, was found to be a widespread survival strategy among textile workers in South-East Europe.[43] Industrial workers in the Balkans also joined the wide array of citizens who engage in the informal economy in different post-socialist contexts.[44] In her masterful collection of oral history interviews from ordinary post-Soviet citizens, Svetlana Alexievich reports the following story, among many others:

> My mother had worked at a sewing factory. It happened so fast. ... They shut down the factory. ... My mother would sit at home all day sewing underwear. All her friends sewed underwear too, every apartment you walked into, that's what they'd be doing. We lived in a building the factory had built for its workers, so everyone in the whole building was sewing bras and underwear. Swimsuits. En masse, they all cut the labels off all their old clothes. ... And they would ask their friends to do it too, to snip the labels off their clothes – preferably imported clothes – so that they could sew them onto those swimsuits of theirs. Then, in small

---

[42] Adrian Smith, Alison Stenning, Alena Rochovska and Dariusz Swiatek, 'The emergence of a working poor: Labour markets, neoliberalization and diverse economies in post-socialist cities', *Antipode*, 40/2 (2008), pp. 283–311.

[43] Clean Clothes Campaign, *Stitched Up – Poverty Wages for Garment Workers in Eastern Europe and Turkey* (2014). Available at: https://cleanclothes.org/resources/publications/stitched-up-1

[44] See for instance Jeremy Morris and Abel Polese (eds), *The Informal Post-Socialist Economy: Embedded Practices and Livelihoods* (London, 2013). On informality in the Bosnian case, see Stef Jansen, Čarna Brković and Vanja Čelebičić (eds), *Negotiating Social Relations in Bosnia and Herzegovina: Semiperipheral Entanglements* (London, 2017).

groups, the women would travel through Russia with bags full of their homemade goods. They called it 'Underwear Tourism'.[45]

Similarly to seamstresses in the post-Soviet space, seamstresses in the post-Yugoslav space often turned to informal work to survive. As I have underlined in other publications and earlier in the book, the re-traditionalization of gender relations that affected the Balkans was not only a result of neo-conservative, nationalist discourses and practices, but also a consequence of the expulsion of women from secure jobs in the public sector, and of the withdrawal of the socialist welfare state, in combination with shady privatization practices, processes of economic and social dispossession and labour intensification in the private sector.[46] All these elements increased women's precariousness and dependency on informal labour markets and on extended family networks. Scholars of gender relations in other post-socialist contexts have singled out similar phenomena, not just for the industrial sector but also for the public sector more generally.[47] Due to their uncertain working or workless status, many workers and former workers strive to get by as best as they can, mobilizing a wide array of survival strategies and skills, which are rooted in the structure of feeling developed during socialism, during which female workers got used to juggling between productive and reproductive labour, while they could count on some welfare resources provided by the socialist state. According to the narratives I collected, the following strategies seem to be predominant in textile workers' survival kits across the post-Yugoslav region: subsistence agriculture, informal work, migration to Western countries for care work, seasonal work in tourism (in Croatia) and handicraft such as sewing and knitting.

A paradigmatic story is the one of Marina, a former worker of the VIS garment factory in Varaždin until 2004 (for an account on the Varaždin region, see Chapter 3). A single mother of three, and a tenant in post-socialist times, she had to design a wide array of saving and income-generating strategies to provide for her children. Marina also had some experiences of moonlighting in the late socialist period, when she could obtain one month of unpaid leave to keep a stand that sold souvenirs in the city centre. During

---

[45] Svetlana Alexievich, *Secondhand Time: The Last of the Soviets* (London, 2016), location 3140-45, kindle version.
[46] See Bonfiglioli, 'Gender, labour and precarity in the South East European periphery'; Bonfiglioli, 'Gendered citizenship in the global European periphery'.
[47] See, for instance, Alison Stenning and Jane Hardy, 'Public sector reform and women's work in Poland: "Working for juice, coffee and cheap cosmetics!"', *Gender, Work and Organization*, 12 /2 (2005), pp. 503–26. See also Daskalova, Romić, Kaser and Radunović (eds), *Gendering Post-socialist Transition*.

the Yugoslav Wars, when the factory was producing clothes for the army, she engaged in frequent night shifts due to the intensification of labour discipline in the factory, for a wage of around 1,500 kunas (200 euros). She also received a child subsidy of 900 kumas. Most of her wage went on the rent and house expenses, so that she started to engage in informal trade to make ends meet, buying clothes in Zagreb and Austria and reselling them to her colleagues. At that time, as she recounted, she weighed 48 kilograms, because she was moving 'non-stop'. Marina also engaged in subsistence agriculture in her garden, cultivating fruits and vegetables with her son. She recalls that the garden and the *dodatni biznis* (extra business) saved her from hunger.

During the 1990s, Marina waged a constant battle against everyday exploitation and poverty. The factory management constantly attempted to increase piece-rate norms, and allegedly she was even forced to buy some shareholders quota in order not to lose her job. At the same time, the flat owner attempted to trick her with the house bills: 'I was terrorized at work, and terrorized by the house owner, from every side I turned. ... You have to be strong for the children.'[48] Marina's story of daily survival challenges romantic representations of the Croatian war of independence. The immense Croatian flag which was placed in the reconquered town of Knin in 1995, in fact, had been created thanks to Marina's and three other seamstresses' feminized, low-paid and exploited work, far from the gleam of international and local media. As for male blue-collar workers, their symbolic and material position in the 1990s is best summarized by the words of Marina's current partner, a former blue-collar worker at Varteks who was also present during our interview: 'When I had to get an apartment [from the factory], then came 1991 and there went the apartment. The apartment went, and I went to Slavonija [to fight].'[49] Today, after some other extremely exploitative experiences of work in the tourist industry, Marina and her partner have found something else that 'saves' them, namely, the possibility to manage a hostel on the Croatian coast in the summer months. While they receive very little compensation for their work, they nonetheless benefit from new patterns of sociability and from the feeling of being appreciated by the hostel's guests, who are mainly young people. Even if they do not speak any foreign language, they rejoice in being able to meet new youngsters and invite friends over every summer. Their work, thus, is not so significant in terms of income, but it is rather a way to rebuild social relations and meaningful identities after deindustrialization.

---

[48] Marina and partner, Varaždin, April 2016. Interview conducted by the author and by Nikolina Hrga.
[49] Ibid.

Like Marina, other former textile workers in post-Yugoslav settings made use of informal work and subsistence agriculture to make ends meet. Such is the case of one of my narrators from the Dalmatinka factory, who started to collect vegetables for a living while her wage was not paid, or of some of my narrators in Novi, who kept an informal sewing workshop where they provided repairs to the community. Workers' sewing and knitting skills, in particular, came in handy during post-socialist transformations. Already during socialist times, textile and knitwear workers were able to buy some unused yarns from their factory at low prices, knitting sweaters and other clothes for their family members. Traditional knitting and sewing skills became again useful during the post-socialist period, not just as an economic resource but also as a meaningful activity after unemployment. This is the case of Zorica, who is a former supervisor in the knitting department at Arena, whose parents also belonged to the Arena management during the socialist era. As mentioned earlier in the book, Zorica was very attached to the factory and to its humanist values. Zorica left her job at Arena when wages started to be delayed, because she could not stand the sight of other workers 'walking like zombies' due to their uncertain status, as she said. She 'fell ill' because of this situation, and decided to leave, since she realized that it was better to 'have nothing, do nothing', rather than be 'fooled by someone else and to work for free'. Zorica lives with her invalid husband, and gets some economic help from her son. She also lost her savings due to the collapse of the internal bank. In this difficult situation, knitting became part of Zorica's strategy of resilience :

> I always knitted, my dad was knitting and my mum as well, we always had some machines at home for hand knitting. And I was always sewing something. ... I do everything by myself, bags and clothes, all on my own. And concerning the food, we will get by, I won't get hungry. There [in the factory] I would have got hungry, and nervous. I got sick precisely from that nervousness. ... I am not the person who can look at someone else's suffering when there is no solution. If it doesn't go, it doesn't go, cross it, turn the page, let's go further.[50]

Zorica is now displaying and selling her knitted creations, from sweaters to bags and slippers, at the main market in Pula. She is also taking part in crafting fairs and events, which provide a new outlet for her skills and new opportunities of social life and appreciation for her work. Other former Arena workers

---

[50] Zorica, Pula, June 2015.

I talked to are engaging in similar handcrafting activities. Dorina, for instance, used to knit the remnants of Arena production for her family, an activity that 'saved her' during socialism. Today she keeps engaging in small repairs for neighbours and acquaintances, to compensate for her small pension, while her friend Božica, also retired, is selling some earrings and other creations in the main marketplace in Pula, like Zorica. Interestingly, Božica managed to pass on some of her crafting skills to her daughter, who is now an emerging fashion designer, and who also bought one of the knitting machines that were for sale at Arena during the bankruptcy procedure for token prices. Božica's daughter also paid homage to the Arena knitwear factory through a fashion collection set in the deindustrialized building of the former factory, expressing her own form of individual solidarity towards her mothers' generation. These examples give an idea of how former seamstresses mobilize their existing skills in the post-socialist context, thanks to the resilience habits formed during the socialist era, which taught women to be hard workers in the productive and reproductive sphere. Activities such as sewing and knitting are not just a reproduction of a traditional female role, but are also a way to reaffirm the dignity of one's work after feeling devalued as industrial workers during the process of deindustrialization.

On the basis of the skills acquired during factory work, but also on the basis of their constant resourcefulness in combining productive and reproductive work, working-class women across the post-Yugoslav space put in place a wide array of survival and resilience strategies that allow them to cope with increasingly uncertain labour markets, low pensions and shrinking welfare states. In the case of former textile workers, these strategies are very much contingent on the place of residence and on the other available opportunities in the area. For instance, former workers in the almost completely deindustrialized town of Novi, in Bosnia-Herzegovina, had much less opportunities than former workers in Štip, Macedonia, where the textile industry is somehow still producing despite its exploitative conditions. Also, for instance, in comparison to other deindustrialized Croatian settings, the border region of Istria provides considerable outlets for middle-aged retired or unemployed women, thanks to the local expanding tourist industry, as well as the proximity of neighbouring Italy, where there is a stable demand for elderly-care workers. Istrian women mostly know Italian due to the history of the area, and thus benefit from an additional cultural capital that can be used to find work across the border. From Istria, thus, there is a stable flow of circular migration towards Italy since the 1990s onwards, with daily early morning bus connections transporting mainly migrant workers on their way to Trieste and Venice – and occasionally, a researcher like myself.

The practices of collective organizing and the individual resilience strategies that I encountered during the research highlight working-class women's attachment to a world in which labour – and especially manual labour – was seen as a source of dignity, respect and deservingness. In his critique of the scholarly literature on post-Fordism and 'the end of work', Strangleman contests the depiction of industrial workers as alienated victims of global capitalism. Instead, he suggests considering the ways in which work 'still provides structure and meaning in people's lives however imperfectly this may occur – one only has to look at the obverse of people without work to see the reality of this'.[51] Through informal work and through new income-generating activities, working-class women in the post-Yugoslav state attempt to replace the structure and meaning provided by factory work during socialism. Their conception of work as a source of dignity, meaning and value (both individual and collective), part of the industrial structure of feeling interiorized within garment factories, lingers on to these days as a form of experiential consciousness through which they read contemporary society and its social injustices. Often depicted in popular culture as the victims or losers of post-socialism, Emina, Rada and the others should be seen instead as both everyday survivors and fighters for a better world based on the universal principles of social justice and dignified labour for all.

[51] Strangleman, 'The nostalgia for permanence at work?'.

Conclusion

The Prvi Maj textile factory in Pirot, in the South-East of Serbia near the Bulgarian border, was considered a model textile factory and was often visited by workers from other factories across Yugoslavia. I found a series of photos of Prvi Maj in the archival collection of the Arena knitwear factory, located in Pula, Croatia, near the border with Italy, over 900 kilometres away from Pirot. Closed in 2013 only a few months short of its fifty-fifth anniversary, Prvi Maj employed up to 7,000 workers during the socialist era. The complex included a childcare facility, a library of 20,000 volumes to which over a thousand workers subscribed,[1] a museum, an art collection of 200 paintings, sport fields and subsidized resorts. Its long-term director, Dragan Nikolić, was a promoter of the 'working mother' gender contract in its most advanced form, stating that working mothers had to be able to cast a look on the kindergarten and park, and to see that their child was playing nearby in all safety (Figure 15).[2]

The book argues that factories such as Prvi Maj were fundamental in building workers' industrial structure of feeling during socialist times, the legacy of which lives on in the present post-socialist era. Despite the end of Yugoslavia and factory closures, and despite the loss of hundreds of thousands of jobs in the textile industry since 1989, the socialist industrial structure of feeling continues to inhabit workers' narratives and imaginations, providing a generational, gendered and class-based framework through which the economic, political and social transformations of the 1990s and 2000s are interpreted. The concept of the structure of feeling, coined by Raymond Williams and adopted by scholars of deindustrialization to understand the lasting effect of Fordism and of industrial labour on post-industrial communities,[3] is here applied for the very first time to the post-Yugoslav context. On the basis of a polyphonic assemblage of working-class women's

---

[1] 'Blago u knjigama I.O. "Prvi Maj" koje propada – video', 10 February 2015. Available at: http://www.pikanal.rs/2015/02/10/blago-i-o-prvi-maj-koje-propada/ (accessed 20 January 2018).
[2] V. Ćirić, '"Prvi Maj" fabrika koja je stvorila grad', 2 March 2013. Available at: http://www.novosti.rs/vesti/naslovna/ekonomija/aktuelno.239.html:422390-Prvi-maj-fabrika-koja-je-stvorila-grad (accessed 20 January 2018).
[3] Williams, *Marxism and Literature*; Byrne, 'Industrial culture in a post-industrial world'; Strangleman, 'Deindustrialisation and the historical sociological imagination'; High, MacKinnon and Perchard (eds), *The Deindustrialized World*.

Figure 15 The kindergarten in Prvi Maj, Pirot. Reproduced with permission from the Arena factory archive in 2015.

narratives collected in Croatia, Macedonia, Bosnia-Herzegovina, Slovenia and Serbia, the book investigates the fundamental intersection between gender, class and labour history in socialist and post-socialist times. While indebted to previous scholarly works on industrialization, deindustrialization and memory in socialist and post-socialist settings,[4] as well as to existing studies of gender, labour and memory in the post-Yugoslav region,[5] this book is the first to combine archive material, visual material and oral history narratives to encompass women's experiences of industrial work in the traditionally feminized textile industry from 1945 until the present, taking into account both the industrialization and deindustrialization processes and their ideological and material effects on workers' lived experience.

The important social and economic gains made by women after 1945 – as well as individual paths of self-realization and empowerment in the public sphere, including industrial labour – are generally undermined in the existing literature on gender relations in the post-Yugoslav region, where the socialist emancipation project is commonly defined as a top-

---

[4] Fidelis, *Women, Communism, and Industrialization in Postwar Poland*; Pozniak, *Nowa Huta*.
[5] Vodopivec, 'On the Road to Modernity'; Vodopivec, 'Past for the present'; Jambrešić-Kirin and Blagaić, 'The ambivalence of socialist working women's heritage'.

down process of 'emancipation from above' and 'state patriarchy',[6] and is even at times blamed for current young women's passivity in post-socialist times.[7] The history of the Antifascist Women's Front of Yugoslavia (1945–53) is also read in many cases as a failed opportunity for women to autonomously organize in the socialist era,[8] while the wide-ranging impact of the organization on the lives of working-class and peasant rank-and-file members is only starting to be fully explored.[9] Throughout this book, I argue for the need to look at women's lives during the socialist era in a more complex and nuanced way, which acknowledges the multiple articulations of women's agency in the productive and reproductive sphere. Together with other scholars, I previously stressed the importance of overcoming normative categories inherited from Cold War divides when researching women's lives under socialism. This book aims to be a further contribution to this new, and contested, strand of research.[10]

Working-class women and their structure of feeling

The industrial structure of feeling developed within socialist factories was based on the specific values of the Yugoslav regime itself, namely, work as a central building block of society. The values of intergenerational solidarity and of individual sacrifice for the collective good were also prominent. Balancing productivity with the needs of human reproduction was another fundamental part of the 'social pact' established between socialist elites and ordinary citizens. The socialist factory itself represented not just a centre of production, but also a key point of welfare redistribution, thanks to the

---

[6] Ramet (ed.), *Gender Politics in the Western Balkans*.
[7] Drakulić, 'How women survived (post-) communism (and didn't laugh)'.
[8] Jancar-Webster, *Women & Revolution in Yugoslavia*; Sklevicky, *Konji, Žene, Ratovi*; Batinić, *Women and Yugoslav Partisans*.
[9] See Dugandžić and Okić (eds), *Izgubljena revolucija*. See also Bonfiglioli, 'Women's political and social activism'.
[10] See the following recent discussion on women's agency in socialist regimes: Nanette Funk, 'A very tangled knot: Official state socialist women's organizations, women's agency and feminism in Eastern European state socialism', *European Journal of Women's Studies*, 21/4 (2014), pp. 344–60; Kristen Ghodsee, 'Untangling the knot: A response to Nanette Funk', *European Journal of Women's Studies*, 22/2 (2015), pp. 248–52; Nanette Funk, '(K)not so: A response to Kristen Ghodsee', *European Journal of Women's Studies*, 22/3 (2015), pp. 350–5; De Haan (ed.), 'Forum: Ten years after, communism and feminism revisited', including my contribution 'On Vida Tomšič, Marxist feminism and agency', pp. 145–51.

wide array of welfare services (canteens, subsidized housing and holidays, scholarships and credits) that were distributed by managers and trade unions in a paternalist fashion.[11] Factory life also strengthened working-class sociability due to the variety of leisure activities (notably sports and cultural associations) present within the workplace. The ideology of workers' self-management, developed since the early 1950s after the Soviet–Yugoslav split, increased workers' loyalty to their specific factory, as well as their feeling of working for their own collective good, due to the designation of the factory as social property, and due to workers' involvement in decision-making concerning factory profits and investments.[12]

The self-management system has been widely studied by local and foreign scholars from a theoretical perspective, but few empirical studies are available when it comes to workers' lived experience of industrial work through the socialist era. As argued in the first chapter, the process of rapid socialist industrialization happened in parallel with women's first obtainment of equal political, social and economic rights in the 1946 Yugoslav Constitution. In a prevailingly rural country, where peasants were turned into industrial workers, young peasant girls also biked for the first time to their night shifts, creating a wave of moral panic among local rural communities, whose traditional patriarchal norms were suddenly being challenged. Working-class women witnessed a rapid change in their living standards and immediate surroundings from the late 1950s onwards, experiencing an increase in economic independence, purchasing power and available consumer goods as well as the possibility to engage in cross-border travels and paid holidays on the Adriatic coast.

At the same time, due to Yugoslavia's uneven development, female workers acutely experienced the gap between theories of women's emancipation and the reality on the ground. Despite the fact that the protection of working mothers was inscribed in the Yugoslav Constitution, and that social reproduction was supposed to be taken care of by the state in a socialized manner, welfare services for working-class women such as maternity leaves and kindergartens were slow to develop, and women's ability to combine productive and reproductive work required enormous sacrifices. As in the 1966 documentary movie *Od 3 do 22* by Zagreb-based director Krešimir Golik, whose heroine's double working day lasted from 3.00 am to 10.00 pm, working women were subjected to an extremely heavy combination of

---

[11] Woodward, 'The political economy of ethno-nationalism in Yugoslavia'; Archer and Musić, 'Approaching the socialist factory'.
[12] Musić, 'Yugoslavia'; Unkovski-Korica, *The Economic Struggle for Power in Tito's Yugoslavia*.

productive and reproductive labour, which included night shifts and piece-rate work (*norma*) in the factory, but also domestic tasks carried out mostly by hand, and without appliances such as washing machines, at least until the late socialist period.

As I made clear in Chapter 2, women's double burden was widely discussed and reported in the press, rather than silenced. The constant valorization and praise of working-class women as 'granite-like' and endlessly resilient, however, was also simultaneously a naturalization of the gendered division of labour within the family, especially in the workplace periodicals published within socialist factories, which somehow reinforced the expectation that a modern woman had to be a mother, a worker and a housewife (*majka, radnica, domaćica*), carrying out all these tasks with equal efficiency. Women coped with these collective difficulties by looking for individual and private solutions, especially when it came to childcare, which was mostly delegated to other female relatives such as mothers, mothers-in-law or elderly neighbours. At the same time, the official recognition of women's double burden allowed them to claim a number of welfare benefits and provided them with the ability to eschew what has been defined as the 'triple burden', namely political activism inside the factories, which usually was not framed as an imposition in socialist Yugoslavia, especially for low-skilled female workers. Solidarity practices in working-class communities also provided an important buffer when it came to everyday social reproduction. While I analysed women's double burden in socialist garment factories throughout the book, I nonetheless challenged the widespread usage of the term as a shorthand for the failure of socialist gender politics among feminist scholars, and as the final balance sheet of women's (lack of) emancipation in the socialist era.[13] Socialist textile factories were not just sites of hardship and oppression; they simultaneously provided female workers with a high degree of personal agency. Not only social mobility, economic independence and social protection, but also working-class sociability and community networks were fundamental aspects of factory life.

This becomes especially clear when looking at archival sources and documentaries from the socialist era, as well as when listening to the ways in which socialist factories are remembered in today workers' narratives. The socialist times are mostly remembered as a moment of potentiality and agency, against current times of uncertainty and stasis.[14] Undoubtedly,

---

[13] Corrin (ed.), *Superwomen and the Double Burden*; Einhorn, *Cinderella Goes to Market*.
[14] Spasić, 'Jugoslavija kao mesto normalnog života'; Petrović, 'Towards an affective history of Yugoslavia'; Jansen, *Yearnings in the Meantime*.

post-socialist economic and social precariousness plays a major role in shaping workers' nostalgic vision of the socialist era. At the same time, I believe that workers' narratives should not be read as a naïve, idealized picture of past workers' lives. Current and former textile workers, those who are still employed and those who are unemployed, recall the socialist period as a benchmark of normality and social welfare, during which work was also hard and low paid, but compensated through a variety of additional welfare services and through job security. Post-Yugoslav textile workers do not miss an idealized socialist utopia that never existed, but rather the very material social rights they enjoyed only some decades beforehand, during the heydays of Fordism, when workers felt that they could aspire to steady material progress for themselves and for the future generations. At the same time, the power inequalities that existed within socialist factories are clearly remembered by blue-collar workers, whose nostalgia for the socialist past is tempered by class awareness. Workers' nostalgia for socialist welfare, thus, appears to be a form of reflective nostalgia,[15] aware of the limits of both the socialist and the post-socialist era. Nostalgic attachments are embedded in workers' structure of feeling as it developed within socialist factories, whose organization was tied to the wider project of alternative socialist modernization.

Post-Yugoslav textile production between the local and the global

The process of deindustrialization and economic de-development that is still ongoing in the region had devastating effects on ordinary citizens, together with the material and civilian losses caused by the Yugoslav Wars. The book addresses the many ways in which textile workers were heavily affected by deindustrialization, criminal privatization and new elites' pillage of social property in their daily lives. While newspapers frequently report on workers' unpaid wages and social contributions, as well as on widespread bankruptcies, the issue of industrial workers' social citizenship remains deeply silenced and obscured in contemporary post-Yugoslav societies on a political level. Željka, a Croatian woman who helped me with some of the transcriptions remotely (we never met in person), could not retain herself

---

[15] Strangleman, 'The nostalgia for permanence at work?'; Boym, *The Future of Nostalgia*.

after hearing some twenty hours of recorded material. She wrote to me in an email: 'The interviews are very depressing. All that is said in them is a public secret, but it is terrible to listen to all of it at once.' Industrial workers' stories of dispossession and marginalization are indeed terrible, and kept as a 'public secret', as they challenge the dominant local and international teleological narratives of national awakening, Europeanization and democratization, as well as the vision of neoliberal capitalism as the only possible economic system. As Kideckel, Stenning and other authors have argued, the former working classes were placed at the bottom of the social scale after 1989, and they were stigmatized alongside the old socialist system for not being able to adapt to new circumstances.[16]

Alongside deindustrialization, workers in the post-Yugoslav region had to face new forms of labour intensification and exploitation. Textile factories' closures happened in parallel to the worsening of labour and social rights in remaining sites of garment production. Central, Eastern and South-Eastern European textile and garment production is now competing with textile and garment production located in the global South. Even if textile workers in Yugoslavia were already producing for foreign clients within the framework of market socialism, they were nonetheless partially sheltered from the extreme 'race to the bottom' that was to follow during the transition to market capitalism. The recognition of women's productive and reproductive tasks also allowed for a certain flexibility in women's working schedule during socialism, while today, working time is totally subsumed to the logic of profit, at the expense of private life. In Chapter 3, I address some cases of neoliberal exploitation, focusing on precarious and low-paid textile production in Štip, Macedonia, and Osijek, Croatia. Poverty wages, precarious contracts, excessive working hours and widespread mobbing practices are common among employees of private factories, who produce subcontracted goods for major European brands.

While the case of the post-Yugoslav textile industry has broader implications for global labour history, working-class women's narratives in the region also prove significant for the growing literature on gender and citizenship in post-socialist settings.[17] This book challenges earlier scholarly representations of female industrial workers as ready to get back home and abandon their workplace after the end of socialism, due to their untenable double burden.[18] Many of my narrators freely decided to stay in

---

[16] Kideckel, 'The unmaking'; Stenning, 'Where is the post-socialist working class?'.
[17] Daskalova, Hornstein Romić, Kaser and Radunović (eds), *Gendering Post-socialist Transition*.
[18] Verdery, 'From parent-state to family patriarchs'.

employment during the socialist era, even when their husbands insisted that they would be better off at home, since the factory represented a space of personal fulfilment, independence and sociability that many were not keen to give up on. Consequently, like female industrial workers in France and Poland, as shown in Chapter 4, female workers in the Balkans miss their industrial workplace after deindustrialization.[19] Workers tend to challenge the devaluation of women's industrial labour, which is a key feature, I argue, of the process of re-traditionalization of gender relations in the region, alongside the revival of national ideologies, which promoted a new gender regime founded on women as 'mothers of the nation'.[20]

When pushed out of the industrial workforce and into precarity, former industrial workers show considerable resilience skills. Informal work, subsistence agriculture and traditional skills such as sewing and knitting are used as survival strategies, but also as a way to engage in new meaningful activities and in new sociability networks. The memory of past working rights and social welfare is often mobilized against processes of privatization and speculation. During the Kamensko workers' hunger strike of 2010 and during the Arena workers' strike of 2014, analysed in Chapter 5, the recollections of the prestige and success of their firm, and the value placed in manual labour during the socialist era, were mobilized as discursive resources, to stress workers' agency, dignity and deservingness against growing social injustices. In order to resist their material and symbolic marginalization, moreover, former workers also engage in the intergenerational transmission of their past memories of work under socialism, reaching out to the younger generations, who are more and more interested in discovering the forgotten voices of former industrial workers through documentaries, exhibitions, art projects and research. New radical alliances between workers, students and activists have been made during the different social mobilizations that have emerged in the Balkans in the past ten years.[21] These mobilizations are tackling issues of poverty, social justice, labour rights and precariousness, and are openly contesting neoliberal capitalism, as shown by the slogan of the 2014 Bosnian Spring, 'We are hungry in three languages,' which challenges the ethnicization of the social sphere in post-Dayton Bosnia, or by a more recent slogan used during the 2017 anti-government protest in Serbia: 'We won't be a cheap labour force,'

---

[19] Clarke, 'Closing Time'; Pine, 'Retreat to the household? Gendered domains in postsocialist Poland'.
[20] Iveković and Mostov, *From Gender to Nation*.
[21] Štiks, '"New left"'. See also Musić, 'Between Facebook and the picket line'; Arsenijević (ed.), *Unbribable Bosnia Herzegovina*.

which contest Serbia's orientation towards foreign direct investments, at the expense of local labour.

Even if industrial workers' experiences are often highlighted within new social mobilizations and within many new publications quoted throughout the book, the voices of working-class women suffer from a double marginalization in post-socialism, not just because of class, but also because of a gendered focus on industrial masculinities in the literature on industrialization and deindustrialization. This book aims to open up new avenues of research in women's history and labour history during the socialist and post-socialist era. Further empirical comparison across different historical phases of the socialist regime, across different republics and across industrial sectors are needed in order to understand the specificities and ambivalences of the socialist modernization process in the field of gender relations, and the femininities and masculinities that were shaped by socialist factories as community and welfare centres. Factory case studies from a gendered perspective are also particularly urgent to better understand the changing ideological paradigms of the 1980s and 1990s, and how they affected workers' everyday lives.[22] The phenomenon of post-socialist deindustrialization in the Balkans also deserves much wider, comparative attention and more thorough empirical research beyond single case studies, especially since it is an ongoing phenomenon that has been changing the geographical and social landscapes of the region in the past three decades. The study of the post-Yugoslav case can productively contribute to global scholarly discussions of deindustrialization, while benefiting from the interdisciplinary insights of the existing literature.[23]

Finally, through the usage of workers' narratives and through feminist oral history, I strived to shed new light on ordinary women and men's everyday lives, and on their struggle for decent living and working conditions, inviting the reader to go beyond the 'ethnic' paradigm that still persists in Western media and scholarly literature when dealing with the Balkans. Hopefully, this book will contribute to the preservation and valorization

---

[22] On this, see the exhibition and research project by Centar za mirovne studije/Baza za radničku inicijativu i demokratizaciju, 'Kome treba poduzeće? Borovo 1988. – 1991'. For a reflection on class, labour and national identities by its authors, see Sven Cvek, Jasna Račić and Snježana Ivčić, 'Sfera rada u interpretacijama Jugoslavenskih sukoba', in Goran Tepšić, Radmila Nakarada i Nemanja Džuverović (eds), *Interpretacije jugoslovenskih sukoba i njihove posledice: između suštinskog neslaganja i dijaloga* (Belgrade, 2016). See also the research project led by Rory Archer and Goran Musić, 'Between class and nation: Working class communities in 1980s Serbia and Montenegro', Available at: https://yulabour.wordpress.com/ (accessed 20 January 2018).

[23] High, MacKinnon and Perchard (eds), *The Deindustrialized World*.

of the local past and present history of women's industrial labour, and will open up new gendered pathways for intergenerational transmission and education, as well as new forms of social awareness and inspiration for the many who are currently fighting for social justice and decent work across the post-Yugoslav region.

Bibliography

Primary sources

Archival sources

Vaska Duganova, 'Problemi zaposlene žene u novim industriskim naseljima preradjivačke industrije u Makedoniji', Titov Veles, 25 March 1961. The Archives of the Republic of Slovenia, Ljubljana, Vida Tomšič collection, AS 1413, box 193.

Zapisnik IV Plenuma Glavnog Odbora AFŽ-a, Sarajevo, 13 March 1948. The Archives of Bosnia-Herzegovina, Sarajevo, box 5, 2912/32.

Zapisnik sa sastanka Upravnog odbora Ženskih društava Jugoslavije, Belgrade, 6 March 1954. The Archives of Yugoslavia, Belgrade, collection 354, SŽDJ, box 1: Zapisnici i stenografske sa sastanaka upravnog odbora i sekretariata SŽDJ i sa savetovanja SŽDJ 1954–1961.

Periodicals

Dalmatinka: list radnih ljudi predionice i tvornice konca – Sinj.
Duga Resa: list radnog kolektiva Pamučne industrije.
Glasnik: list radnika RO Kamensko Zagreb.
Makedonka: bilten na Pamučna industrija 'Makedonka'.
RIO: list kolektiva Riječke industrije odjeće.
Pobjeda: list radnog kolektiva tekstilne industrije 'Pobjeda' Zagreb.
Vuteks: list Vukovarske tekstilne industrije 'Vuteks' Vukovar.
Sana: list RO Tvornica trikotaže i konfekcije 'Sana' Bosanski Novi.
Žena: Časopis za znastvena, društvena i kulturna pitanja o mjestu i ulozi žene i porodice u društvu (published by the Konferencija za Društvenu Aktivnost Žena).

Audiovisual sources

Cenzura (emission on the Kamensko case), 11 March 2011, part one. Available at: https://www.youtube.com/watch?v=4R-WXPMdAWU (accessed 20 January 2018).

Cenzura (emission on the Kamensko case), 11 March 2011, part two. Available at: https://www.youtube.com/watch?v=fjx9HsDT0RA (accessed 20 January 2018).

Dalmatinka Sinj (Dragana Modrić, Jelena Pavlinušić, Nikola Križanac, 2014). Available at: https://vimeo.com/104534639 (accessed 20 January 2018).

Firma (Hladno Pivo, official video, 2015). Available at: https://www.youtube.com/watch?v=uFQIPl5kT-k (accessed 20 January 2018).
Najbolji muž (Vera Jocić, 1967). Available at: https://vimeo.com/134070626 (accessed 20 January 2018).
Od 3 do 22 (Krešimir Golik, 1966). Available at: https://www.youtube.com/watch?v=avaas3e37T4 (accessed 20 January 2018).
Priče iz Fabrike (Vojislav Milašević, 1985). First episode available at: https://www.youtube.com/watch?v=Ukm9bKwC2oc (accessed 20 January 2018).
Projekt višegodišnjeg nasada jabuka (Dario Juričan, 2016). Trailer available at: https://vimeo.com/169520373 (accessed 20 January 2018).
Radnice u gladovanju (Goran Ferčeg, 2013/2014). Text available at: http://drame.hr/drame/358-radnice-u-gladovanju (accessed 20 January 2018).
Revija u štrajku – Arena trikotaža – Pula, 8 March 2014 (Pulska Grupa). Available at: https://www.youtube.com/watch?v=dKkYDd6YWNM&t=1s (accessed 20 January 2018).
Spolitika, (Radio Maestral Pula), 26 February 2014, and 30 April 2014. Digital copy in possession of the author.
The Seamstresses (Biljana Garvanlieva, 2010). Extract available at: https://vimeo.com/54517757 (accessed 20 January 2018).
Vera i Eržika (Želimir Žilnik, 1981). Digital copy in possession of the author.

Secondary sources

Adizes, Ichak, *Industrial Democracy: Yugoslav Style* (Los Angeles, 1977).
Alexievich, Svetlana, *Secondhand Time: The Last of the Soviets* (London, 2016).
Alinčić, Mira, 'Law and the status of women in Yugoslavia', *The Columbia Human Rights Law Review*, 8 (1976–7), pp. 345–72.
Angé, Olivia and David Berliner (eds), *Anthropology and Nostalgia* (New York, 2014).
Antić, Milica, 'Yugoslavia: The transitional spirit of the age', in C. Corrin (ed.), *Superwomen and the Double Burden* (London, 1992), pp. 155–79.
Arandarenko, Mihail, 'Waiting for the workers: Explaining labor quiescence in Serbia', in S. Crowley and D. Ost (eds), *Workers after Workers' States: Labor and Politics in Postcommunist Eastern Europe* (London, 2001), pp. 159–80.
Archer, Rory, '"Paid by the workers, occupied by the bureaucrats": Housing inequalities in 1980s Belgrade', in R. Archer, I. Duda and P. Stubbs (eds), *Social Inequalities and Discontent in Yugoslav Socialism* (Farnham, 2016), pp. 58–76.
Archer, Rory, 'The moral economy of home construction in late socialist Yugoslavia', *History and Anthropology*, 29/2 (2018), pp. 141–62.
Archer, Rory and Goran Musić, 'Approaching the socialist factory and its workforce: Considerations from fieldwork in (former) Yugoslavia', *Labor History*, 58/1 (2017), pp. 44–66.

Archer, Rory, Igor Duda and Paul Stubbs (eds), *Social Inequalities and Discontent in Yugoslav Socialism* (Farnham, 2016).
Arena, 'Naših Prvih 50 Godina', commemorative catalogue (Pula, 1998).
Arsenijević, Damir (ed.), *Unbribable Bosnia Herzegovina: The Fight for the Commons* (Baden-Baden, 2014).
Avdić, Selvedin, *Moja Fabrika* (Zenica, 2013).
Baker, Catherine, *The Yugoslav Wars of the 1990s* (London, 2015).
Batinić, Jelena, *Women and Yugoslav Partisans: A History of World War II Resistance* (Cambridge, 2015).
Begić, Sandina and Boriša Mraović, 'Forsaken monuments and social change: The function of socialist monuments in the post-Yugoslav space', in S. L. Moeschberger and R. A. Phillips De Zalia (eds), *Symbols that Bind, Symbols that Divide: The Semiotics of Peace and Conflict* (Switzerland, 2014), pp. 13–38.
Bernard, Sara, *The Return of the Gastarbeiter in Socialist Yugoslavia, 1965–1991*. PhD dissertation (Regensburg University, 2016).
Bieber, Florian, Armina Galijaš and Rory Archer (eds), *Debating the End of Yugoslavia* (London, 2014).
Blagojević, Jelisaveta, Katerina Kolozova and Svetlana Slapšak (eds), *Gender and Identity: Theories from and/or on Southeastern Europe* (Belgrade, 2006).
Bohle, Dorothee, 'Neoliberal Hegemony, transnational capital and the terms of EU's eastward expansion', *Capital & Class*, 30/1 (2006), pp. 57–86.
Bokovoy, Melissa. *Peasants and Communists: Politics and Ideology in the Yugoslav Countryside, 1941–1953* (Pittsburgh, 1998).
Bonfiglioli, Chiara, 'Gendering social citizenship: Textile workers in post-Yugoslav states', *CITSEE Working Papers Series*, School of Law, University of Edinburgh, 30 (2013), pp. 1–33.
Bonfiglioli, Chiara, 'Gender, labour and precarity in the South East European periphery: The case of textile workers in Štip', *Contemporary Southeastern Europe*, 1/2 (2014), pp. 7–23.
Bonfiglioli, Chiara, 'Women's political and social activism in the early Cold War era: The case of Yugoslavia', *Aspasia*, 8 (2014), pp. 1–25.
Bonfiglioli, Chiara, 'Gendered citizenship in the global European periphery: Textile workers in post-Yugoslav states', *Women's Studies International Forum*, 49 (2015), pp. 57–65.
Bonfiglioli, Chiara, Katja Kahlina and Adriana Zaharijević, 'Transformations of gender, sexuality and citizenship in South East Europe', *Women's Studies International Forum*, 49 (2015), pp. 43–7.
Borojević, Rajka, *Iz Dubca u svet* (Belgrade, 2006), first edition 1964.
Boym, Svetlana, *The Future of Nostalgia* (London, 2001).
Bracewell, Wendy, 'Eating up Yugoslavia: Cookbooks and consumption in socialist Yugoslavia', in P. Bren and M. Neuburger (eds), *Communism Unwrapped: Consumption in Cold War Eastern Europe* (Oxford, 2012), pp. 169–96.

Bren, Paulina and Mary Neuburger, 'Constructive criticism', in P. Bren and M. Neuburger (eds), *Communism Unwrapped: Consumption in Cold War Eastern Europe* (Oxford, 2012), pp. 321–24.

Brunnbauer, Ulf, 'From equality without democracy to democracy without equality? Women and transition in southeast Europe', *South-East Europe Review for Labour and Social Affairs*, 3 (2000), pp. 151–68.

Bryman, Alan, *Social Research Methods* (Oxford, 2008).

Byrne, David, 'Industrial culture in a post-industrial world: The case of the North East of England', *City*, 6/3 (2002), pp. 279–89.

Calic, Marie-Janine, 'The beginning of the end – The 1970s as a historical turning point in Yugoslavia', in M. Calic, D. Neutatz and J. Obertreis (eds), *The Crisis of Socialist Modernity: The Soviet Union and Yugoslavia in the 1970s* (Göttingen, 2011), pp. 66–86.

Castellina, Luciana, *Discovery of the World: A Political Awakening in the Shadow of Mussolini* (London, 2014).

Center for Research and Policy Making, *The History of the Macedonian Textile Industry with a Focus on Shtip* (Skopje, 2005).

Cepić, Dražen, 'The crisis of working class sociability in Croatia: Challenges of de-unionization', *Ethnologia Balkanica*, 18 (2015), pp. 337–53.

Clarke, Jackie, 'Closing time: Deindustrialisation and nostalgia in contemporary France', *History Workshop Journal*, 79/1 (2015), pp. 107–25.

Comisso, Ellen Turkish, *Workers' Control Under Plan and Market: Implications of Yugoslav Self-management* (New Haven, 1979).

Corrin, Chris (ed.), *Superwomen and the Double Burden: Women's Experiences of Change in Central and Eastern Europe and the Former Soviet Union* (Great Britain/Canada, 1992).

Cowie, Jefferson and Joseph Heathcott (eds), *Beyond the Ruins: The Meaning of Deindustrialisation* (Ithaca, 2003).

Crowley, Stephen and David Ost, *Workers after Workers' States: Labor and Politics in Postcommunist Eastern Europe* (London, 2001).

Cvek, Sven, Jasna Račić and Snježana Ivčić, 'Sfera rada u interpretacijama Jugoslavenskih sukoba', in G. Tepšić, R. Nakarada and N. Džuverović (eds), *Interpretacije jugoslovenskih sukoba i njihove posledice: između suštinskog neslaganja i dijaloga* (Belgrade, 2016), pp. 109–30.

Damachi, Ukandi G., Hans D. Seibel and Jeroen Scheerder, *Self-Management in Yugoslavia and the Developing World* (London, 1982).

Daskalova, Krassimira, Caroline Hornstein Romić, Karl Kaser and Filip Radunović (eds), *Gendering Post-socialist Transition: Studies of Changing Gender Perspectives* (Vienna, 2012).

Deacon, Bob, 'Eastern European welfare states: The impact of the politics of globalization', *Journal of European Social Policy*, 10/2 (2000), pp. 146–61.

Đilas, Maja, *Prostori reprezentacije moći alternativnih kulturnih praksi u Jugoslaviji: 1945–1980*, PhD dissertation (University of Novi Sad, 2014).

Dimova, Rozita, 'Between borderlines, betwixt citizenship: Gender, agency and the crisis in the Macedonia/Greece border region', *Women's Studies International Forum*, 49 (2015), pp. 66–72.

Dobrivojević, Ivana, 'Industrijalizacija kao imperativ. Ekonomska politika Partije 1945-1955', in L. Duraković and A. Matošević (eds), *Socijalizam na klupi. Jugoslavensko društvo očima nove postjugoslavenske humanistike* (Pula-Zagreb, 2013), pp. 17-46.

Dolenec, Danijela, Karin Doolan and Tomislav Tomašević, 'Contesting neoliberal urbanism on the European semi-periphery: The right to the city movement in Croatia', *Europe Asia-Studies*, 69/9 (2017), pp. 1401-29.

Draganić, Ilija, 'Neki problemi i pravci razvoja tekstilne industrije Jugoslavije', *Ekonomika preduzeća*, 39/7-8 (1991), pp. 391-404.

Dragović, Sonja, 'Tailors turned activists: Surviving the demise of the Croatian textile industry', *Intersections*, 2/1 (2016), pp. 32-53.

Duda, Igor, *U potrazi za blagostanjem. O povijesti dokolice i potrošačkog društva u Hrvatskoj 1950-ih I 1960-ih* (Zagreb, 2005).

Duda, Igor, 'Adriatic for all: Summer holidays in Croatia', in B. Luthar and M. Pušnik (eds), *Remembering Utopia: The Culture of Everyday Life in Socialist Yugoslavia* (Washington, 2010), pp. 289-311.

Duda, Igor (ed.), *Stvaranje socijalističkoga čovjeka. Hrvatsko društvo i ideologija jugoslavenskoga socijalizma* (Zagreb and Pula, 2017).

Dugandžić, Andreja and Tijana Okić (eds), *Izgubljena revolucija: AFŽ između mita i zaborava* (Sarajevo, 2016).

Dunn, Elizabeth C., *Privatizing Poland: Baby Food, Big Business, and the Remaking of Labor* (Ithaca, 2004).

Einhorn, Barbara, 'Where have all the women gone? Women and the women's movement in East Central Europe', *Feminist Review*, 39 (1991), pp. 16-36.

Einhorn, Barbara, *Cinderella Goes to Market. Citizenship, Gender, and Women's Movements in East Central Europe* (London, 1993).

Erdei, Ildiko, 'Stepeni tuge: ekonomska devastacija i društveni zaborav', *Issues in Ethnology Anthropology*, 9/2 (2014), pp. 351-69.

Erlich, Vera Stein, *Family in Transition: A Study of 300 Yugoslav Villages* (Princeton, 1966).

Fidelis, Malgorzata, *Women, Communism, and Industrialization in Postwar Poland* (Cambridge and New York, 2010).

Fodor, Eva, *Working Difference: Women's Working Lives in Hungary and Austria, 1945-1995* (Durham, 2003).

Funk, Nanette, 'A very tangled knot: Official state socialist women's organizations, women's agency and feminism in Eastern European state socialism', *European Journal of Women's Studies*, 21/4 (2014), pp. 344-60.

Funk, Nanette, '(K)not so: A response to Kristen Ghodsee', *European Journal of Women's Studies*, 22/3 (2015), pp. 350-5.

Gal, Susan and Gail Kligman, *The Politics of Gender after Socialism: A Comparative-Historical Essay* (Princeton, 2000).

Ghodsee, Kristen, 'Untangling the knot: A response to Nanette Funk', *European Journal of Women's Studies*, 22/2 (2015), pp. 248-52.

Ghodsee, Kristen and Kateřina Lišková, 'Bumbling idiots or evil masterminds? Challenging Cold War stereotypes about women, sexuality and state socialism', *Filozofija i Društvo*, 27/3 (2016), pp. 489-503.

Gluck, Sherna B. and Daphne Patai (eds), *Women's Worlds: The Feminist Practice of Oral History* (New York, 1991).

Grandits, Hannes and Karin Taylor, *Yugoslavia's Sunny Side: A History of Tourism in Socialism (1950s–1980s)* (Budapest, 2010).

Grdešić, Marko, 'Mapping the paths of the Yugoslav model: Labour strength and weakness in Slovenia, Croatia and Serbia', *European Journal of Industrial Relations*, 14/2 (2008), pp. 133–51.

Grdešić, Marko, 'Workers and Unions after Yugoslavia', in S. Horvat and I. Štiks (eds), *Welcome to the Desert of Post-Socialism* (Brooklyn, NY, 2015), pp. 65–81.

Haan, Francisca de (ed.), 'Forum: Ten years after, communism and feminism revisited', *Aspasia*, 10 (2016), pp. 102–68.

Hale, Angela and Jane Wills (eds), *Threads of Labour: Garment Industry Supply Chains from the Workers' Perspective* (Hoboken, 2005).

Haney, Lynne, *Inventing the Needy: Gender and the Politics of Welfare in Hungary* (Oakland, 2002).

Hanzl-Weiss, Doris, 'Enlargement and the textiles, clothing and footwear industry', *World Economy*, 27/6 (2004), pp. 923–45.

Harvey, David, 'The "new" imperialism: Accumulation by dispossession', *Socialist Register*, 40 (2009), pp. 63–87.

Hassenstab, Christina and Sabrina Petra Ramet (eds), *Gender (In)equality and Gender Politics in South-Eastern Europe: A Question of Justice* (London, 2014).

Heerma van Voss, Lex, Els Hiemstra-Kuperus and Elise van Nederveen Meerkerk (eds), *The Ashgate Companion to the History of Textile Workers, 1650–2000* (London, 2010).

Helms, Elissa, *Innocence and Victimhood: Gender, Nation, and Women's Activism in Postwar Bosnia-Herzegovina* (Madison, 2013).

Herbst, Natalja, 'Women in socialist Yugoslavia in the 1950s: The example of Rajka Borojević and the Dragačevo women's cooperative', in R. Kersten-Pejanić, S. Rajilić and C. Voß (eds), *Doing Gender-Doing the Balkans* (München, Berlin, Washington DC, 2012), pp. 209–20.

High, Steven, 'Beyond aesthetics: Visibility and invisibility in the aftermath of deindustrialisation', *International Labor and Working-Class History*, 84 (2013), pp. 140–53.

High, Steven, '"The wounds of class": A historiographical reflection on the study of deindustrialisation', *History Compass*, 11/11 (2013), pp. 1–14.

High, Steven and David Lewis, *Corporate Wasteland: The Landscape and Memory of Deindustrialisation* (Toronto, 2007).

High, Steven, Lachlan MacKinnon and Andrew Perchard (eds), *The Deindustrialized World: Confronting Ruination in Postindustrial Places* (Vancouver, Toronto, 2017).

Hodges, Andrew, 'Worker narratives of blame and responsibility during the 2018 crisis: The case of the Uljanik Shipyard, Croatia', IOS Working Paper,

November 2018. Available at: https://www.dokumente.ios-regensburg.de/publikationen/mitteilungen/mitt_67.pdf (accessed 20 January 2018).

Hofman, Ana, *Novi život partizanskih pesama* (Belgrade, 2016).

Hofman, Ana and Polona Sitar, '"Buy me a silk skirt, Mile!" Celebrity culture, gender and social positioning in socialist Yugoslavia', in R. Archer, I. Duda and P. Stubbs (eds), *Social Inequalities and Discontent in Yugoslav Socialism* (Farnham, 2016), pp. 155–72.

Hormel, Leontina M., 'A case study of gender, class, and garment work reorganization in Ukraine', *Gender: Journal for Gender, Culture and Society*, 1 (2011), pp. 10–25.

Horvat, Srećko and Igor Štiks (eds), *Welcome to the Desert of Post-Socialism: Radical Politics after Yugoslavia* (Brooklyn, 2015).

Hozić, Aida A., 'The Balkan Merchants: Changing borders and informal transnationalization', *Ethnopolitics*, 5/3 (2006), pp. 243–56.

Hunter, Janet and Helen Macnaughtan, 'Gender and the global textile industry', in L. Heerma van Voss, E. Hiemstra-Kuperus and E. van Nederveen Meerkerk (eds), *The Ashgate Companion to the History of Textile Workers, 1650–2000* (London, 2010), pp. 703–24.

Ivandić, Marina and Igor Livada, *Lines of (Dis)Continuity: Forms and Methods of Labour Struggle in Croatia 1990–2014* (Belgrade, 2015).

Iveković, Rada and Julie Mostov, *From Gender to Nation* (Ravenna, 2002).

Jambrešić-Kirin, Renata and Marina Blagaić, 'The ambivalence of socialist working women's heritage: A case atudy of the Jugoplastika factory', *Narodna Umjetnost*, 50/1 (2003), pp. 40–73.

Jancar-Webster, Barbara, *Women & Revolution in Yugoslavia – 1941–1945* (Denver, 1990).

Jansen, Stef, *Yearnings in the Meantime: 'Normal Lives' and the State in a Sarajevo Apartment Complex* (Oxford and New York, 2014).

Jansen, Stef, Čarna Brković and Vanja Čelebičić (eds), *Negotiating Social Relations in Bosnia and Herzegovina: Semiperipheral Entanglements* (London, 2017).

Jovanović, Nebojša, *Gender and Sexuality in the Classic Yugoslav Cinema*, PhD dissertation (CEU Budapest, 2014).

Kalb, Don, 'Introduction: Class and the new anthropological holism', in J. G. Carrier and D. Kalb (eds), *Anthropologies of Class: Power, Practice and Inequality* (Cambridge, 2015), pp. 1–10.

Kazandziska, Milka, Marija Risteska and Verena Schmidt, 'The gender pay gap in the former Yugoslav Republic of Macedonia', ILO Decent Work Technical Support Team and Country Office for Central and Eastern Europe (Skopje, 2012).

Kečman, Jovanka, *Žene Jugoslavije u radničkom pokretu i ženskim organizacijama 1918–1941* (Belgrade, 1978).

Kideckel, David A., 'The unmaking of an East-Central European working class', in C. M. Hann (ed.), *Postsocialism: Ideals, Ideologies, and Practices in Eurasia* (London and New York, 2002), pp. 141–57.

Kirk, John, Sylvie Contrepois and Steve Jefferys (eds), *Changing Work and Community Identities in European Regions: Perspectives on the Past and Present* (Basingstoke, 2012).

Kojanić, Ognjen, 'Nostalgia as a Practice of the Self in Post-socialist Serbia', *Canadian Slavonic Papers*, 57/3–4 (2015), pp. 195–212.

Kojanić, Ognjen, 'Countering Dispossession with Worker-Ownership: The Case of ITAS in Neoliberal Croatia', unpublished conference paper (EASA, 2016).

Kokanović, Marina, 'The Cost of Nationalism: Croatian Labour, 1990–1999', in S. Crowley and D. Ost (eds), *Workers after Workers' States: Labor and Politics in Postcommunist Eastern Europe* (London, 2001), pp. 43–74.

Komlosy, Andrea, 'Austria and Czechoslovakia: The Habsburg Monarchy and Its Successor States', in L. Heerma van Voss, E. Hiemstra-Kuperus and E. van Nederveen Meerkerk (eds), *The Ashgate Companion to the History of Textile Workers, 1650–2000* (London, 2010), pp. 135–58.

Korintus, Marta and Nada Stropnik, 'Hungary and Slovenia: Long leave or short?', in S. B. Kamerman and P. Moss (eds), *The Politics of Parental Leave Policies: Children, Parenting, Gender and the Labour Market* (Bristol, 2009), pp. 195–213.

Kulcsar, Rozsa, 'The socioeconomic condition of women in Hungary', in S. L. Wolchik and A. G. Meyer (eds), *Women, State and Party in Eastern Europe* (Durham, 1985), pp. 351–73.

Le Normand, Brigitte, 'The house that socialism built: Reform, consumption and inequality in postwar Yugoslavia', in P. Bren and M. Neuburger (eds), *Communism Unwrapped: Consumption in Cold War Eastern Europe* (Oxford, 2012), pp. 351–71.

Lowinger, Jake, *Economic Reform and the 'Double Movement' in Yugoslavia: An Analysis of Labor Unrest and Ethno-nationalism in the 1980s*, PhD dissertation (John Hopkins University, Baltimore, 2009).

Luthar, Breda, 'Shame, desire and longing for the West: A case study of consumption', in B. Luthar and M. Pušnik (eds), *Remembering Utopia: The Culture of Everyday Life in Socialist Yugoslavia* (Washington, 2010), pp. 341–78.

Luthar, Breda and Maruša Pušnik (eds), *Remembering Utopia: The Culture of Everyday Life in Socialist Yugoslavia* (Washington, 2010).

Mah, Alice, *Industrial Ruination, Community, and Place: Landscapes and Legacies of Urban Decline* (Toronto, 2012).

Makovicky, Nicolette (ed.), *Neoliberalism, Personhood, and Postsocialism: Enterprising Selves in Changing Economies* (London and New York, 2016).

Maksić, Maja, *Trikotaža Arena Pula. Etnologija Ženskog Rada*, MA dissertation (University of Pula, 2016).

Mara, *Mara, 1909–1984*, commemorative publication (Osijek, 1984).

Marinković, Darko, 'Strike at Kolubara – A Case Study', *South-East Europe Review for Labour and Social Affairs*, 6 (2003), pp. 41–72.
Matjašić, Marjan, *Jugoslovanski Manchester: mariborska tekstilna industrija – The Manchester of Yugoslavia: Maribor textile industry* (Maribor, 2016).
Matošević, Andrea, 'Omladinske radne akcije: kontinuiteti i odmaci iz iskustva akcijaša', *Traditiones*, 44/3 (2015), pp. 93–111.
Matošević, Andrea, *Socijalizam s udarničkim licem. Etnografija radnog pregalaštva* (Zagreb, 2015).
McIvor, Arthur, *Working Lives: Work in Britain since 1945* (Basingstoke, 2013).
Merunka-Golubić, Mirka, 'Reprodukcijska Prava', in D. Dijanić Dijana, M. Merunka-Golubović, I. Niemčić and D. Stanić (eds), *Ženski biografski leksikon. Sjećanje žena na život u socijalizmu* (Zagreb, 2004), pp. 341–45.
Mesarić Žabčić, Rebeka and Perić Kaselj, Marina, 'Žene i Industrijska Baština: primjer "Dalmatinke" Sinj', in A. Černelić Krošelj and H. Rožman (eds), *Kulturna dediščina industrijskih panog i industrijska kulturna baština* (Ljubljana, 2011), pp. 286–300.
Meszmann, Tibor, 'The lingering constituency: Discourses of class in postsocialist Serbia', *East European Politics and Society*, 29/3 (2015), pp. 672–84.
Meurs, Mieke and Rasika Ranasinghe, 'De-development in post-socialism: Conceptual and measurement issues', *Politics & Society*, 31 (2003), pp. 31–53.
Mežnarić, Silva, 'Theory and reality: The status of employed women in Yugoslavia', in S. L. Wolchik and A. G. Meyer (eds), *Women, State and Party in Eastern Europe* (Durham, 1985), pp. 214–20.
Mihovilović, Miro A. i suradnici, *Žena između rada i porodice: utjecaj zaposlenosti žene na strukturu i funkciju porodice* (Zagreb, 1975).
Milan, Chiara, 'Reshaping citizenship through collective action: Performative and prefigurative practices in the 2013–2014 cycle of contention in Bosnia & Hercegovina', *Europe-Asia Studies*, 69/9 (2017), pp. 1346–61.
Milić, Anđelka, 'Women and work in former Yugoslavia and their present situation', in Barbara Łobodzińska (ed.), *Family, Women, and Employment in Central-Eastern Europe* (Westport, 1995), pp. 237–44.
Miškovska Kajevska, Ana, *Feminist Activism at War: Belgrade and Zagreb Feminists in the 1990s* (London and New York, 2017).
Molyneux, Maxine, 'Gendered transitions in Eastern Europe', *Feminist Studies*, 21/3 (1995), pp. 637–45.
Morris, Jeremy and Abel Polese (eds), *The Informal Post-Socialist Economy: Embedded Practices and Livelihoods* (London, 2013).
Muehlebach, Andrea and Nitzan Shoshan, 'Introduction, special collection on post-Fordist affect', *Anthropological Quarterly*, 85/2 (2012), pp. 317–43.
Musić, Goran, 'Yugoslavia: Workers' self-management as state paradigm', in Dario Azzellini (ed.), *Ours to Master and to Own: Workers' Control from the Commune to the Present* (Chicago, 2011), pp. 172–90.
Musić, Goran, 'Between Facebook and the picket line: Street protests, labour strikes and the New Left in the Balkans', *Debatte*, 21/2–3 (2013), pp. 321–35.

Musić, Goran, *Serbia's Working Class in Transition, 1988–2013* (Belgrade, 2013).
Musić, Goran, *The Self-Managing Factory after Tito: the Crisis of Yugoslav Socialism on the Shop Floor*. PhD dissertation (EUI, 2016).
Musiolek, Bettina, 'Tools for enforcing labour rights and ensuring corporate social responsibility in the garment sector: The South-East European context', *South-East Europe Review for Labour and Social Affairs*, 3/3 (October 2000), pp. 123–35.
Ost, David, 'Class after communism: Introduction to the special issue', *East European Politics and Societies and Cultures*, 29/3 (2015), pp. 543–64.
Palmberger, Monika, 'Nostalgia matters: Nostalgia for Yugoslavia as a potential vision for a better future', *Sociologija*, L/4 (2008), pp. 355–70.
Papić, Žarana, 'Women in Serbia: Post-communism, war and nationalist mutations', in S. P. Ramet (ed.), *Gender Politics in the Western Balkans: Women and Society in Yugoslavia and the Yugoslav Successor States* (University Park, 1999), pp. 153–69.
Pascall, Gillian and Jane Lewis, 'Emerging Gender Regimes and Policies for Gender Equality in a Wider Europe', *Journal of Social Policy*, 33/3 (2004), pp. 373–94.
Patterson Patrick Hyder, *Bought & Sold: Living and Losing the Good Life in Socialist Yugoslavia* (Ithaca, 2011).
Penn, Shana and Jill Massino (eds), *Gender Politics and Everyday Life in State Socialist Eastern and Central Europe* (Basingstoke, 2009).
Petrović, Tanja, '"When we were Europe": Socialist workers in Serbia and their nostalgic narratives', in. M. N. Todorova (ed.), *Remembering Communism: Genres of Representation* (New York, 2010), pp. 127–53.
Petrović, Tanja, 'Towards an affective history of Yugoslavia', *Filozofija i društvo*, 27/3 (2016), pp. 504–20.
Pine, Frances, 'Retreat to the household? Gendered domains in postsocialist Poland', in C. M. Hann (ed.), *Postsocialism: Ideals, Ideologies, and Practices in Eurasia* (London and New York, 2002), pp. 95–113.
Pokret za slobodu, *Deindustrijalizacija i Radnički Otpor. Borbe i Inicijative za Očuvanje Radnih Mesta u Periodu Tranzicije* (Belgrade, 2011).
Pokret za slobodu, *Borba za Budućnost. Ka Balkanskom Pokretu Otpora. Otpor Deindustrijalizaciji i Otimanju Zemlje* (Belgrade, 2013).
Portelli, Alessandro, *They Say in Harlan County: An Oral History* (Oxford, 2012).
Potkonjak, Sanja and Tea Škokić, '"In the world of iron and steel": On the ethnography of work, unemployment and hope', *Narodna umjetnost*, 50/1 (2013), pp. 74–95.
Pozniak Kinga, *Nowa Huta: Generations of Change in a Model Socialist Town* (Pittsburg, 2014).
Premuž Đipalo, Vedrana, 'Žene u Doba Socijalizma: Slučaj "Dalmatinka"', *Ethnologica Dalmatica*, 23/1 (2016), pp. 159–92.
Radenković, Ivan, *Foreign Direct Investments in Serbia* (Belgrade, 2016).

Radović, Srđan, 'Politike simbola na gradskim ulicama: obrasci preimenovanja javnih prostora u postjugoslovenskim zemljama', *Narodna Umjetnost*, 51/2 (2014), pp. 117–32.

Rakić-Vodinelić, Vesna, Saša Gajin and Mario Reljanović (eds), *Europa ne stanuje u Babušnici. Građani protiv Srbije pred Sudom u Strazburu* (Belgrade 2013).

Rajković, Ivan, *Struggles for Moral Ground: Problems with Work and Legitimacy in a Serbian Industrial Town*, PhD dissertation (Manchester University, 2015).

Ramet, Sabrina Petra (ed.), *Gender Politics in the Western Balkans: Women and Society in Yugoslavia and the Yugoslav Successor States* (University Park, 1999).

Reeves, Joy B., 'Women, work and family in former Yugoslavia', in Barbara Łobodzińska (ed.), *Family, Women, and Employment in Central-Eastern Europe* (Westport, 1995), pp. 245–58.

Regulska, Joanna and Bonnie G. Smith (eds), *Women and Gender in Postwar Europe: From Cold War to European Union* (New York, 2012).

Rofel, Lisa, *Other Modernities: Gendered Yearnings in China after Socialism* (Berkeley, 1999).

Rusac, Nikolina, *Pazinka. Kulturnoantropološki i muzeološki pristupi tematizaciji industrijsko nasljeđa socijalizma*, MA dissertation (University of Zagreb, 2014).

Rusinow, Dennison, *The Yugoslav Experiment, 1948–1974* (London, 1977).

Rutar, Sabine, 'Towards a Southeast European history of labour: Examples from Yugoslavia', in S. Rutar (ed.), *Beyond the Balkans, Towards an Inclusive History of Southeastern Europe* (Vienna and Berlin, 2014), pp. 325–56.

Saveski, Zdravko, 'The process of the reduction of workers' rights in Macedonia in the period 1993–2003', *South-East Europe Review*, 2 (2005), pp. 95–109.

Schierup, Carl Ulrik, *Migration, Socialism and the International Division of Labour: The Yugoslavian Experience* (Aldershot, 1990).

Schierup, Carl Ulrik, 'Quasi-proletarians and a patriarchal bureaucracy: Aspects of Yugoslavia's re-peripheralisation', *Soviet Studies*, 44/1 (1992), pp. 79–99.

Schult, Ulrike, *Zwischen Stechuhr und Selbstverwaltung: Eine Mikrogesschichte sozialer Konflikte in der jugoslawischen Fahrzeugindustrie 1965–1985* (Vienna, 2017).

Siegle, Lucy and Jason Burke, *We Are What We Wear: Unravelling fast fashion and the collapse of Rana Plaza* (London, 2014).

Šimončić-Bobetko, Zdenka, 'Razvoj tekstilne industrije u Hrvatskoj u razdoblju između dva svjetska rata (1918-1941)', *Povijesni Prilozi*, 1 (Zagreb, 1982), pp. 101–203.

Sklevicky, Lydia, *Konji, Žene, Ratovi* (Zagreb, 1996).

Škokić, Tea and Sanja Potkonjak, '"Working class gone to heaven": From working class to middle class and back', *Narodna Umjetnost*, 53/1 (2016), pp. 117–32.

Smith, Adrian, John Pickles, Robert Begg, Poli Roukova and Milan Buček, 'Outward processing, EU enlargement and regional relocation in the European textile and clothing industry: Reflections on the European Commission's communication on "The Future of The Textiles and Clothing Sector in the enlarged European Union"', *European Urban and Regional Studies*, 12/1 (2005), pp. 83–91.

Smith, Adrian, Alison Stenning, Alena Rochovska and Dariusz Swiatek, 'The emergence of a working poor: Labour markets, neoliberalisation and diverse economies in post-socialist cities', *Antipode*, 40/2 (2008), pp. 283–311.

Spasić, Ivana, 'Jugoslavija kao mesto normalnog života: sećanja običnih ljudi u Srbiji', *Sociologija*, LIV/4 (2012), pp. 577–94.

Spaskovska, Ljubica, 'The Yugoslav chronotope – histories, memories and the future of Yugoslav studies', in F. Bieber, A. Galijas and R. Archer (eds), *Debating the Dissolution of Yugoslavia* (London, 2014), pp. 241–53.

Spaskovska, Ljubica, *The Last Yugoslav Generation: The Rethinking of Youth Politics and Cultures in Late Socialism* (Manchester, 2017).

Srećković, Milenko, *Corporate Imperialism: The Zones of Exploitation in Serbia* (Belgrade, 2015).

Srigley, Katrina, Stacey Zembrzycki and Franca Iacovetta, *Beyond Women's Words, Feminisms and Practices of Oral History in the Twenty-First Century* (London and New York, 2018).

Stambolieva, Marija, *Welfare State Transformation in the Yugoslav Successor States: From Social to Unequal* (London, 2016).

Stambolieva, Marija and Stefan Dehnert (eds), *Welfare States in Transition: 20 Years after the Yugoslav Welfare Model* (Sofia, 2011).

Stanić, Igor, 'Društveno-ekonomski položaj radničke klase u Hrvatskoj 1950-ih', in I. Duda, A. Buhin and I. Stanić (eds), *Radionica za suvremenu povijest* (Pula-Zagreb, 2013), pp. 27–48.

Stenning, Alison, 'Where is the post-socialist working class? Working class lives in the spaces of (post)socialism', *Sociology*, 39/5 (2005), pp. 983–99.

Stenning, Alison, 'Re-placing work: Economic transformations and the shape of a community in post-socialist Poland', *Work, Employment and Society*, 19/2 (2005), pp. 235–59.

Stenning, Alison and Jane Hardy, 'Public sector reform and women's work in Poland: "Working for juice, coffee and cheap cosmetics!"', *Gender, Work and Organization*, 12/2 (2005), pp. 503–26.

Štiks, Igor, '"New Left" in the post-Yugoslav space: Issues, sites, and forms', *Socialism and Democracy*, 29/3 (2015), pp. 135–46.

Strangleman, Tim, *Work Identity at the End of the Line: Privatisation and Culture Change in the UK Rail Industry* (Basingstoke, 2004).

Strangleman, Tim, 'The nostalgia for permanence at work? The end of work and its commentators', *The Sociological Review*, 55/1 (2007), pp. 81–103.

Strangleman, Tim, 'Deindustrialisation and the historical sociological imagination: Making sense of work and industrial change', *Sociology*, 51/2 (2017), pp. 466–82.
Strangleman, Tim, James Rhodes and Sherry Linkon, 'Introduction to Crumbling cultures: Deindustrialisation, class, and memory', *International Labor and Working-Class History*, 84 (2013), pp. 7–22.
Ströhle, Isabel, 'Of social inequalities in a socialist society: The creation of a rural underclass in Yugoslav Kosovo', in R. Archer, I. Duda and P. Stubbs (eds), *Social Inequalities and Discontent in Yugoslav Socialism* (Farnham, 2016), pp. 112–31.
Suvin, Darko, 'On Class Relationships in Yugoslavia 1945–1974, with a Hypothesis about the Ruling Class', *Journal of Contemporary Central and Eastern Europe (Debatte)*, 20/1 (2012), pp. 37–71.
Tivadar, Blanka and Andreja Vezovnik, 'Cooking in socialist Slovenia: Housewives on the road from a bright future to an idyllic past', in B. Luthar and M. Pušnik (eds), *Remembering Utopia: The Culture of Everyday Life in Socialist Yugoslavia* (Washington, 2010), pp. 379–405.
Todorova, Maria N. and Zsuzsa Gille (eds), *Post-communist Nostalgia* (New York, 2010).
Tomić-Koludrović, Inga and Marko Petrić, 'Class in Yugoslav socialism and in the post-Yugoslav societies: Toward a Bourdieuan repositioning of the issue (Part 1)', *Revija za sociologiju*, 44/2 (2014), pp. 107–37.
Toplišek, Alen and Lasse Thomassen, 'From protest to party: Horizontality and verticality on the Slovenian left', *Europe-Asia Studies*, 69/9 (2017), pp. 1383–400.
True, Jacqui, *Gender, Globalization, and Postsocialism: The Czech Republic After Communism* (New York, 2003).
Unkovski-Korica, Vladimir, *The Economic Struggle for Power in Tito's Yugoslavia: From World War II to Non-alignment* (London, 2016).
Upchurch, Martin and Darko Marinković, 'Serbia from the October 2000 revolution to the crash', in G. Dale (ed.) *First the Transition, Then the Crash – Eastern Europe in the 2000s* (London, 2011), pp. 229–50.
Varteks, *90 priča za 90. rođendan Varteksa*, commemorative publication (Varaždin, 2008).
Velikonja, Mitja, *Titostalgia: A Study of Nostalgia for Josip Broz* (Ljubljana, 2008).
Velikonja, Mitja, 'Lost in transition: Nostalgia for socialism in post-socialist countries', *East European Politics and Societies*, 23/4 (2009), pp. 535–51.
Verdery, Katherine, 'From parent-state to family patriarchs: Gender and nation in contemporary Eastern Europe', *East European Politics and Societies*, 8/2 (1994), pp. 225–55.
Vodopivec, Nina, 'Past for the present: The social memory of textile workers in Slovenia', in M. N. Todorova (ed.), *Remembering Communism: Genres of Representation* (New York, 2010), pp. 213–34.
Vodopivec, Nina, 'On the road to modernity: Textile workers and post-socialist transformations in Slovenia', *History*, 97/328 (2012), pp. 609–29.

Volčič, Zala, 'The notion of "the West" in the Serbian national imaginary', *European Journal of Cultural Studies*, 8/2 (2005), pp. 155–75.

Volgyes, Ivan, 'Blue-collar working women and poverty in Hungary', in S. L. Wolchik and A. G. Meyer (eds), *Women, State and Party in Eastern Europe* (Durham, 1985), pp. 221–33.

Wachtel, Howard M., *Workers' Management and Workers' Wages in Yugoslavia: The Theory and Practice of Participatory Socialism* (Ithaca, 1973).

Walkerdine, Valerie and Luiz Jimenez, *Gender, Work and Community After De-Industrialisation: A Psychosocial Approach to Affect* (Basingstoke, 2012).

Williams, Raymond, *Marxism and Literature* (Oxford and New York, 1978).

Woodward, Susan L., 'The rights of women: Ideology, policy and social change in Yugoslavia', in S. L. Wolchik and A. G. Meyer (eds), *Women, State and Party in Eastern Europe* (Durham, 1985), pp. 234–56.

Woodward, Susan L., *Socialist Unemployment: The Political Economy of Yugoslavia, 1945–1990* (Princeton, 1995).

Woodward, Susan L., 'The political economy of ethno-nationalism in Yugoslavia', *Socialist Register*, 39 (2003), pp. 73–92.

Žarkov, Dubravka, *The Body of War: Media, Ethnicity, and Gender in the Break-up of Yugoslavia* (Durham and London, 2007).

Zhurzhenko, Tatiana, 'Free market ideology and new women's identities in post-socialist Ukraine', *European Journal of Women's Studies*, 8/1 (2001), pp. 29–49.

Zimmermann, Susan, 'Gender regime and gender struggle in Hungarian state socialism', *Aspasia*, 4 (2010), pp. 1–24.

Živković, Andreja, 'From the market…to the market: The debt economy after Yugoslavia', in Srećko Horvat and Igor Štiks (eds), *Welcome to the Desert of Post-Socialism* (Brooklyn, NY, 2015), pp. 54–78.

Zukin, Sharon, *Beyond Marx and Tito: Theory and Practice in Yugoslav Socialism* (London and New York, 1975).

Zukin, Sharon, 'The representation of working-class interests in socialist society: Yugoslav Labor Unions', *Politics & Society*, 10/3 (1981), pp. 281–316.

Online sources and press

Alijodžić, Daliborka, 'Dobila Otkaz Telefonom: U "Juri" otpustili samohranu majku, koja se na bolovanju leči od raka!', *Novosti.rs*, 1 December 2016. Available at: http://www.novosti.rs/vesti/naslovna/reportaze/aktuelno.293.html:637692-DOBILA-OTKAZ-TELEFONOM-U-Juri-otpustili-samohranu-majku-koja-se-na-bolovanju-leci-od-raka (accessed 20 January 2018).

Arbutina, Paulina, 'Unska Slagalica Strave', *Novosti*, 29 October 2010. Available at: http://arhiva.portalnovosti.com/2010/10/unska-slagalica-strave/ (accessed 20 January 2018).

Archer, Rory and Goran Musić, *Between Class and Nation: Working Class Communities in 1980s Serbia and Montenegro*. Available at: https://yulabour.wordpress.com/ (accessed 20 January 2018).
Birač, Dimitrije, 'TOKG iznevjerio radnike', 15 September 2016. Available at: https://www.radnicki.org/tokg-iznevjerio-radnike/ (accessed 20 January 2018).
Birač, Dimitrije, 'Ponižavanje radnica Orljave', 6 February 2017. Available at: https://www.radnicki.org/ponizavanje-radnica-orljave/ (accessed 20 January 2018).
Capital.ba, 'Nakon poslova štrajkaju gladu', 25 September 2010. Available at: http://www.capital.ba/nakon-posla-strajkuju-gladu/ (accessed 20 January 2018).
Centar za mirovne studije / Baza za radničku inicijativu i demokratizaciju, 'Kome treba poduzeće? Borovo 1988. – 1991'. Available at: http://borovo1988.radnickaprava.org/ (accessed 20 January 2018)
Ćirić, V. '"Prvi Maj" fabrika koja je stvorila grad', 2 March 2013. Available at: http://www.novosti.rs/vesti/naslovna/ekonomija/aktuelno.239.html:422390-Prvi-maj-fabrika-koja-je-stvorila-grad (accessed 20 January 2018).
Clean Clothes Campaign, *Made in Europe: Swiss, Austrian and German Workwear Suppliers Profit from Macedonian Workers' Poverty and Fear*, 2012. Available at: http://www.sachsen-kauft-fair.de/wp-content/uploads/2012/08/madeineurope_engl.pdf (accessed 20 January 2018).
Clean Clothes Campaign, *Stitched Up – Poverty Wages for Garment Workers in Eastern Europe and Turkey*, 2014. Available at: https://cleanclothes.org/resources/publications/stitched-up-1 (accessed 20 January 2018).
Clean Clothes Campaign, *Country Profile Serbia*, 2017. Available at: https://cleanclothes.org/livingwage/europe/country-profiles/serbia/view (accessed 20 January 2018).
Delo, 'Adijo Tovarna'. Available at: http://www.delo.si/adijo-tovarna (accessed 20 January 2018).
Dokovska Natasha, 'Sweatshops Producing Big Western Brands in Macedonia Continue Unchecked Leaving Twenty Women Dead This Summer'. *The Wip*, 18 August 2007. Available at: http://thewip.net/2007/08/18/sweatshops-producing-big-western-brands-in-macedonia-continue-unchecked-leaving-twenty-women-dead-this-summer/ (accessed 20 January 2018).
Drakulić, Slavenka, 'How women survived (post-) communism (and didn't laugh)', *Eurozine*, 5 June 2015. Available at: http://www.eurozine.com/how-women-survived-post-communism-and-didnt-laugh/ (accessed 20 January 2018).
Džokić, Ana, *Taking Common Matter into Your Own Hands* (research archive, 2010). Available at: http://www.stealth.ultd.net/stealth/25_taking.common.matter.into.your.own.hands.html (accessed 20 January 2018).
Fair Wear Foundation, *Macedonia Country Study*, 2010. Available at: https://www.fairwear.org/resource/macedonia-country-study-2010/ (accessed 20 January 2018).

'Invest in Macedonia', official website. Available at: www.investinmacedonia.com (accessed 20 January 2018).

Isović Dobrijević, Maja, 'Emina Busuladžić o 40 godina rada u "Diti": Radnik u BiH nikad nije bio u goroj situaciji', *Buka*, 6 February 2017. Available at: http://www.6yka.com/novost/120369/emina-busuladzic-o-40-godina-rada-u-diti-radnik-u-bih-nikad-nije-bio-u-goroj-situaciji (accessed 20 January 2018).

Jakovljević Marija and Luka Matić, 'Osijek i Kruševac: postranzicijsko ogledalo', 23 December 2015. Available at: http://www.osijek031.com/osijek.php?topic_id=60210 (accessed 20 January 2018).

Jugmedia, '*Žena koja se udala za svoje preduzeće*', 4 May 2013. Available at: http://jugmedia.rs/zena-koja-se-udala-za-svoje-preduzece/ (accessed 20 January 2018).

Jukic, Elvira M., 'Workers' takeover saves iconic Bosnian firm', *Balkan Insight*, 1 July 2015. Available at: http://www.balkaninsight.com/en/article/workers-takeover-saves-tuzla-s-iconic-detergent-company (accessed 20 January 2018).

Kirn, Gal, 'Slovenia's social uprising in the European crisis: Maribor as periphery from 1988 to 2012', *Stasis*, 24 January 2014. Available at: http://www.stasisjournal.net/all-issues/24-1-2014-revolutions-and-protest-movements/60-slovenia-s-social-uprising-in-the-european-crisis-maribor-as-periphery-from-1988-to-2012 (accessed 20 January 2018).

Kocić, Danilo, 'Protest radnika konfekcije "Inkol"', *Juznevesti*, 9 January 2012. Available at: https://www.juznevesti.com/Drushtvo/Protest-radnika-konfekcije-Inkol.sr.html (accessed 20 January 2018).

Landeka, Nada, 'Nenad Leček; Uvoz i loša politika uništili su domaće tekstilce', 9 May 2014. Available at: http://www.hazud.hr/nenad-lecek-uvoz-i-losa-politika-unistili-su-domace-tekstilce/ (accessed 20 January 2018).

Maas, Peter, 'Muslims forced to leave Bosnia', *Washington Post*, 25 July 1992. Available at: https://www.washingtonpost.com/archive/politics/1992/07/25/muslims-forced-to-leave-bosnia/f81d0b25-4e0c-4bb2-80f5-bc6d09715c56/?utm_term=.4ea44972254b (accessed 20 January 2018).

Mašina, 'What is the real price of Geox shoes?', 16 March 2017. Available at: http://www.masina.rs/eng/real-price-geox-shoes/ (accessed 20 January 2018).

Mašina, 'Working for GEOX in the 21° century – The case of Serbia', 12 April 2017. Available at: http://www.masina.rs/eng/working-geox-21-century-case-serbia/ (accessed 20 January 2018).

Mihaljević, Domagoj, 'Tržište rada kao faktor rodne nejednakosti u zemljama bivše Jugoslavije', *Bilten*, 16 December 2015. Available at: www.bilten.org/?p=10776 (accessed 20 January 2018).

Milat, Andrea, 'Pobuna radnica Kamenskog i kako se oduprijeti kapitalizmu (I.)', *Slobodni Filosofski*, 20 September 2012. Available at: http://slobodnifilozofski.com/2012/09/andrea-milat-pobuna-radnica-kamenskog-i.html (accessed 20 January 2018).

Munjin, Bojan, 'Goran Ferčeg, Kapitalizam je ucjenjivački mehanizam', *Novosti*, 28 June 2017. Available at: http://www.portalnovosti.com/goran-fercec-kapitalizam-je-ucjenjivacki-mehanizam (accessed 20 January 2018).

Muzej Jugoslavije, 'Jugo moja Jugo'. Available at: http://www.mij.rs/izlozbe/442/jugo-moja-jugo-.html (accessed 20 January 2018).

Palibrk, Duška, 'Bili smo proizvođači, bankari i trgovci - tvornica je bila naša kuća', *Glas Istre*, 24 April 2015.

Pepić, Anđela, 'Reclaiming the factory: A story from Bosnia', *Open Democracy*, 15 June 2015. Available at: https://www.opendemocracy.net/can-europe-make-it/andjela-pepic/reclaiming-factory-story-from-bosnia (accessed 20 January 2018).

Perić, Vito, 'Umrlo si ti, umrla je tvornica, a ni mi nismo baš najbolje', *Slobodna Dalmacija*, 23 March 2009. Available at: http://www.slobodnadalmacija.hr/dalmacija/split-zupanija/clanak/id/45434/umro-si-ti-umrla-je-tvornica-a-ni-mi-nismo-bas-najbolje (accessed 20 January 2018).

Pikanal.rs, 'Blago u knjigama I.O. "Prvi Maj" koje propada – video', 10 February 2015. Available at: http://www.pikanal.rs/2015/02/10/blago-i-o-prvi-maj-koje-propada/ (accessed 20 January 2018).

Powers, Charles T., 'Serbs accused of "blackmail" on refugees', *Los Angeles Times*, 29 July 1992. Available at: http://articles.latimes.com/1992-07-29/news/mn-4653_1_refugee-problem (accessed 20 January 2018).

Pulska Grupa, 'We were destroyed by capitalism! Interview with worker from Kamensko who wishes to stay anonimous and student Jelena Miloš', 15 August 2012. Available at: http://praksa.hr/kamensko/ (accessed 20 January 2018).

Savez samostalnih sindikata Kragujevca, 'Saopštenje za javnost', 2016. Available at: http://www.sindikat-kragujevac.org.rs/novi/wp-content/uploads/2017/03/Pobuna-radnica-u-Fori-Textile.pdf (accessed 20 January 2018).

Šimpraga, Saša, 'Dalmatinka, Sinj', *H-Alter*, 10 September 2014. Available at: http://www.h-alter.org/vijesti/dalmatinka-sinj (accessed 20 January 2018).

Spaic, Igor, 'Bosnia's "hero town" dies on its feet', *Balkan Insight*, 23 October 2017. http://www.balkaninsight.com/en/article/bosnia-s-hero-town-dies-on-its-feet-10-20-2017 (accessed 20 January 2018).

Stojaković, Gordana, 'Povodom međunarodnog praznika rada. Po drugi put o slučaju tekstilne radnice Ljubice Ljubičić i nešto malo o Klari Cetkin', 27 April 2016. Available at: http://pravonarad.info/?p=909 (accessed 20 January 2018).

Tomčić, Ladislav, 'Zašto su Raznici Zgaženi 90-IH: "Tada su sindikalci bili izdajnici domovine, strani plaćenici, jugonostalgičari, četnici"', *Lupiga*, 21 May 2014. Available at: http://www.lupiga.com/vijesti/zasto-su-radnici-izgubili-borbu-sa-najezdom-skakakavaca-koji-su-opustosili-hrvatsko-gospodarstvo (accessed 20 January 2018).

Vukliš, Vladan, 'Štrajk tekstilnih radnica 1969. u retrospektivi (1)', *Glas Sprske*, 2 March 2015. Available at: https://www.glassrpske.com/plus/istorija/

Zapisi-iz-Arhiva-Republike-Srpske-54-Strajk-tekstilnih-radnica-1969-u-retrospektivi-1/lat/176456.html (accessed 20 January 2018).

Women in Black, Belgrade, *Leskovac iz ženskog ugla* (Belgrade, 2012). Available at: http://zeneucrnom.org/pdf/Leskovac.pdf (accessed 20 January 2018).

World Bank, 'Yugoslavia – Industrial restructuring study: Overview, issues and strategy for restructuring', 1991. Available at: http://documents.worldbank.org/curated/en/839571468304234506/Yugoslavia-Industrial-restructuring-study-overview-issues-and-strategy-for-restructuring (accessed 20 January 2018).

Index

abortion   10, 48–9
academic realm, industrial workers' struggles in   163–9
AFŽ, *see* Antifascist Women's Front (*Antifašistički front žena*)
aktiv žena   62, 69
Alargić, Judita   63
alienation   62, 91, 134, 184
Amazon depots   121
Anđelić and others v. Serbia (court case)   111
Antifascist Women's Front (*Antifašistički front žena*, or AFŽ)   32–5, 56, 63, 187
Arena knitwear factory (*Arena Trikotaža*)   47–51, 126–7, 133, 136, 139–40, 182–3, 185, 186
   strike of 2014   71, 71 n.46, 175–8, 192
Article 24, Yugoslav Constitution of 1946   57
artistic realm, industrial workers' struggles in   163–9
Astibo garment factory   96–7, 97 n.33
Astra shoe factory   47
atomization   115
Austria   104

bankruptcy   1, 15, 17, 106, 112, 115, 117, 123, 128, 130, 141, 142, 165, 175, 176
Beko garment factory   97 n.33
blue-collar workers   15, 18, 29, 41, 47, 52, 53, 68, 69, 71–3, 101, 108, 115–16, 120, 122, 132, 134–7, 147, 154, 155, 156, 157, 159, 181, 190
Borojević, Rajka   34–5

Borovo industrial complex   167
Bosnia-Herzegovina   1, 13, 15, 22, 25, 37, 72 n.51, 94 n.27, 124, 131, 145, 151, 165, 170, 183, 186
   post-socialist transformations   89
Bosnian Spring of 2014   162, 168, 192
brotherhood and unity   7, 26
   nostalgia for   146–52
Brotherhood and Unity Highway   27
Broz, Jovanka   136
Bulatović, Zoran   115
Buljan, Vice   37, 142
Butorac, Anka   26

canteens   9, 16, 40, 42, 48, 51, 58, 60, 64, 83, 84, 97, 101, 121, 130, 131, 140, 144, 149, 169, 188
Čateks textile factory   116, 117
Central Europe   13 n.32, 59 n.15, 91
childcare facilities   40, 58, 60, 62–7, 95–7, 103, 135, 160, 185, 189
civil marriage   33
class   1, 2, 9, 10, 18–20, 26, 31, 34–7, 56, 57, 67, 78, 90, 137, 153–60, 162, 174
   analysis   14
   belonging   18, 157, 159
   consciousness   12
   domination   71
   equality   1
   formation   153
   inequality   90, 134, 135

positioning 153, 157, 159
relations 4, 179
Clean Clothes Campaign 94 n.28, 98
collective organizing 169–78
Communist Party of Yugoslavia (KPJ) 24
community networks 124, 189
commuting expenses 101
Conference for the Social Activity of Women (*Konferencija za Društvenu Aktivnost Žena* or KDAŽ) 36, 68
coupon privatization (*kuponska privatizacija*) 116
credit repayments 42
credits 50, 73, 78, 102, 145, 188
criminal privatization 14, 14 n.36, 113, 125, 142, 162, 165, 169, 170 n.29, 174, 176, 190
Croatia 1, 6, 13, 15, 22–5, 186
  job losses in 94 n.27
  Labour Law 108, 178
  labour unions 113–14
  maternity leave 58
  maternity leave provision 109–10
  post-socialist transformations 89
  working conditions in subcontracting firms 111
Croatian Democratic Party (HDZ) 114, 116, 142, 170
cultural capital 91, 158, 183
cultural realm, industrial workers' struggles in 163–9

Dalmatinka spinning mill 38, 91, 130, 131, 142–5, 147 n.37, 166, 182
de-development 89
deindustrialization 3–7, 14, 17, 58, 59, 81, 88, 90, 97, 111, 139, 146, 160, 186, 190, 191, 193

deindustrialized landscapes, across post-Yugoslav space 124–32
democratization 191
deskilling 101
devaluation 9, 10, 17, 89, 90, 101, 104, 107, 120–2, 141, 142, 144, 155, 163, 178, 183, 192
Dioki petrolchemical factory 165
DITA detergent factory 162, 168, 178
double burden 9, 10, 19, 20, 55–61, 63, 67, 74, 95, 132, 145, 160, 189, 191
Dragačevo weaving cooperative 35
DTR textile factory, strike 161 n.3
Duga Resa textile factory 22, 23, 25, 36, 68, 69
Duganova, Vaska 64–6

East-Central Europe 91
Eastern Europe 56, 91, 92
  trade unions in 112
ECHR, *see* European Courts of Human Rights
economic accumulation 14
education 31, 35, 36, 41, 47, 59, 67, 68, 70, 71, 73, 76, 95, 119 n.73, 116 n.56, 168, 194
EEC, *see* European Economic Community
'emancipation from above' 8–9 n.18, 9, 187
equality 25, 33, 39, 63, 65
  gender 1, 56, 57
Estare Culto factory, protest 161 n.3
ethnicity 7, 10, 12, 26, 75, 114, 146, 147, 151, 158
EU, *see* European Union
European Courts of Human Rights (ECHR) 111
European Economic Community (EEC) 92
European Union (EU) 89, 92, 93, 104

Europeanization 191
everyday survival strategies 179–84

factory, as second home 132–8
Fair Wear Foundation 98
Falke textile factory 112
FDI, *see* foreign direct investment
Fordism 121, 138, 185, 190
foreign direct investment (FDI) 90, 93, 112
fragmentation 30, 115, 133
France 192
free association of producers 29
free export zones 90, 93
Freedom Fight Movement (*Pokret za Slobodu*) 162

Gastarbeiters (migrant workers) 167
gender 153–60
  domination 71
  equality 1, 56, 57
  history between socialism and post-socialism 7–12
  inequality 90, 124, 135
  regimes 2, 9, 56, 95, 192
  relations 4, 8 n.17, 9 n.19, 10, 11, 180, 186, 192, 193
  see also 'working mother' gender contract
gender-based violence 10
gendered division of labour 33, 34, 75, 189
gendered modernization 2, 39
gendered segregation of jobs 59
gendered warfare 11, 90
generations 1, 5, 7, 12 n.30, 15, 18, 20, 32, 34, 46, 75, 86, 95–107, 115, 124, 128, 132, 133, 140–2, 149, 162, 166, 167, 183, 190, 192
gentrification 124, 129, 176
GEOX shoe factory 111
Germany 104
Glas Istre (newspaper) 50

global economic crisis of 2008 12, 87
global garment industry 22, 88, 92, 93, 98, 107, 140, 190–194
global textile production 190–4
Golden Deer (*Zlatna Košuta*) award 128, 129
Golik, Krešimir 61, 188
Grabar-Kitarović, Kolinda 137
Gredelj metal factory 165
green field companies 119

HDZ, *see* Croatian Democratic Party (HDZ)
health clinics 58, 60, 140
Hladno Pivo (music band) 164
holidays 16, 30, 40, 44, 49, 104, 145, 156, 157, 188
  allowance 42
  public 66, 67
  subsidized 3, 44, 49, 75, 103, 149
  summer 66, 67, 101, 172
housing 42, 58, 60, 70 n.43, 75, 78–80, 96, 97, 103, 104, 144, 152, 156, 157, 166
  cheap 3
  social 78–80, 169
  subsidized 40, 188
  unhealthy conditions 63
humanisation of work (*humanizacija rada*) 51

IDS, *see* Istrian Democratic Party
ILO Convention of 1948 77
IMF, *see* International Monetary Fund
IMK Slavonija 104–6, 130
Independent Trade Union of Workers in the Textile, Clothing, Leather and Rubber Industry (*Samostalni sindikat tekstila, obuće, kože, gume Hrvatske*) 117, 171

industrialization 2–5, 16, 17, 22, 26, 27, 30, 31, 43, 46, 57, 58, 63, 66, 81, 96, 126, 138, 186, 188, 193
informal economy 113, 179
informal work 10, 20, 150, 163, 180, 182, 184, 192
informalization 88, 95
Inkol textile factory 112
INKOP shoe factory 122 n.78
insecurity 103, 137, 139, 141
interethnic solidarity 148
intergenerational solidarity 103, 124, 133, 138–45, 187
intergenerational transmission 163, 166, 192, 194
International Monetary Fund (IMF) structural adjustment programmes 89
intersubjectivity 81
Istrian Democratic Party (IDS) 126
ITAS metal factory 162
Ivančića shoe factory 28, 118

Javor factory, strike 161 n.3
job security 2, 7, 109, 138, 145, 160, 166, 190
Jugoremedija pharmaceutical factory 162

Kamensko garment factory 122 n.78, 129, 161–2, 164
  hunger strike of 2010 9, 70, 169–78, 192
KDAŽ, see Conference for the Social Activity of Women (Konferencija za Društvenu Aktivnost Žena or KDAŽ)
kindergartens 9, 48, 62, 70 n.43, 80, 135, 149, 185, 186, 188
Ključ stockings factory 25
Klupko garment factory 130
Kožara leather factory 104

KPJ, see Communist Party of Yugoslavia (KPJ)
Krivokuća, Milan 114
KTK garment factory, strike 161 n.3
Kutle, Miroslav 170

labour intensification 91
labour measurement (norma) 7, 41, 42, 134
labour quiescence 113
labour rights 1, 2, 7, 10, 11, 90
labour shortages 29
labour strength 116
labour weakness 112, 116
laundries 9, 43, 65
League of Communists 72 n.51
leisure 40–6
Leteks textile factory 111, 147 n.37
LIO garment factory 104
local textile production 190–4
Lohn work 88
lon poslovi 60
low productivity 29
low wages 24, 42, 71, 87, 98, 111, 119, 132, 176

Macedonia 1, 13, 15, 25, 27, 64, 183, 186
  foreign direct investment 93
  post-socialist transformations 89
Makedonka textile factory 65, 66, 97, 98, 101, 102, 130, 131
Mara knitwear factory 104, 105
Maribor uprisings of 2012 162
market socialism 13, 21–53, 95, 157, 191
material deprivation 43, 46, 75, 79
maternity leave 10, 58, 60, 101, 104
Međimurska trikotaža Čakovec (MTČ) 116
Meiso shoe factory 118

Metka textile factory   43–6
Milašević, Vojislav   82
Milošević government   114
mismanaged privatization   17
mobbing   18, 87, 104, 106, 111, 119, 191
Montenegro   96
   post-socialist transformations   89
'Movement for high productivity'   28
MTČ, *see* Međimurska trikotaža Čakovec
multi-ethnic coexistence   20, 124, 146, 148, 150, 152
Mura textile factory   93, 130, 131

Nada Dimić textile factory   28
nationalism   10–12, 126
nationhood   12
neo-capitalism   91
neoliberal capitalism   13, 95, 105, 191, 192
neoliberal productivity   109
night shift   7, 38, 41, 58, 59, 65–8, 77, 84, 85, 101, 108, 134–6, 181, 188, 189
Nikola Tesla textile factory, strike   161 n.3
Nikolić, Dragan   185
Non-Aligned Movement   96
normality   2, 81, 148, 169, 190
North America   3
nostalgia   2, 13, 14 n.39, 20, 124, 146–52
   Yugo-nostalgia   153–60

Od 3 do 22 (movie)   61–2, 188–9
Olga Ban knitwear factory   47, 50
OPT, *see* outward processing trade
oral history   3–7, 15–17, 19, 46, 60, 73–4, 131, 153, 166, 179, 186, 193
Orljava textile factory   122 n.78, 137

outward processing trade (OPT)   88
overtime   24, 87, 98, 100, 101, 103, 104, 107, 109, 110, 140 n.28, 170

paid work   57, 67, 172
part-time work   10, 58, 60
party membership   72–3
paternalism   46, 49, 113, 115, 122, 134, 156, 158
paternalist management, in socialism   46–53
People's University, Duga Resa   36, 37
Petrokemija petrolchemical factory   162, 163 n.7
Planinc, Milka   52, 137
Pobjeda textile factory   61, 62
Poland   57, 166, 192
   double burden in   10 n.22
   everyday life in   73
   post-socialist transformations   91
post-Fordist capitalism   14
post-socialism   4, 5, 13 n.32, 14, 19, 87–122, 154, 158, 165, 179, 184, 193
   and socialism, gender history between   7–12
post-socialist deindustrialization   2, 10, 18
post-socialist transformations   88–95, 105–6
precarity/precarization   3, 6, 11, 12, 19, 61, 88, 91, 95, 97, 99, 103, 105, 110, 138, 139, 192
Priče iz Fabrike (TV series)   81, 83, 85, 147, 150
privatization   89–91, 94, 146, 160, 180
   coupon (*kuponska privatizacija*)   116
   criminal   14, 14 n.36, 113, 125, 142, 162, 165, 169, 170 n.29, 174, 176, 190
   mismanaged   17

prizes   28, 51, 102, 106, 127, 128, 135, 172
productive labour   2, 10, 32, 180
productivity and welfare, balancing   46–53
Prvi Maj textile factory   185, 186

'race to the bottom'   6, 88, 93, 191
Radmilović, Zoran   82
Rana Plaza building collapse   107
Rašica knitwear factory   49
Raška textile factory, hunger strike   115
rate of employment   58
rebranding   129
re-peripheralization   89
reproductive labour   10, 180
reproductive rights   11
resilience   7, 12, 19, 20, 78, 80, 116, 161, 163, 168, 169, 175, 178, 179, 182–4, 192
retirement pensions   75
RIO textile factory   70, 70 n.43, 74
Romania   91, 121
   working conditions in subcontracting firms   110

Sana garment factory   72, 81–3, 124, 130, 146–8, 150
scholarships   12, 30, 40, 71, 188
seamstresses   7, 9–11, 19, 59, 61–7, 74, 81–7, 134, 135, 158, 159, 176, 180, 181, 183
self-management   26–32, 58, 68, 69, 70 n.43, 71, 72, 88, 112, 113, 154, 188
self-sacrifice   7, 46, 77, 78
Serbia   112, 125, 186
   deindustrialization   111
   foreign direct investment   93
   post-socialist transformations   89
   trade unions   112–13

working conditions in subcontracting firms   110
Seventh Congress of the League of Communists (1958)   30–1
shock work   26–32
sick leaves (*bolovanje*)   48, 60, 101, 104
sick pay   112
single mothers (*samohrane majke*)   47–9, 70 n.43, 76, 111, 170, 173, 180
Škrinjarić, Ivan   50–2
Slobodna Dalmacija (newspaper)   142
Slovenia   1, 12, 13, 15, 22, 23, 25, 27, 43, 49, 186
   job losses in   94 n.27
   maternity leave   58
   trade unions   115
sociability networks   2, 192
social capital   91
social housing   78–80, 169
social inequalities   14, 89, 119
social justice   20, 82, 115, 162, 184, 185, 192, 194
social and labour history, after Yugoslavia   12–15
social mobility   7, 41, 70, 133, 189
'social motherhood'   57
social security payments   112
social stratification   59, 78, 81
social welfare   30, 145, 166, 190, 192
socialism and post-socialism, gender history between   7–12
socialist gendered pedagogies   36, 37
socialist industrialization   2
socialist microcosm, factory as   40–6
solidarity   2, 65, 81, 83, 105, 121–2, 132, 135, 136, 149, 150, 162, 166, 168, 171, 174–6, 178, 183, 189
   civil society   163

collective 75, 152
  funds 40
  interethnic 148
  intergenerational 103, 124, 133, 138–45, 187
South-Eastern Europe 92
Soviet Constitution of 1936 57
Soviet Union 22, 26, 28–31, 53, 57, 58, 75, 117, 125, 180
Soviet-Yugoslav split 3, 22, 169, 188
sport associations 68
Stakhanovism 28
state control 8, 29
state patriarchy 9, 34, 187
state sovereignty 2
stigmatization 121
Story of a Factory (movie) 28
strike 5, 9, 26, 70, 71, 161, 169–78
structure of feeling 4, 5, 22, 29, 31, 32, 39, 46, 52, 55, 74, 75, 80, 81, 85, 86, 88, 102, 105, 112, 113, 115, 120–60, 187–90
subalternization of labour 91
subcontracting 103–12
subsidized holiday centres (*odmarališta*) 44, 58
subsidized holidays 3, 44, 49, 75, 103, 149
subsidized housing 188
summer camps for children 112
Svilana garment factory 104
sweatshops 6, 93, 107
symbolic awards 106
SŽD, *see* Union of Women's Societies (*Savez ženskih društava*)

technical training schools 64
Tekos childwear factory 104, 105
textile factories, in interwar era 22–6
Tito, Josip Broz 81, 136, 137
Tivar textile factory, strike 24–6, 117, 157

trade unions, in post-Yugoslav states 112–22
triple burden 56, 58–9, 67–74, 189
Trudbenik textile factory, strike 71, 83
Tuđman, Franjo 164

Uljanik shipyard 48, 48 n.86, 126, 129, 130, 157
Umberto Gorjan textile factory 50
Union of Independent Trade Unions of Croatia (*Savez Samostalnih Sindikata Hrvatske*) 114
Union of Women's Societies (*Savez ženskih društava* or SŽD) 32–3, 63, 68
unpaid work 67, 87
unsafe working conditions 87

Varaždinska Industrija Svila (VIS) 116, 117, 180
Vardar textile factory 25
Vareško, Marija 127, 129
Varteks textile factory 21 n.1, 49 n.89, 93, 97 n.33, 116–19, 137, 156, 181
Vera i Eržika (movie) 83, 85
VIS, *see* Varaždinska Industrija Svila
vocational schools 64
voluntary firefighter brigades 68
voluntary work (*radne akcije*) 27
Vuteks textile factory 75–8

welfare 40–6
  entitlements 2, 19, 47, 56, 132, 145
  facilities 75
  and productivity, balancing 46–53
  redistribution 46, 86, 157, 187
  rights 1–3, 7, 10, 16, 20, 39, 90, 117

services   9, 29, 36, 40, 44, 57, 58, 63–5, 67, 68, 75, 97, 120, 122, 133, 140, 157, 158–60, 188, 190
Western Europe   3, 53, 58, 97, 121, 129, 147, 169, 170, 172
white-collar workers   6–7, 18, 41, 42, 44, 46, 47, 52, 67, 72, 78, 99, 101, 129, 132, 134, 155, 156, 157
Women's Day   36, 70, 75, 80, 120, 136, 144, 147
women's emancipation through labour   32–40
work   40–6
   across generations   95–103
   see also individual entries
workers' councils   3, 29, 30, 33, 40, 65, 72, 112, 154, 155
workers' education, *see* education
workers' portraits, in factory press   74–81
workers' pride   133, 140, 174
workers' recognition   7, 20, 69, 74, 84, 102, 103, 119, 136, 189, 191
workers' representations, in popular culture   81–6
workers' sacrifice   7, 39, 43, 46, 74, 75, 79, 133, 134, 140–2, 149, 152, 172, 187, 188

workers' shame   144, 178
working camps (*radni logori*)   118
'working mother' gender contract   3, 9–11, 55–86
working relations   2
working-class families   78
working-class sociability   81
working-class women   2, 7, 10–12, 17, 56, 78, 80, 145, 160, 184, 187–90
workplace periodicals   16, 19, 74, 80, 189
World Trade Organization (WTO)   92
WTO, *see* World Trade Organization (WTO)

Yugo-nostalgia   153–60
Yugoslav Constitution of 1946   55, 188
   Article 24   57
   working mothers' equal rights and protection   63
Yugoslav socialist system   1–2
Yugoslav Wars   3, 12, 89, 146, 181
Yura cable factory   111

Zbor Praksa (choir)   177
Žena (magazine)   68
Žilnik, Želimir   83

www.ingramcontent.com/pod-product-compliance
Lightning Source LLC
Chambersburg PA
CBHW052038300426
44117CB00012B/1878